D1635855

William Shakespeare

RICHARD III

Edited with a Commentary by E. A. J. Honigmann
Introduced by Michael Taylor
The Play in Performance by Gillian Day

PENGUIN BOOKS

PENGUIN BOOKS

Published by the Penguin Group
Penguin Books Ltd, 80 Strand, London WC2R ORL, England
Penguin Group (USA) Inc., 375 Hudson Street, New York, New York 10014, USA
Penguin Group (Canada), 10 Alcorn Avenue, Toronto, Ontario, Canada M4V 3B2
(a division of Pearson Penguin Canada Inc.)
Penguin Ireland, 25 St Stephen's Green, Dublin 2, Ireland (a division of Penguin Books Ltd)
Penguin Group (Australia), 250 Camberwell Road, Camberwell, Victoria 3124, Australia
(a division of Pearson Australia Group Pty Ltd)
Penguin Books India Pvt Ltd, 11 Community Centre, Panchsheel Park, New Delhi – 110 017, India
Penguin Group (NZ), cnr Airborne and Rosedale Roads, Albany, Auckland 1310, New Zealand
(a division of Pearson New Zealand Ltd)
Penguin Books (South Africa) (Pty) Ltd, 24 Sturdee Avenue, Rosebank 2196, South Africa

Penguin Books Ltd, Registered Offices: 80 Strand, London WC2R ORL, England

www.penguin.com

This edition first published in Penguin Books 1968
Reissued in the Penguin Shakespeare series 2005

7

This edition copyright © Penguin Books, 1968
Account of the Text and Commentary copyright © E. A. J. Honigmann, 1968, 1995
General Introduction and Chronology copyright © Stanley Wells, 2005
Introduction and Further Reading copyright © Michael Taylor, 2005
The Play in Performance copyright © Gillian Day, 2005

All rights reserved

The moral right of the editors has been asserted

Set in 11.5/12.5 PostScript Monotype Fournier
Typeset by Palimpsest Book Production Limited, Polmont, Stirlingshire
Printed in England by Clays Ltd, St Ives plc

ISBN-13: 978-0-141-01303-9

www.greenpenguin.co.uk

Penguin Books is committed to a sustainable future
for our business, our readers and our planet.
The book in your hands is made from paper
certified by the Forest Stewardship Council.

Contents

General Introduction

Every play by Shakespeare is unique. This is part of his greatness. A restless and indefatigable experimenter, he moved with a rare amalgamation of artistic integrity and dedicated professionalism from one kind of drama to another. Never shackled by convention, he offered his actors the alternation between serious and comic modes from play to play, and often also within the plays themselves, that the repertory system within which he worked demanded, and which provided an invaluable stimulus to his imagination. Introductions to individual works in this series attempt to define their individuality. But there are common factors that underpin Shakespeare's career.

Nothing in his heredity offers clues to the origins of his genius. His upbringing in Stratford-upon-Avon, where he was born in 1564, was unexceptional. His mother, born Mary Arden, came from a prosperous farming family. Her father chose her as his executor over her eight sisters and his four stepchildren when she was only in her late teens, which suggests that she was of more than average practical ability. Her husband John, a glover, apparently unable to write, was nevertheless a capable businessman and loyal townsfellow, who seems to have fallen on relatively hard times in later life. He would have been brought up as a Catholic, and may have retained

Catholic sympathies, but his son subscribed publicly to Anglicanism throughout his life.

The most important formative influence on Shakespeare was his school. As the son of an alderman who became bailiff (or mayor) in 1568, he had the right to attend the town's grammar school. Here he would have received an education grounded in classical rhetoric and oratory, studying authors such as Ovid, Cicero and Quintilian, and would have been required to read, speak, write and even think in Latin from his early years. This classical education permeates Shakespeare's work from the beginning to the end of his career. It is apparent in the self-conscious classicism of plays of the early 1590s such as the tragedy of *Titus Andronicus*, *The Comedy of Errors*, and the narrative poems *Venus and Adonis* (1592–3) and *The Rape of Lucrece* (1593–4), and is still evident in his latest plays, informing the dream visions of *Pericles* and *Cymbeline* and the masque in *The Tempest*, written between 1607 and 1611. It inflects his literary style throughout his career. In his earliest writings the verse, based on the ten-syllabled, five-beat iambic pentameter, is highly patterned. Rhetorical devices deriving from classical literature, such as alliteration and antithesis, extended similes and elaborate wordplay, abound. Often, as in *Love's Labour's Lost* and *A Midsummer Night's Dream*, he uses rhyming patterns associated with lyric poetry, each line self-contained in sense, the prose as well as the verse employing elaborate figures of speech. Writing at a time of linguistic ferment, Shakespeare frequently imports Latinisms into English, coining words such as abstemious, addiction, incarnadine and adjunct. He was also heavily influenced by the eloquent translations of the Bible in both the Bishops' and the Geneva versions. As his experience grows, his verse and prose become more supple,

the patterning less apparent, more ready to accommo-
date the rhythms of ordinary speech, more colloquial in
diction, as in the speeches of the Nurse in *Romeo and
Juliet*, the characterful prose of Falstaff and Hamlet's
soliloquies. The effect is of increasing psychological
realism, reaching its greatest heights in *Hamlet*, *Othello*,
King Lear, *Macbeth* and *Antony and Cleopatra*. Gradually
he discovered ways of adapting the regular beat of the
pentameter to make it an infinitely flexible instrument for
matching thought with feeling. Towards the end of his
career, in plays such as *The Winter's Tale*, *Cymbeline* and
The Tempest, he adopts a more highly mannered style,
in keeping with the more overtly symbolical and emblem-
atical mode in which he is writing.

So far as we know, Shakespeare lived in Stratford till
after his marriage to Anne Hathaway, eight years his
senior, in 1582. They had three children: a daughter,
Susanna, born in 1583 within six months of their marriage,
and twins, Hamnet and Judith, born in 1585. The next
seven years of Shakespeare's life are virtually a blank.
Theories that he may have been, for instance, a school-
master, or a lawyer, or a soldier, or a sailor, lack evidence
to support them. The first reference to him in print, in
Robert Greene's pamphlet *Greene's Groatsworth of Wit* of
1592, parodies a line from *Henry VI*, *Part III*, implying
that Shakespeare was already an established playwright.
It seems likely that at some unknown point after the birth
of his twins he joined a theatre company and gained
experience as both actor and writer in the provinces and
London. The London theatres closed because of plague
in 1593 and 1594; and during these years, perhaps recognizing the need for an alternative career, he wrote and
published the narrative poems *Venus and Adonis* and *The
Rape of Lucrece*. These are the only works we can be

certain that Shakespeare himself was responsible for putting into print. Each bears the author's dedication to Henry Wriothesley, Earl of Southampton (1573–1624), the second in warmer terms than the first. Southampton, younger than Shakespeare by ten years, is the only person to whom he personally dedicated works. The Earl may have been a close friend, perhaps even the beautiful and adored young man whom Shakespeare celebrates in his *Sonnets*.

The resumption of playing after the plague years saw the founding of the Lord Chamberlain's Men, a company to which Shakespeare was to belong for the rest of his career, as actor, shareholder and playwright. No other dramatist of the period had so stable a relationship with a single company. Shakespeare knew the actors for whom he was writing and the conditions in which they performed. The permanent company was made up of around twelve to fourteen players, but one actor often played more than one role in a play and additional actors were hired as needed. Led by the tragedian Richard Burbage (1568–1619) and, initially, the comic actor Will Kemp (d. 1603), they rapidly achieved a high reputation, and when King James I succeeded Queen Elizabeth I in 1603 they were renamed as the King's Men. All the women's parts were played by boys; there is no evidence that any female role was ever played by a male actor over the age of about eighteen. Shakespeare had enough confidence in his boys to write for them long and demanding roles such as Rosalind (who, like other heroines of the romantic comedies, is disguised as a boy for much of the action) in *As You Like It*, Lady Macbeth and Cleopatra. But there are far more fathers than mothers, sons than daughters, in his plays, few if any of which require more than the company's normal complement of three or four boys.

The company played primarily in London's public playhouses – there were almost none that we know of in the rest of the country – initially in the Theatre, built in Shoreditch in 1576, and from 1599 in the Globe, on Bankside. These were wooden, more or less circular structures, open to the air, with a thrust stage surmounted by a canopy and jutting into the area where spectators who paid one penny stood, and surrounded by galleries where it was possible to be seated on payment of an additional penny. Though properties such as cauldrons, stocks, artificial trees or beds could indicate locality, there was no representational scenery. Sound effects such as flourishes of trumpets, music both martial and amorous, and accompaniments to songs were provided by the company's musicians. Actors entered through doors in the back wall of the stage. Above it was a balconied area that could represent the walls of a town (as in *King John*), or a castle (as in *Richard II*), and indeed a balcony (as in *Romeo and Juliet*). In 1609 the company also acquired the use of the Blackfriars, a smaller, indoor theatre to which admission was more expensive, and which permitted the use of more spectacular stage effects such as the descent of Jupiter on an eagle in *Cymbeline* and of goddesses in *The Tempest*. And they would frequently perform before the court in royal residences and, on their regular tours into the provinces, in non-theatrical spaces such as inns, guildhalls and the great halls of country houses.

Early in his career Shakespeare may have worked in collaboration, perhaps with Thomas Nashe (1567–c. 1601) in *Henry VI, Part I* and with George Peele (1556–96) in *Titus Andronicus*. And towards the end he collaborated with George Wilkins (*fl.* 1604–8) in *Pericles*, and with his younger colleagues Thomas Middleton (1580–1627), in *Timon of Athens*, and John Fletcher (1579–1625), in *Henry*

VIII, *The Two Noble Kinsmen* and the lost play *Cardenio*. Shakespeare's output dwindled in his last years, and he died in 1616 in Stratford, where he owned a fine house, New Place, and much land. His only son had died at the age of eleven, in 1596, and his last descendant died in 1670. New Place was destroyed in the eighteenth century but the other Stratford houses associated with his life are maintained and displayed to the public by the Shakespeare Birthplace Trust.

One of the most remarkable features of Shakespeare's plays is their intellectual and emotional scope. They span a great range from the lightest of comedies, such as *The Two Gentlemen of Verona* and *The Comedy of Errors*, to the profoundest of tragedies, such as *King Lear* and *Macbeth*. He maintained an output of around two plays a year, ringing the changes between comic and serious. All his comedies have serious elements: Shylock, in *The Merchant of Venice*, almost reaches tragic dimensions, and *Measure for Measure* is profoundly serious in its examination of moral problems. Equally, none of his tragedies is without humour: Hamlet is as witty as any of his comic heroes, *Macbeth* has its Porter, and *King Lear* its Fool. His greatest comic character, Falstaff, inhabits the history plays and *Henry V* ends with a marriage, while *Henry VI*, *Part III*, *Richard II* and *Richard III* culminate in the tragic deaths of their protagonists.

Although in performance Shakespeare's characters can give the impression of a superabundant reality, he is not a naturalistic dramatist. None of his plays is explicitly set in his own time. The action of few of them (except for the English histories) is set even partly in England (exceptions are *The Merry Wives of Windsor* and the Induction to *The Taming of the Shrew*). Italy is his favoured location. Most of his principal story-lines derive from printed writings; but the structuring and translation of these narratives into dramatic terms is Shakespeare's own, and he invents much additional material. Most of the plays contain elements of myth and legend, and many derive from ancient or more recent history or from romantic tales of ancient times and faraway places. All reflect his reading, often in close detail. Holinshed's *Chronicles* (1577, revised 1587), a great compendium of English, Scottish and Irish history, provided material for his English history plays. The *Lives of the Noble Grecians and Romans* by the Greek writer Plutarch, finely translated into English from the French by Sir Thomas North in 1579, provided much of the narrative material, and also a mass of verbal detail, for his plays about Roman history. Some plays are closely based on shorter individual works: *As You Like It*, for instance, on the novel *Rosalynde* (1590) by his near-contemporary Thomas Lodge (1558–1625), *The Winter's Tale* on *Pandosto* (1588) by his old rival Robert Greene (1558–92) and *Othello* on a story by the Italian Giraldi Cinthio (1504–73). And the language of his plays is permeated by the Bible, the Book of Common Prayer and the proverbial sayings of his day.

Shakespeare was popular with his contemporaries, but his commitment to the theatre and to the plays in performance is demonstrated by the fact that only about half of his plays appeared in print in his lifetime, in slim paperback volumes known as quartos, so called because they were made from printers' sheets folded twice to form four leaves (eight pages). None of them shows any sign that he was involved in their publication. For him, performance was the primary means of publication. The most frequently reprinted of his works were the nondramatic poems – the erotic *Venus and Adonis* and the more moralistic *The Rape of Lucrece*. The *Sonnets*, which appeared in 1609, under his name but possibly without his consent, were less successful, perhaps because the vogue for sonnet sequences, which peaked in the 1590s, had passed by then. They were not reprinted until 1640, and then only in garbled form along with poems by other writers. Happily, in 1623, seven years after he died, his colleagues John Heminges (1556–1630) and Henry Condell (d. 1627) published his collected plays, including eighteen that had not previously appeared in print, in the first Folio, whose name derives from the fact that the printers' sheets were folded only once to produce two leaves (four pages). Some of the quarto editions are badly printed, and the fact that some plays exist in two, or even three, early versions creates problems for editors. These are discussed in the Account of the Text in each volume of this series.

Shakespeare's plays continued in the repertoire until the Puritans closed the theatres in 1642. When performances resumed after the Restoration of the monarchy in 1660 many of the plays were not to the taste of the times, especially because their mingling of genres and failure to meet the requirements of poetic justice offended against the dictates of neoclassicism. Some, such as *The Tempest* (changed by John Dryden and William Davenant in 1667 to suit contemporary taste), *King Lear* (to which Nahum Tate gave a happy ending in 1681) and *Richard III* (heavily adapted by Colley Cibber in 1700 as a vehicle for his own talents), were extensively rewritten; others fell into neglect. Slowly they regained their place in the repertoire, and they continued to be reprinted, but it was not until the great actor David Garrick (1717–79) organized a spectacular jubilee in Stratford in 1769 that Shakespeare began to be regarded as a transcendental genius. Garrick's idolatry prefigured the enthusiasm of critics such as Samuel Taylor Coleridge (1772–1834) and William Hazlitt (1778–1830). Gradually Shakespeare's reputation spread abroad, to Germany, America, France and to other European countries.

During the nineteenth century, though the plays were generally still performed in heavily adapted or abbreviated versions, a large body of scholarship and criticism began to amass. Partly as a result of a general swing in education away from the teaching of Greek and Roman texts and towards literature written in English, Shakespeare became the object of intensive study in schools and universities. In the theatre, important turning points were the work in England of two theatre directors, William Poel (1852–1934) and his disciple Harley Granville-Barker (1877–1946), who showed that the application of knowledge, some of it newly acquired, of early staging conditions to performance of the plays could render the original texts viable in terms of the modern theatre. During the twentieth century appreciation of Shakespeare's work, encouraged by the availability of audio, film and video versions of the plays, spread around the world to such an extent that he can now be claimed as a global author.

The influence of Shakespeare's works permeates the English language. Phrases from his plays and poems – 'a tower of strength', 'green-eyed jealousy', 'a foregone conclusion' – are on the lips of people who may never have read him. They have inspired composers of songs, orchestral music and operas; painters and sculptors; poets, novelists and film-makers. Allusions to him appear in pop songs, in advertisements and in television shows. Some of his characters – Romeo and Juliet, Falstaff, Shylock and Hamlet – have acquired mythic status. He is valued for his humanity, his psychological insight, his wit and humour, his lyricism, his mastery of language, his ability to excite, surprise, move and, in the widest sense of the word, entertain audiences. He is the greatest of poets, but he is essentially a dramatic poet. Though his plays have much to offer to readers, they exist fully only in performance. In these volumes we offer individual introductions, notes on language and on specific points of the text, suggestions for further reading and information about how each work has been edited. In addition we include accounts of the ways in which successive generations of interpreters and audiences have responded to challenges and rewards offered by the plays. The Penguin Shakespeare series aspires to remove obstacles to understanding and to make pleasurable the reading of the work of the man who has done more than most to make us understand what it is to be human.

Stanley Wells

The Chronology of Shakespeare's Works

A few of Shakespeare's writings can be fairly precisely dated. An allusion to the Earl of Essex in the chorus to Act V of *Henry V*, for instance, could only have been written in 1599. But for many of the plays we have only vague information, such as the date of publication, which may have occurred long after composition, the date of a performance, which may not have been the first, or a list in Francis Meres's book *Palladis Tamia*, published in 1598, which tells us only that the plays listed there must have been written by that year. The chronology of the early plays is particularly difficult to establish. Not everyone would agree that the first part of *Henry VI* was written after the third, for instance, or *Romeo and Juliet* before *A Midsummer Night's Dream*. The following table is based on the 'Canon and Chronology' section in *William Shakespeare: A Textual Companion*, by Stanley Wells and Gary Taylor, with John Jowett and William Montgomery (1987), where more detailed information and discussion may be found.

The Two Gentlemen of Verona	1590–91
The Taming of the Shrew	1590–91
Henry VI, Part II	1591
Henry VI, Part III	1591

Introduction

ANTECEDENTS

William Shakespeare's *Richard III* does not stand alone.
It was the last in a series of four connected plays, a
tetralogy, dealing ambitiously with two huge subjects: the
so-called Hundred Years War between the English and
the French (1337–1453), and the civil war in England
between the Houses of York and Lancaster, known popularly as the Wars of the Roses, which came to an end at
the battle of Bosworth Field in 1485 with the death of
Richard III. All four plays were probably written in the
first three years of the 1590s but not necessarily in the
order in which they deal with history. (It is thought, for
instance, that the first part of *Henry VI* was written after
its 'predecessors', the second and third parts.) In this fourth
play, *Richard III*, the horrors often gruesomely dramatized in the first three – the wars against the French in
Henry VI, Part I, and the 'dire division' (*Richard III*, V.5.28)
among the English themselves (the subject of the second
and third parts of *Henry VI*) – come to an exhausted end
in the defeat of the satanically depraved Yorkist, Richard
III, by his God-fearing Tudor antagonist, Henry, Earl of
Richmond, the future Henry VII, grandfather of Elizabeth
I. For the Elizabethans, then, the plays were a kind of

serial in the theatre, with *Richard III* as the culminating
episode in which, after much bloodshed, right finally
triumphed and ushered in the Tudor line of godly
monarchs. It is hardly surprising, given this political
mandate, that Richard himself should be conceived in the
fiendish terms we encounter in *Richard III*.

For modern-day audiences and readers, however,
Richard III usually comes detached from the plays that
supply its pre-history. No doubt this is because it is a much
greater play than they are (though the *Henry* plays have
been persistently underrated) with Richard's part almost
as seductive for actors, audiences and readers as Hamlet's.
And although it is helpful for audiences and readers to
have some knowledge of what went on in the three parts
of *Henry VI* – hence the explanatory prologue written
especially for Michael Bogdanov's English Shakespeare
Company production of *Richard III* in 1988 (available on
video) – it is not an essential requirement for the enjoy-
ment of this final play. As an aesthetic and theatrical experience *Richard III* manages very well on its own. Lines
such as 'Now is the winter of our discontent' and 'A
horse, a horse, my kingdom for a horse' have joined 'To
be or not to be – that is the question' and 'Tomorrow,
and tomorrow, and tomorrow' in the lexicon of all-time
favourite Shakespeare quotations. In short, *Richard III*
may well be closer in quality as well as in length to *Hamlet*
than it is to its immediate predecessor, *Henry VI, Part III*.

Yet, especially for Elizabethan audiences, *Richard III*
does not stand alone in another sense. It came to them
mediated through a host of influences and sources. Its
story of the royal crook-backed ogre that actors loved to
play and audiences to hate had long been established
as a favourite in the pantheon of cautionary tales from
English history, however distorted interpretations of that

history may have been (see Further Reading). It is the sixteenth-century version of today's urban myth with Richard as a bugaboo figure constructed out of tendentious legend rather than real history. Many in Shakespeare's audience would have read his story in the sources that Shakespeare himself used, as they were as popular with the Elizabethan reading public as *Richard III* proved to be with both reading and playgoing publics. (There were five reprints of the 1597 Quarto before the printing of the 1623 Folio. For a discussion of the relationship of Quartos and Folio, see An Account of the Text.) Standing behind Shakespeare's main sources for his play – Edward Hall's *Union of the Noble and Illustre Families of Lancaster and York* (1548) and Rafael Holinshed's *Chronicles of England, Scotland, and Ireland* (1577 and 1587) – lies the enormously entertaining distortion of Richard's real history in Sir Thomas More's *History of King Richard III* (1543). It was so highly regarded by Hall and Holinshed that they quoted chunks of it (always respectfully acknowledging them). A passage chosen almost at random conveys its author's command of a virile English idiom. Here More talks of Richard's desperately bad character:

He was close and secret, a deep dissimulator, lowly of countenance, arrogant of heart, outwardly companionable where he inwardly hated, not letting to kiss whom he thought to kill, dispiteous and cruel, not for evil will always, but often for ambition, and either for the surety or increase of his estate.

One can see even from this short extract just how hard More was on Richard, and his view was endorsed, even exaggerated, by the later writers.

Richard III is a good early illustration of Shakespeare's

habits as a writer, especially his magpie-like tendency to collect bits of stuff from other writers. The play glitters with remnants and influences. Christopher Marlowe's presence, for instance, can be felt in the rhythm of the lines and, more specifically, in the example of a character like Barabas in *The Jew of Malta* (*c.* 1590) who, like Richard, opens his play with a soliloquy. Thomas Kyd's *The Spanish Tragedy*, published in 1592, had been in the London theatres for a number of years and was a useful model for Shakespeare for his adaptation of a Senecan framework. Seneca himself, the Roman playwright and philosopher (*c.* 4 BC–AD 65), is an important influence on *Richard III* (and on *Titus Andronicus*, *Julius Caesar* and *Hamlet*). Behind Kyd and Marlowe looms the tradition of the medieval morality play whose Vice figure, both sinister and comic, is so important for an understanding of the sinister wit of Richard III or of Iago in *Othello* (see Further Reading). John Jowett in his Oxford edition of the play widens the net to include Edmund Spenser's *Faerie Queene* (published in 1590) and traces of Thomas Sackville, Philip Sidney and John Lyly. To take a micro-instance: editors of *Richard III* have established impressive credentials for the range of reading behind the linguistic *tour de force* that is Clarence's dream (I.4.9–63). It is an imaginative fusion and recreation of elements from Seneca, Arthur Golding's translation of Ovid's *Metamorphoses* (1565–7), Thomas Sackville's *The Mirror for Magistrates* (1563, etc.), *The Spanish Tragedy* and, above all, the episode of the Cave of Mammon and the sea-episodes in the first three books of *The Faerie Queene*.

TRAGIC HISTORY

Although, in many senses of the word, *Richard III* does
not stand alone, its protagonist thinks *he* does. 'I am
myself alone', Richard boasts at the end of the third
part of *Henry VI*, the play that comes immediately before
Richard III; and as though to underscore this scandalous
repudiation of family and community Shakespeare
begins *Richard III* with the stage direction, '*Enter
Richard, Duke of Gloucester, alone*'. The sardonic narcis-
sist then delivers one of the most famous soliloquies in
Shakespeare: an irresistible combination of wit, bravado,
self-mockery and scorn for King Edward IV's effete
court. (Richard speaks five soliloquies in all, four of
them in the first three scenes.) The next time we see
him alone onstage after the bravura performances of
Act I the direction reads: '*Richard starts out of his dream*'.
We are now in the fifth act and the soliloquy that he
then delivers, lame and inchoate, measures the distance
we have come from his earlier speeches in Act I, as
though the dream Richard starts out of is everything
that has happened to him since he was 'determined to
prove a villain' (I.1.30).

Richard's tragic trajectory prefigures Macbeth's
written some twenty years later in 1606. Late in *Richard
III* Ratcliffe, a Richard supporter, talks of Richard's
'many doubtful, hollow-hearted friends' (IV.4.435) –
though Ratcliffe is not himself one of them – and Blunt
comments: 'He hath no friends but what are friends for
fear' (V.2.20). As a result of the breakdown of community Richard is forced into an alliance with its marginal-
ized members:

> I will converse with iron-witted fools
> And unrespective boys. None are for me
> That look into me with considerate eyes. (IV.2.28–30)

Richard believes he can only trust those around him who lack the intellectual acumen to see him as he truly is: the dull ('iron-witted'), the disrespectful ('unrespective'), the thoughtless. (It is a measure of Richard's strength of mind that he can speak so objectively about his effect on people who are as intelligent as he is.) Macbeth gloriously expands on this theme:

> And that which should accompany old age,
> As honour, love, obedience, troops of friends,
> I must not look to have; but, in their stead,
> Curses, not loud, but deep, mouth-honour, breath
> Which the poor heart would fain deny and dare not.
>   (V.3.24–8)

In *Macbeth* the poetry of disintegration is equal in power to the poetry of ambition, whereas in *Richard III* the blight that eats away at Richard also corrodes his language. Both plays are tragedies of damnation, and the linguistic falling-off in *Richard III* could simply be a slump in the confidence of Shakespeare writing at the beginning of his career. But there may be another more interesting reason why, as many commentators believe, the last half of the play does not sustain the verve and intensity of the first half. *Richard III* is both a chronicle history play and a tragedy. As the former it is the purgative climax to this series of plays dealing with the Wars of the Roses in which the spirit of fractious individualism, at its most brazenly inventive in Richard, is finally subdued. The play's audiences in the 1590s would have been well aware of this inevitable outcome. As we have seen, Shakespeare's sources constituted popular reading material for many of the London citizenry who came to see Richard Burbage play his namesake in *Richard III*. Yet at the same time *Richard III* is the only chronicle history play in the 1623 Folio to be designated also as a tragedy (not even *Richard II* warranted the accolade apparently). How well, then, in this early play – recent research suggests 1592–3 as a probable date of composition – do the demands of tragedy and chronicle history play cohere?

To begin with, we might notice that throughout the play (but particularly in the second half) the verse is at its flattest when called upon to deliver historical information for, as it were, its own sake (see, for example, III.5.85–91; III.7.5–14; III.7.176–81; IV.2.102–6; IV.4.498–505; IV.4.520–7; IV.5.10–20). Hence the decline in dramatic tension when Shakespeare feels the need in Act III to follow closely Richard's dealings with the London citizenry as recorded in his sources. And hence the elaborate charade that Richard and Buckingham stage for London's citizens in which Buckingham is ordered by Richard to inform the Mayor about the bastardy of Edward's children and how

> Edward put to death a citizen
> Only for saying he would make his son
> Heir to the Crown, meaning indeed his house,
> Which by the sign thereof was termèd so. (III.5.75–8)

The incident described in these undistinguished lines can be found in More and Hall (though not in Holinshed).

At moments like this we might say that the language of the play is buckling under the need to chronicle its history. An argument something along these lines has characterized a great deal of critical commentary on Richard himself (see Further Reading). Many critics picture Richard as somehow unable to break free from the demands of his recorded story. He comes to the play, they argue, shackled by all his previously well-known appearances in works ranging from More and the chroniclers to *The True Tragedy of Richard The Third*, an anonymous English play, published in 1594, but probably composed several years earlier. In all of these appearances Richard exists not only to entertain but to illustrate the workings of a providence that eventually brought Elizabeth I to the throne. As such he has to assume, as we have seen, the demonic characterization of God's scourge; he is there to kill off all those Lancastrians and Yorkists who would have blocked the Tudor line. Without Richard III there would have been no Elizabeth I. It is not for nothing, then, that *Richard III* is full of God-talk, not least, ironically enough, from Richard himself who started talking it early. In *Henry VI, Part II* he threatens Young Clifford: 'you shall sup with Jesu Christ tonight', or if not with him 'you'll surely sup in hell' (V.1.214, 216). 'Jesu' occurs twice in *Richard III*, both times spoken by Richard, once in the first act, and once in that final despairing, Faustian soliloquy in Act V: 'Have mercy, Jesu!' (V.3.179).

Richard III is the second longest of Shakespeare's plays – only *Hamlet* is longer – and some critics think that it wears out its welcome. Even today it is rare to see a completely uncut version in the theatre, and its stage history shows it to be one of the most pillaged of Shakespeare's plays when it is adapted for performance. Characters are liable to disappear – Margaret especially – and anything may go that is not related to Richard's existential tragedy. What tends to get sacrificed is the historical rather than the

tragic (although the two are not always easily divisible).
Without Margaret, for instance, the play's obsessive, ritu-
alized replaying of the events of the three parts of *Henry
VI* largely disappears. What also tends to disappear are
those reflective moments in the play when the nature of
the historical process itself comes under scrutiny. One such
curious, somewhat mysterious moment occurs in an obtru-
sively tangential conversation in III.1.69–88 between
Richard, Buckingham and Prince Edward about the Tower
of London and Julius Caesar (a discussion not mentioned
in the sources). Shakespeare the historian is here also
Shakespeare the historiographer, but Shakespeare as historiographer has little interest for theatre directors – perhaps
rightly so – though considerable interest for literary critics,
as recent work on him demonstrates.

   The dialogue between these three – principally
between Buckingham and Prince Edward – establishes
Edward as one of the first in a long line of voluble,
poignantly astute children in Shakespeare – Macduff's
son in *Macbeth* is one of the best known – whose observations are often dangerously 'Bold, quick, ingenious,
forward, capable' (III.1.155). Through the observations
of Edward here Shakespeare challenges the position he
himself takes in the *Sonnets* and *Measure for Measure*
whereby written 'characters' establish 'A forted residence
'gainst the tooth of time | And razure of oblivion'
(V.1.12–13). Buckingham claims that it is upon record –
that is, it is written down – that Julius Caesar built the
Tower of London. But as far as Prince Edward is
concerned a 'forted residence' can be found just as well
in the oral tradition: even if Julius Caesar's intervention
is not 'registered', it will nonetheless be 'retailed to all
posterity, | Even to the general all-ending day'
(III.1.77–8). Richard quibblingly agrees: 'I say, without

characters fame lives long' (III.1.81). The portentous 'I
say' alerts us to the quibble: Richard's fame will live long
(as Richard III) if the princes, the 'characters', are no
more. Whatever else it may do, this oddly serious, paren-
thetical exchange throws doubt on the authority of the
written record. We have come some way from the obsession in *Henry VI, Part I* with the necessity to record heroic
deeds in order to keep them alive – as the written *Henry
VI, Part I* itself does (though what it also keeps alive are
the characters' acts of treachery, stupidity, arrogance and
lust). Just how unreliable (not to say corrupt) writing can
be is dramatized in another scene in *Richard III* that directors often deem superfluous. Act III, scene 6 consists of
a single speech by a Scrivener who finished writing out
the reasons for Hastings's death before he was accused,
arrested and tried. Yet no one is fooled by this 'palpable
device' (III.6.11), and we can imagine the difference
between what is said (in private) about this sequence of
events – as the Scrivener in his soliloquy privately tells
us – and what is written down. Ironies abound here.
Despite the Scrivener's expostulations he is not only
willing to go along with the deception but, as a profes-
sional writer, takes pride and pleasure in doing the deception well. (Earlier in the play the oral tradition fares just
as badly when the Mayor responds in the manner of the
Scrivener to Richard and Buckingham's oral account of
Hastings's guilt: 'your grace's word shall serve, | As well
as I had seen, and heard him speak' (III.5.61–2).) *Richard
III*, then, dramatizes Shakespeare's growing awareness
of the sinister plasticity of language, written or spoken,
particularly when it is in the service of affairs of state,
when it is dealing with or conveying 'history'.

MYSTERIES

For a play that pivots on an unambiguous contrast between the forces of good and evil, *Richard III* offers readers and performers numerous occasions for different, conflicting interpretative possibilities. In this it differs, I would suggest, from the history plays that precede it, and anticipates the greater work to come. There are mysteries here; at times the characters are provocatively opaque. It is not only language that proves to be plastic. The encounter between Richard and Elizabeth in the fourth act is a good illustration of the open season on interpretation. There is little in Elizabeth's response to Richard's brazen urging that she should act as the go-between in his pursuit of marriage with her daughter to justify his contemptuous belief that she has capitulated. 'Relenting fool, and shallow, changing woman!' (IV.4.431) is his confident verdict on her reticence. Equally, there is nothing that points incontrovertibly to her rejection of his suit, which we hear about casually in the next scene. Shakespeare increases the mysteriousness of the exchange between them by choosing not to dramatize the meeting between mother and daughter. As a consequence Elizabeth's last words to Richard are supremely non-committal: 'Write to me very shortly, | And you shall understand from me her mind' (IV.4.428–9). Lines like these allow the actor much latitude, but many productions make it clear that Elizabeth is toying with Richard. Others, however, make it just as clear that Richard is toying with Elizabeth, so that her change of heart in the next scene is yet another instance of her behaviour as a relenting fool. A popular theatrical tradition takes Richard's view of things by rendering the encounter erotic, making much of Richard's 'Bear her my true love's kiss' (IV.4.430). In Peter Hall's 1963 production, for instance, Elizabeth kissed Richard passionately at this point; in most other productions she runs the gamut of mild distaste to abhorrence. (In some editions Richard's line is followed by the unauthorized stage direction, '*Kissing her*'.)

Minor characters are often impenetrable. Ratcliffe, Lovel and Catesby, Ratcliffe in particular, offer themselves as pliable material for any director. What can be done with Ratcliffe is demonstrated by Jane Howell's 1982 BBC production which plays him as a supremely sinister, omnipresent henchman, the unswervingly loyal yes-man. In the scene where Richard accuses Hastings of treason Shakespeare gives the lords who are seated around the table with him no reaction to the accusation other than to follow Richard on the line, 'The rest that love me, rise and follow me' (III.4.79). We must rely on the expression on their faces, the manner of their leaving, to gauge what they feel about Hastings's fate, and these reactions are in the domain of the director not the writer. Sometimes minor characters say something – often out of the blue – that has no importance for the plot but which in some unstatable way contributes to the occasion. Such are the unexpected remarks by the Second and Third Citizens that end Act II, scene 3: 'Marry, we were sent for to the justices', 'And so was I. I'll bear you company' (46–7). Why they were sent for – why it should be mentioned that they were sent for – is a mystery. Richard himself sometimes says things which are hard to evaluate as to tone and intention. What are we to make of the apparently sincere expression of regret about the treatment of Margaret?

> I cannot blame her. By God's holy Mother,
> She hath had too much wrong, and I repent
> My part thereof that I have done to her. (I.3.305–7)

There is nothing to indicate that this is said ironically, scornfully, contemptuously or with hypocritical piety, though an actor might feel obliged to play it along these lines, especially as, when the stage is cleared, Richard rhapsodizes on the way in which he fools everybody, 'I do beweep to many simple gulls' (I.3.327). He does 'seem a saint, when most I play the devil' (I.3.337). Is Rivers, incidentally, a simple gull in his response to Richard: 'A virtuous and a Christian-like conclusion – | To pray for them that have done scathe to us' (I.3.315–16)? The hesitating dash at the end of the first line suggests, perhaps, that Rivers is neither a simpleton nor a gull. In elusive moments like these much can depend upon the choice of punctuation.

The famous wooing scene between Richard and Anne can be inflected very differently depending on whether Anne is or is not compliant in her responses to him. What she actually says often has a quizzical plasticity: 'To take is not to give' (I.2.202), for instance. What she 'takes' is the ring offered by Richard. How compliant is she in the taking? Just as a piece of punctuation can be important for the meaning of lines, so, too, even more so, can the choice of stage direction. In this edition '*She puts on the ring*'; in the Oxford edition – discussed in Further Reading – the editor hedges his bets, '*She takes the ring on her finger*'. (In the Quartos and Folio, most enigmatically of all, there is no stage direction.) Between 'puts' and 'takes' (and no direction at all) falls the shadow of a number of differently nuanced theatrical productions. In some performances Richard forces the ring on Anne's finger in a symbolic rape; in others Anne willingly takes the ring as though in anticipation of the marriage service. Later Buckingham advises Richard with a line that could almost be a gloss on this incident: 'Play the maid's part: still answer nay, and take it' (III.7.50). Playing the maid's part could be the basis for an actor's entire interpretation of Richmond who, as a character, is pliability itself. The lines he speaks allow him to be played as a colourless representative of historical necessity (as opposed to the vibrant evil of Richard) or as a modest, straight-talking saviour whose language is plain, direct, economical and trustworthy (as opposed to the colourful instability of Richard's language).

And so it goes. Is Tyrrel, Richard's contact for the murders of the princes in the Tower of London, genuinely moved by his recitation of the guilt-ridden account of their murder by Dighton and Forrest, the actual murderers, or is it justifiable to have him repeat their lugubrious sentimentalities semi-sarcastically – as he did in the English Shakespeare Company production in 1988? And what about the relationship between Richard and Buckingham? There is nothing in the text of the play to intimate that Buckingham is closer to Richard than any of the other lords until Richard calls him 'My other self, my counsel's consistory, | My oracle, my prophet, my dear cousin' (II.2.151–2). (Earlier Richard had included Buckingham's name in his list of 'simple gulls' (I.3.327).) In the 1982 BBC performance Buckingham's elevation comes as a surprise to us, though it would not have done so, of course, to anyone familiar with the historical Buckingham (as many in Shakespeare's audience would have been). Going one better, in Michael Bogdanov's ESC production Andrew Jarvis says 'My other self' in a tone of ecstatic incredulity. The revelation comes as much as a surprise to him as it

does to us. In many productions, however, the actors make
it clear by their body language that from the beginning
Richard and Buckingham are in some kind of sinister asso-
ciation. The play seems to be speaking to its exploitation
of the indeterminate when Buckingham, in lines of plan-
gent monosyllables, warns the Bishop of Ely about the
impenetrability of the human heart:

> We know each other's faces; for our hearts,
> He [Richard] knows no more of mine than I of yours;
> Or I of his, my lord, than you of mine. (III.4.10–12)

('I would I knew thy heart' (I.2.192), the hapless Anne
had said to Richard.) A sly little joke emerges from the
fact that Buckingham is talking to the Bishop of Ely whose
heart Buckingham thoroughly knows. But it is certainly
true that Buckingham, as we later learn, does not know
Richard's heart; and it is just as true that the Bishop does
not know Buckingham's heart. Similarly, Hastings does
not know either Buckingham's or Richard's heart, though
he thinks he does. Indeed, Hastings is as innocent and
stupid as the Bishop in his simple idea that Richard is
transparently knowable:

> I think there's never a man in Christendom
> Can lesser hide his love or hate than he,
> For by his face straight shall you know his heart. (III.4.51–3)

Compared with the three parts of *Henry VI*, whose characters generally wear their hearts on their sleeves, *Richard
III* is an intriguingly reticent play. From the actions and
fulminations of Richard in the past – especially in *Henry
VI, Part III* – an Elizabethan audience may well have
anticipated more of the same in *Richard III* (and to quite
some degree they got it). Richard's first appearance in

Henry VI, Part III is just as striking as in *Richard III*. His opening words and action speak volumes for his presence in that play: 'Speak thou for me and tell them what I did' (I.1.16) he says as *'He throws down the Duke of Somerset's head'*. His father conveys the play's ethos and values in his admiring response: 'Richard hath best deserved of all my sons' (I.1.17). Although Hastings's head is brought on stage in *Richard III* – and in some inspired productions kicked around by Richard supporters – Shakespeare by and large declines the invitations in his sources to sensationalize his material. The only death we witness onstage is Richard's own, though Clarence's is begun there, but finished in the offstage malmsey-butt. Most conspicuously, Shakespeare chooses not to stage the deaths of the princes in the Tower of London, perhaps the most notorious murders in English history. Instead we hear of their deaths at two removes: Tyrrel's report of the account of them by the contrite murderers, Dighton and Forrest. The news of Anne's death comes casually at the end of Richard's list of things accomplished, 'And Anne my wife hath bid this world good night' (IV.3.39). With the notable and magnificent exception of the wooing scene between Richard and Anne, Shakespeare also refrains from exploiting the erotic possibilities suggested by his sources. And so, although the person of Jane Shore, mistress to Edward IV and (in this play) Hastings, is mentioned on more than one occasion she is not a character in the play, though this does not prevent modern productions from including her. (She often enters, for example, to give a silent, tender, sometimes passionate demonstration of the preciousness of Hastings's life which he is celebrating in Act III, scene 2.)

The play's openness to differences of interpretation, its ambiguities, hesitations and reticences, have had a

sometimes insidious effect on its life in the theatre. Take
for instance the matter of Richard's death, the only one
we actually witness in its entirety from start to finish,
and therefore in terms of spectacle the climax of the
play. The stage direction is unequivocal: '*Enter King
Richard and Richmond; they fight; Richard is slain.*' It
continues: '*Retreat and flourish. Enter Richmond, the Earl
of Derby bearing the crown, with divers other lords.*'
(Versions of these directions are to be found in all the
Quartos and the Folio.) Richmond then says: 'God and
your arms be praised, victorious friends! | The day is
ours; the bloody dog is dead' (V.5.1–2). The bloody dog
has clearly been put down in single combat by his polar
opposite, the kingly lion Richmond. But many productions will not have it so. In the modern era, directors,
perhaps understandably suspicious of Tudor myth-
ologizing, often find the original texts' instructions old-
fashioned. Perhaps influenced by a critic like Jan Kott,
they substitute endings much more unsettling. In 1967
at Stratford, Ontario, Alan Bates played an alienated,
Brechtian Richard III. In the final battle, Richard effec-
tively committed suicide by tossing his dagger to the
disarmed Richmond. In the 1982 BBC production Ron
Cook as Richard III is killed at least a dozen times – or
so one would have thought – by a ring of anonymous
halberdiers, but doesn't in fact die until he more or less
runs on to Richmond's sword. Richmond appears out of
nowhere for this cynical *coup de grâce*. In Laurence
Olivier's 1955 film Richard is killed by a mob led by
Stanley with Richmond nowhere to be seen.

COPIOUS EXCLAIMS

Reticence is not the first word that springs to mind, however, in any consideration of *Richard III*. Despite the fact that it has no sub-plot and little comic relief – though the murderers of Clarence are amusing and Richard is witty – the play is almost as long-winded as *Hamlet*. In its longest scene the Duchess asks: 'Why should calamity be full of words?' (IV.4.126). It is so in this play largely because it is expressed by women who only have words at their disposal not deeds. Gone are the days when a character like Joan in *Henry VI, Part I* or the Margaret in *Henry VI, Part II* and *Henry VI, Part III* played the role of Amazonian trull, leading their armies on to the field and, in Margaret's case, displacing her husband, Henry VI, from his rightful place as royal commander. All the women in *Richard III*, and not just the women, are awash with words. Not for them Richard's injunction to Derby: 'What need'st thou run so many miles about, | When thou mayst tell thy tale the nearest way?' (IV.4.460–61). No one tells their tale the nearest way in *Richard III*. Even the children are full of words: 'this little prating York' (III.1.151) is the way Buckingham distinguishes Elizabeth's second son from his brother. 'Be copious in exclaims' (IV.4.135) the Duchess advises Elizabeth. So in the name of amplification Elizabeth is full of words – riveting words – to describe words:

> Windy attorneys to their client's woes,
> Airy succeeders of intestate joys,
> Poor breathing orators of miseries,
> Let them have scope! (IV.4.127–30)

'Let them have scope!' could be considered the linguistic
moral of this play, even though — or perhaps especially
as — they are windy and airy, full of poor breathing. (Still
they may, the Duchess believes, acquire a murderous
density: 'in the breath of bitter words let's smother | My
damnèd son that thy two sweet sons smothered'
(IV.4.133–4).)

Richard himself for much of the play is a confident,
flamboyant manipulator of words of all kinds, as well as,
with Buckingham, an inspired theatrical director. His
language is whimsically eclectic: a combination of
colourful imprecation, complicated metaphor, stately
rhetoric, down-to-earth colloquialism, and those lines of
trenchant, threatening monosyllables that are one of the
hallmarks of Shakespeare's style throughout his career:

> Let me put in your minds, if you forget,
> What you have been ere this, and what you are;
> Withal, what I have been, and what I am. (I.3.130–32)

How breathtaking it is, even late in the play, when Richard
is 'plain': 'Shall I be plain? I wish the bastards dead'
(IV.2.18). When Richard isn't plain he occasionally sounds
like a typical lyric poet of the sixteenth century such as
those found in the standard anthology *Silver Poets of the
Sixteenth Century*. 'Our aery buildeth in the cedar's top |
And dallies with the wind and scorns the sun' (I.3.263–4),
he says in praise of his lineage. Shades of the occasional
pastoral outburst from him in *Henry VI, Part III*:

> See how the morning opes her golden gates,
> And takes her farewell of the glorious sun!
> How well resembles it the prime of youth,
> Trimmed like a younker prancing to his love! (II.1.21–4)

In *Richard III* Richard's example is contagious.
Richmond's style of speaking – usually unadorned and
to the point – takes on a new vitality with Richard as its
subject; he describes Richard, for example, as the
'usurping boar' who 'Swills your warm blood like wash,
and makes his trough | In your embowelled bosoms'
(V.2.9–10). Richard seems to bring out the language in
people; he is the cause of metaphor in other men. (And
women, too, when we think of the change in Anne's
language in Act I, scene 2 from stately lament to colloquial execration.)

  Richard III is, then, in fits and starts an impressive
literary artefact. And an equally impressive piece of
theatre. How impressive may best be sampled in scenes
that seem to come directly from Shakespeare's imagination. The famous wooing scene, Act 1, scene 2, between
Anne and Richard has often aroused questions as to its
plausibility. As with Iago's seduction of Othello there has
been an inclination in the critical literature simply to
accept the whole unlikely performance as a theatrical
given, a convention of the drama that bypasses the need
to be psychologically convincing. Yet a response to the
power and passion of its writing and to what the actors
do with their bodies makes it just as easy to bypass any
dependence on convention and rely in the main on those
windy attorneys to their client's woes, the words. There
need be no willing or unwilling suspension of disbelief.
A look at this scene's artistry might persuade us that
Richard III is at its finest when it is at its most fictional,
untethered to historical obligation. In establishing its
powerful evocation of a claustrophobic sensuality, we
notice how the vocabulary of this scene is full of body
parts: lips, eyes, tongues, cheeks, mouths, throats, shoulders, nails, knees, hearts, hands. And of what these parts

do: eyes that pour a 'helpless balm' (I.2.13) or 'kill me
with a living death' (I.2.152); hands that 'made these holes'
(I.2.14); mouths and tongues that curse, exclaim and
moan; faces that blush; nails that rend beauty. Such an
emphasis climaxes in action, in a startling *coup de théâtre*,
when Anne spits in Richard's face which he then gallantly
turns into an erotic intimacy: 'Never came poison from
so sweet a place' (I.2.146). Even Anne's attempt to redi-
rect his meaning – 'Never hung poison on a fouler toad'
(I.2.147) – reinforces the intimacy of the gesture as
Richard presumably has not as yet wiped away Anne's
saliva which must be hanging there for the audience to
see (or for some of them anyway) as it was in Bogdanov's
1988 ESC production: Andrew Jarvis in 1988 savoured
it on his extended tongue. (Antony Sher in 1984 at
Stratford-upon-Avon made much of this moment,
running his finger through the saliva then wiping it on
Anne's face and her half-exposed breasts). It is a quite
extraordinary moment in the play, a startling breakdown
in aristocratic decorum. (Olivier was so enamoured of it
that he had Claire Bloom spit on him twice, and in
Bogdanov's production Anne spits on Richard again when
she appears as a ghost in the fifth act.)

Is it so surprising, then, given this emphasis on the
concupiscent flesh, in language and in action, that Richard
should successfully switch the subject from the body as
antagonist to the body as erotic performer: 'Teach not
thy lip such scorn; for it was made | For kissing, lady,
not for such contempt' (I.2.171–2)? And Richard's invitation to Anne to kill him with his sword, or to tell him
to kill himself with his sword, takes on an obvious erotic
dimension: 'I lay it naked to the deadly stroke' (I.2.177).
Through all of this, Anne is no passive observer, no mere
speechless victim of a sexual predator. Her opening

invitation to Richard throbs with self-defeating com-
plicity: 'If thou delight to view thy heinous deeds, |
Behold this pattern of thy butcheries' (I.2.53–4). Olivier
reinforced the compliance factor in this scene by having
Richard kiss Anne passionately twice (to match the
number of times she spits on him in his production) when
he asks her to 'Bid me farewell' (I.2.222). In *The Taming
of the Shrew* Shakespeare exploits the comedy of a
knowing collusion on Katherine's part with Petruchio's
demands; here, the antiphonal exchanges between Anne
and Richard are begun by Anne when she responds to
Richard's 'Lady, you know no rules of charity' with
'Villain, thou know'st nor law of God nor man' (I.2.68,
70). Responding to his cues, echoing his constructions,
she seems to be a more than willing partner in their verbal
dance. Or if not completely willing, she cannot seem to
prevent what she says from betraying what she means.
So when Richard seizes upon her curse that he know no
rest in his bedchamber with 'So will it, madam, till I lie
with you' (I.2.113), Anne's reply 'I hope so' (I.2.113–14)
is treacherously equivocal.

In its masterly control of tone and mood, the scene
anticipates later encounters in Shakespeare between lovers
in crisis: between Othello and Desdemona, Antony and
Cleopatra, Leontes and Hermione in *The Winter's Tale*.
It is not surprising perhaps in *Richard III* that Anne should
return obsessively to this scene of courtship, recounting
it again and at length in Act IV, this time to the supportive
women around her. When Elizabeth begs Anne not to
wish herself harm, Anne can only recount the encounter
as an overwhelming illustration of why she should do so.
And as though anticipating future critical controversy,
Shakespeare seizes on the occasion to spell out the reason
for Anne's compliance: 'Within so small a time, my

woman's heart | Grossly grew captive to his honey words'
(IV.1.78–9). That 'so small a time', especially, reveals
Shakespeare's understanding of the magical element in
the encounter; it is a phrase that Othello could well
have used in describing how quickly he succumbed to
Iago. Yet there is an element here of special pleading
even though Anne is accusing herself; she could accuse
herself of a greater degree of cooperation from her
woman's heart – as we have witnessed – than merely
having allowed it to fall under the spell of Richard's
seductive words.

As in the *Henry VI* plays, the political and the sexual
are inseparable. Hastings is guilty of treason, it seems,
because of his liaison with Jane Shore: this is his 'open
guilt' (III.5.30) according to Richard – 'his conversation
with Shore's wife' (III.5.31). Buckingham chimes in: 'I
never looked for better at his hands | After he once fell
in with Mistress Shore' (III.5.49–50). One of Richard's
hastily assembled accusations against Edward is his
'bestial appetite in change of lust' (III.5.80). Anne's praise
of her husband Edward, Henry VI's son, at the expense
of Richard, sounds, given her admiration for conventional masculine virtues, like praise of Richard at the
expense of Edward: 'O, he was gentle, mild, and virtuous!'
(I.2.104). When Richard appeals to his troops just before
Bosworth he does so in terms of their virility: 'Shall these
enjoy our lands? Lie with our wives? | Ravish our daugh-
ters?' (V.3.337–8). And when he tells Catesby to tell
Hastings that the latter's enemies 'are let blood at Pomfret
Castle' (III.1.183), he suggests that the news of this blood-
letting should be celebrated erotically: Hastings should
'for joy of this good news, | Give Mistress Shore one
gentle kiss the more' (III.1.184–5). In this play murder
and violence are frequently eroticized; but they are also,

in Richard's mind, coupled with other appetites. When
he is on the brink of demanding Hastings's head he asks
the Bishop of Ely for strawberries (this incident can be
found in More); in the 1921 production at Stratford-upon-
Avon Balliol Holloway ostentatiously sorted out the most
luscious of the strawberries immediately after the
command, 'Off with his head!' (III.4.76). Hastings's head
and Richard's dinner inhabit the same menu: 'Now by
Saint Paul I swear | I will not dine until I see the same!'
(III.4.76–7). (In some performances of the 1989 Royal
National Theatre production, Ian McKellen tasted the
blood from Hastings's severed head.) When Richard
wants to hear the details of the young princes' death, it
is as an after-supper story: 'Come to me, Tyrrel, soon at
after-supper, | When thou shalt tell the process of their
death' (IV.3.31–2). (Richard was avid for such detail in
Henry VI, Part III.) Edward cannot bear to hear of his
father's death: 'O, speak no more, for I have heard too
much' (II.1.48). Richard replies: 'Say how he died, for I
will hear it all' (II.1.48–9). Death seems, then, in this
play to stimulate appetite and aid digestion (at least in
Richard's case). And reproduction. In a spectacularly
inappropriate image, Richard transmutes the substance
of Elizabeth's accusation, 'Yet thou didst kill my children', into a kind of compost in Anne's womb to enable
his seed to germinate: 'But in your daughter's womb I
bury them, | Where, in that nest of spicery, they will
breed | Selves of themselves, to your recomforture'
(IV.4.423–5).

Nests of spicery would not be an inappropriate image
to describe many of Richard's sentences. But there is
another kind of language in the play that opposes itself
to that spoken by him. Monumental, liturgical, incanta-
tory, the vehicle of oracular pessimism and painful

memory, it flows unstoppably from the mouths of the
women characters in the play. Either singly or as a chorus
they fill the air with lamentation. Their grave interrup-
tions are irresistible even for Richard whose 'bustle'
(V.3.290) – a word used in Shakespeare only by Richard
– must make way for their intrusive moralizing. He
cannot drown out, for instance, their roll-call of the
names of the persons he has had murdered – 'gentle
Rivers, Vaughan, Grey', 'kind Hastings' etc. – though
he tries:

> A flourish, trumpets! Strike alarum, drums!
> Let not the heavens hear these tell-tale women
> Rail on the Lord's anointed. Strike, I say! (IV.4.149–51)

The tell-tale trademark of the women's railing is its
ponderous mass – both imposing and oppressive – as in
the Duchess's lamentation earlier in this scene:

> Dead life, blind sight, poor mortal-living ghost,
> Woe's scene, world's shame, grave's due by life usurped,
> Brief abstract and record of tedious days,
> Rest thy unrest on England's lawful earth,
> Unlawfully made drunk with innocents' blood!
> (IV.4.26–30)

It is impossible for any actor to speak these lines quickly.
In this particular instance, to make her oratory more
impersonal and all-inclusive, it is not clear to whom the
Duchess is speaking. The frequent insertion in various
editions of the play of the stage direction '*Sits down*'
between lines 29 and 30 makes it seem as though she is
talking to herself. But she could just as well be addressing
Elizabeth. No matter who, really, as they are all examples

of those sententious contradictions: dead lives, blind sights, poor mortal-living ghosts.

When Margaret comes forward to add her voice to the chorus of lamentation, the names of the dead become interchangeable and, for the moment, indistinguishable. Later in the scene we lose our bearings again in a cascading inventory of Edwards: Edward the Prince of Wales, Edward IV, Edward V. One Plantagenet, as Margaret says, quits another, but we are never quite sure who is quitting who, however well we think we know the play. Although the names do of course refer to specific individuals whose stories we have experienced in the tetralogy, and although each woman is being precise in her use of them, the effect of these interchangeable names is to make it seem as though through them we are remembering in a vague and disturbing way dozens of de-individualized deaths, all those hapless victims of the Wars of the Roses. The use of the indefinite article here helps in this effect:

> I had an Edward, till a Richard killed him;
> I had a Harry, till a Richard killed him:
> Thou hadst an Edward, till a Richard killed him;
> Thou hadst a Richard, till a Richard killed him.
>   (IV.4.40–43)

Shakespeare establishes the connection between women and oracular pessimism early in the play when we first meet Queen Elizabeth, Edward's wife, who refuses to be comforted: 'Would all were well! But that will never be. | I fear our happiness is at the highest' (I.3.40–41). At the death of her husband Elizabeth is suicidal: 'I'll join with black despair against my soul | And to myself become an enemy' (II.2.36–7). As so often in this play, we are dealing here with a masochistic prophet: 'Welcome destruction, blood, and massacre! | I see, as in a map, the end of all' (II.4.53–4). We sense in her, as in Anne, a desire for catastrophe, as though, in an extreme version of the workings of individual conscience, the punishment to come is to be welcomed for the sins of the past. Later in the play Anne is violently masochistic; she wants the crown to be made of 'red-hot steel, to sear me to the brains!', or 'Anointed let me be with deadly venom | And die ere men can say, "God save the Queen!"' (IV.1.60–62). Until she disappears in the middle of the play's longest scene (IV.4), however, it is Margaret who assumes the role of chief avenging Fury, Hecate to the other women's Witches. She tutors them in the art of lamentation, though she has to compete in a sometimes almost comic manner with Richard's mother, the Duchess of York, who believes herself to be in this area the role model for others: 'I am your sorrow's nurse, | And I will pamper it with lamentation' (II.2.87–8). The women pamper each other with lamentation in a curious kind of fractious solidarity. At one point Margaret orchestrates the new alliance:

> If sorrow can admit society,
> *Sits down with them*
> Tell over your woes again by viewing mine. (IV.4.38–9)

With an apologetic 'Bear with me!' (IV.4.61), she repeats her *cri de coeur*, 'cloying' (i.e. gorging) herself and us with her extended litany of abuses. However apologetic she may be, she repeats herself again – with variations – in her triumphing over Elizabeth: 'Where is thy husband now? Where be thy brothers?' (IV.4.90).

In some ways Margaret is an awkward, alien presence, and not only for her tormented interlocutors. Directors have no compunction about discarding her as a character. The historical figure of Margaret never left France, the country to which Shakespeare's character returns in Act IV. But it is of course extraordinarily reductive to abandon this Cassandra of choruses, especially for those audiences who have experienced her in the three previous plays of the tetralogy, the only character to appear in all of the plays. As they listen to her strident utterances in *Richard III*, they might well remember that she entered the tetralogy as a purveyor of words, although of a very different kind from those she now speaks. In *Henry VI, Part I* Suffolk is ravished as much by her words as by her beauty: 'Words sweetly placed and modestly directed' (V.3.179). In the next two plays the words are no longer sweet, and are murderously directed. For *Richard III* she establishes a magnificent line in cursing: 'Thou elvish-marked, abortive, rooting hog!' (I.3.227) she says to Richard; 'this poisonous bunch-backed toad' (I.3.245) she says of him to Queen Elizabeth, a vein of invective adopted by the other women, as in Elizabeth's 'That bottled spider, that foul bunch-backed toad!' (IV.4.81). No doubt Richard wishes he had not been prevented by his brother in *Henry VI, Part III* from killing her for the words he finds intolerable in her: 'Why should she live to fill the world with words?' (*Henry VI, Part III*, V.5.44).

By *Richard III* her words have become prescient. After having called up the horrors of the past, Margaret invokes a terrible future for the participants in her son's killing, reserving of course the worst for Richard, 'the troubler of the poor world's peace!' (I.3.220). She wants him — as he becomes — friendless, sleepless, or, if asleep, tormented by bad dreams. But it is her opening curse in this sequence which both taps into the play's deep structure and startles us as to its seeming unlikelihood: 'The

worm of conscience still begnaw thy soul!' (I.3.221).
How can she believe this to be possible if Richard truly
is how she then describes him: 'Thou that wast sealed in
thy nativity | The slave of nature and the son of hell!'
(I.3.228–9)? She leaves the play appropriately enough
after an exchange with Elizabeth about words. 'My words
are dull. O, quicken them with thine!' Elizabeth pleads.
To which on exiting Margaret replies: 'Thy woes will
make them sharp and pierce like mine' (IV.4.125).

CONSCIENCE

The worm of conscience has in fact burrowed deep in
this play, gnawing the souls of many of its characters.
With 'guilt' and 'despair' and, above all, 'God',
'conscience' is a word used more often in *Richard III*
than in any other of Shakespeare's works (apart from a
glut of it in *Henry VIII*). (The commentary in John
Jowett's Oxford edition of the play is stuffed with biblical
allusion and reference.) If 'Conscience is but a word that
cowards use' (V.3.310), as Richard maintains, then the
play is full of cowards. Indeed, it manifests itself most
dramatically in a hesitation, 'some certain dregs of
conscience' (I.4.122–3), before the performance of a
despicable act. It holds up the play's action momentarily
as the women's poetry retards the pace of the play's
spoken word. Some moments are more momentary than
others. When Buckingham asks Richard what should be
done about Hastings, Richard replies: 'Chop off his head!
Something we will determine' (III.1.193). Doesn't
Richard have to pause and change tack in mid-line when
he sees the expression on Buckingham's face? Is this not
a presaging instance of the later time when, as Richard

believes, Buckingham's 'kindness freezes' (IV.2.22) over the projected murder of the princes? And when on this latter occasion in Act IV we think of the delight that both Richard and Buckingham have taken in all that is involved in Richard's evocation of 'bustle', Buckingham's reply not only unexpectedly shatters his characterization but seems to anticipate a change of direction for the whole play. 'Give me some little breath, some pause, dear lord,' he says – no doubt pausing all the while – 'Before I positively speak in this' (IV.2.24–5). Catesby too must pause – even Catesby – when Richard confides to him his chilling plans for Anne, and he incurs Richard's impatience: 'Look how thou dream'st! I say again, give out | That Anne, my Queen, is sick and like to die' (IV.2.55–6).

In what turns out to be a routine move in later Shakespeare plays – Falstaff's anatomy of 'honour' in *Henry IV, Part I* (V.1.129–40), published in 1598, is a much-quoted example – the efficacy of this procrastinating conscience gets a comic treatment. In this instance, the murderers assigned to stab a sleeping Clarence pause in their commission to allow the Second Murderer a prose disquisition on the topic of conscience: ''Tis a blushing shamefaced spirit that mutinies in a man's bosom. It fills a man full of obstacles' (I.4.139–41). Catching for a moment his companion's squeamishness, the First Murderer's conscience too is 'even now at my elbow, persuading me not to kill the Duke' (I.4.147–8). It takes a comic reconsideration by the Second Murderer, as they keep exchanging debating positions, to convince his companion to stay the course. When Clarence wakes up he aligns the pity he spies in the look of the Second Murderer explicitly with the Christian prohibition against murder:

> The great King of kings
> Hath in the table of His law commanded
> That thou shalt do no murder. Will you then
> Spurn at His edict, and fulfil a man's?
> Take heed; for He holds vengeance in His hand
> To hurl upon their heads that break His law.
>   (I.4.198–203)

After they have killed Clarence, it is the Second Murderer who, reverting to type, once again repents: 'Take thou the fee, and tell him what I say, | For I repent me that the Duke is slain' (I.4.280–81). This gesture on his part surely undermines the suggestion by some critics that the murderers are only pretending to be conscience-stricken.

The murderers' comic fluctuations of conscience, and Clarence's serious talk of God, have their echoes throughout the play. Despite the fact that Dighton and Forrest, according to Tyrrel, are 'fleshed villains, bloody dogs' they 'Wept like to children in their death's sad story', overcome 'with conscience and remorse' (IV.3.6, 8, 20) before smothering the princes in the Tower. And what remorse! Unlike their social equals, Clarence's murderers, these two, via Tyrrel – who is, however, quoting them verbatim – reveal an unexpected aptitude for a vein of sentimental poetry caught best by Forrest's lines describing the spectacle of the princes sleeping in each other's arms: 'Their lips were four red roses on a stalk, | Which in their summer beauty kissed each other' (IV.3.12–13). This is comedy of a kind, especially as their poetic flights don't prevent them from carrying out their mission. Tyrrel himself seems almost as moved as his henchmen – though an actor may play it differently – but there is nothing to indicate in what he then says to

Richard that he has any moral reservations about the murders. There are no pauses indicated in the text here, though an actor could convey Tyrrel's disapproval of Richard in the manner in which he speaks lines of a conspicuous neutrality. At all events by the end of the play, in response to Richmond's opening exhortation to the leaders of his army, Oxford can call upon conscience as a kind of secret weapon in the armoury of the rebels: 'Every man's conscience is a thousand men, | To fight against this guilty homicide' (V.2.17–18).

Appeals to, or expressions of, a working conscience are only one of a number of manifestations of the moral high ground that many of the play's characters take or are forced to take. If Richard's 'diffused infection of a man' (I.2.78) has a varied aetiology, symptoms of its opposite – the 'divine perfection' (I.2.75) that Richard claims to see in Anne – are just as varied. It is not just the women characters, for example, who are commentators on the vanity of human wishes, especially the wish for men (and women) to be lords of all they survey. At any given moment both minor and major characters of either sex may swell the ranks of those moralizing on the decadence of the times or on the human condition. Take Brakenbury, for instance: he joins Elizabeth and Margaret in lamenting the distinction between outward glory and inward unhappiness (a familiar theme in Shakespeare's history plays): 'Princes have but their titles for their glories, | An outward honour for an inward toil' (I.4.78–9). Richard himself is a sardonic social commentator, anticipating those Jacobean malcontents Vindice in Thomas Middleton's *The Revenger's Tragedy* (1606) and Malevole in John Marston's *The Malcontent* (1603) who comment bitterly on their corrupt Italian courts. When Rivers, Grey and Vaughan are being taken to their deaths

Vaughan predicts, 'You live that shall cry woe for this hereafter' (III.3.6). (This is the only line that he speaks in the play as a living person; as a ghost he has two lines.) When Hastings contemplates his own peculiar version of the vanity of human wishes he joins this moralizing chorus, addressing England and Richard: 'I prophesy the fearfull'st time to thee | That ever wretched age hath looked upon' (III.4.104–5).

It is in this context that we must read the extended narrative of Clarence's dream (I.4.9–63) which gains added force when we recall that *Richard III* may have been written at the time of one of the worst outbreaks of plague in Elizabethan London. The vanity of human wishes in Clarence's underwater landscape lies strewn in the drowned treasure of 'a thousand fearful wracks' (I.4.24) that takes on a kind of meretricious life and eerie sexuality in contrast with the skeletons of the drowned sailors. While some jewels lay scattered on the seabed, others

> lay in dead men's skulls, and in the holes
> Where eyes did once inhabit, there were crept,
> As 'twere in scorn of eyes, reflecting gems,
> That wooed the slimy bottom of the deep
> And mocked the dead bones that lay scattered by.
>   (I.4.29–33)

A. P. Rossiter's famous essay, 'Angel with Horns: The Unity of *Richard III*', argues that any interpretation of Clarence's dream should include all of the play's major characters, whom he describes as 'desperate swimmers' in the tide of history.

A quasi-comic rendition of the Hastings/Vaughan/ Brakenbury position can be found in the representatives of London's citizenry in Act II. They are the decent counterweights to their criminal social equals, Dighton and Forrest and Clarence's murderers, and their foreboding commentary comes from them as free men unlike that from Rivers and company. (Although, to return to that strange moment at the scene's end, the citizens 'were sent for to the justices' (II.3.46) – perhaps to answer for some criminal act?) We imagine them to have been among those London citizens in the next act, the 'breathing stones' who 'spake not a word' and 'looked deadly pale' (III.7.25, 24, 26) when urged by an angry Buckingham to show their support for Richard. Although all three citizens 'fear 'twill prove a giddy world' as the Second Citizen puts it, it is the Third who is the most outspoken, changing the Second's 'giddy' to 'troublous', and forthrightly condemning his superiors: 'O, full of danger is the Duke of Gloucester, | And the Queen's son and brothers haught and proud' (II.3.5, 27–8). His response to the First Citizen's facile 'All will be well' is a homely version of the aristocratic women's lofty enumeration of signs and portents:

> When clouds are seen, wise men put on their cloaks;
> When great leaves fall, then winter is at hand;
> When the sun sets, who does not look for night?
> (II.3.32–4)

However, he ends piously: 'But leave it all to God' (II.3.45).

Leaving it all to God may well be, in the last analysis, what the play would have us do. Such a fatalistic attitude, however, whether or not dependent on a mysterious final benevolence – especially if it is so dependent – does not sit well with modern critics. Many would like to be able to claim for Shakespeare a secular humanism which this play resists. Instead, the play presses forward inexorably,

religiously, to Richard's despair in Act V in which his
subsequent bravery in battle and renewed colloquial
eloquence, like Macbeth's, remind us of what has been
crushed in the drive to the pax Britannica. 'Crushed' may
be an appropriate word to describe an action of the God
of this play, who is the *deus absconditus*, the hidden,
implacable God of the Old rather than the New
Testament. He is the Calvinist precursor, perhaps, of Jan
Kott's Grand Mechanism, that juggernaut of a historical
process which mows down all before it. God's character
in this play may best be summed up in Dorset's elabo-
rately unfeeling rebuke for Elizabeth's grief over the death
of her husband:

> Comfort, dear mother; God is much displeased
> That you take with unthankfulness His doing.
> In common worldly things 'tis called ungrateful
> With dull unwillingness to repay a debt
> Which with a bounteous hand was kindly lent;
> Much more to be thus opposite with heaven
> For it requires the royal debt it lent you. (II.2.89–95)

For Richard's partner in conspiracy, the Duke of
Buckingham – my other self as Richard calls him – it is
only too clear who has done the crushing. Act V, scene
1 is the last we see of him. It is 2 November, All Souls'
Day, as Buckingham himself portentously notes, the day
when God is petitioned on behalf of the souls of the
faithful dead. And this is the day when Buckingham's
own prediction about his fate comes true at the hands of
the 'high All-seer which I dallied with' (V.1.20). It is a
predestined day, then, one that 'to my fearful soul | Is
the determined respite of my wrongs' (V.1.18–19). (Of
course an impending death tends to focus the mind on

God as it did for Hastings (III.4.96–7) and Rivers
(III.3.17–25).) 'Determined' is another word used more
frequently in *Richard III* than in any other of
Shakespeare's plays and its range of application takes in
Buckingham's belief in manifest destiny and Richard's
in free agency. In retrospect, Richard's confident 'I am
determined to prove a villain' (I.1.30) may be closer in
meaning to Buckingham's than Richard could ever have
imagined.

Richard's other other self – his shadow self – is the
one we experience in the play's last two acts. In the first
three he is in his Machiavellian prime; in the last two he
is a shadow of this former self, and his new state of mind
is heralded in his wife's scornful account of his 'timorous
dreams' (IV.1.84), the product of his own fearful soul.
Rivalling in frequency its theological vocabulary, the
play is full of references to mirrors, glasses, play-acting,
shadows – the vocabulary of the theatre – commenting
self-referentially on Richard's (and Buckingham's) ability
to add 'colours to the chamelion' (*Henry VI, Part III*
III.2.191). In *Richard III* one such performance involves
Richard and Buckingham constructing an elaborate
charade for the benefit of London's Mayor in which
Richard plays the role of unworldly saint, appearing on
the balcony accompanied by two bishops and carrying a
holy book. The bishops are described by Buckingham as
'two props of virtue for a Christian prince' (III.7.95).
('Props' in its theatrical sense is not recorded until 1841;
but 'property' and 'properties' as theatrical terms were
available.) This playlet – casually blasphemous – merges
Richard's two 'shadows': player and other self. His frac-
tured soliloquy in the next act in response to the shadows
visiting him from the past – the ghosts of his victims –
reveals him to have been all along playing a part in a

compellingly theological play heavily influenced by the typology of medieval drama. In this final soliloquy Richard debates with himself, as the Murderers had debated with each other, arguments for and against obeying his conscience. In his case, as in theirs, it doesn't sufficiently beggar his spirit. If it fills him with obstacles, as it did momentarily the Second Murderer, he is too despairing – the ultimate sin – for Jesu to be able to work in him, however much he may desire it. Richard starts out of his dream only to fall back into it as the nightmare in which his kingdom is worth no more than a horse.

His tragic despair, however, is not the play's final word. True to its Tudor obligations, *Richard III* gives us an ending in which the kingly lion, Richmond, with a free and easy conscience speaks the words that Richard is tortured by: 'God', 'sacrament', 'heaven', 'smooth-faced peace', 'smiling plenty', 'fair prosperous days'. (We hear in these last words an echo of Richard's opening soliloquy in which he was so contemptuous of 'this weak piping time of peace', its 'merry meetings' in 'these fair well-spoken days'.) Richmond anticipates the fair and prosperous days of a united England in which the 'White Rose and the Red' make up a 'fair conjunction' (V.5.19–20). An Elizabethan audience would well understand the point of Richmond's insistence on the significance of the legitimacy of his marriage with Elizabeth:

> And let their heirs, God, if Thy will be so,
> Enrich the time to come with smooth-faced peace,
> With smiling plenty, and fair prosperous days! (V.5.32–4)

The 'time to come', that is, of the reigns of Henry VIII and Elizabeth I. But in this final speech the play is just

as true to its obligations as an unsettling work of art as
it is to its function as Tudor propaganda. Richmond's
and the play's last two lines seem perilously fragile, their
blend of empirical statement and personal wish almost
overwhelmed by the nagging worry in the lines that
expansively introduce them:

> Abate the edge of traitors, gracious Lord,
> That would reduce these bloody days again
> And make poor England weep in streams of blood!
> Let them not live to taste this land's increase
> That would with treason wound this fair land's peace!
> Now civil wounds are stopped, peace lives again;
> That she may long live here, God say amen! (V.5.35–41)

Given this rhetorical structure, God's 'amen' – his 'let
that be so' – may be as problematic in the long term as
Richard's 'Have mercy, Jesu' was in the short. Indeed,
although Shakespeare did not live to see it, the civil
wounds were reopened with the onset of the English Civil
War in 1642 making poor England, as Richmond
presciently feared, weep again in streams of blood.

Michael Taylor

The Play in Performance

Richard III has one of the longest uninterrupted performance histories in the Shakespeare canon. Yet for much of that theatrical life *Richard* was really only Richard, and he was more alone onstage than Shakespeare ever proposed. The chief architect of his isolation was Colley Cibber, whose adaptation sustained the play's popularity on the English stage for almost two centuries, from 1700 to 1870. Cibber fashioned the piece into Richard's private tragedy. Removing its historical dimension, he replaced 80 per cent of the original with material, partly drawn from other Shakespeare plays, that dramatized an inner struggle between Richard's villainous ambition, fed by deprivation and jealousy, and his troubled virtue. No wonder, then, that David Garrick (1741) and Edmund Kean (1814) played Cibber's Richard as if he were Macbeth.

Cibber's influence survived the return to Shakespeare's text. Actor-managers such as Henry Irving (Lyceum Theatre, 1877) proudly revived the 'authentic' Shakespeare, but they shaped his words to Cibber's frame and held the dramatic focus firmly on Richard – the role, after all, that most of them chose to play. Chronicle detail was minimized; scenes of court wrangling in which Richard did not feature were removed; out went the figures of the citizens and Scrivener, along with

the seemingly anachronistic interventions of Queen
Margaret, a role which was rarely seen on a regular basis
until the 1960s (Irving restored her, briefly, in his 1897
revival). The ghosts spoke solely to Richard, and
appeared more as the promptings of his conscience than
heralds of an inevitable history. Waking from this nightmare, Irving's Richard fell to his knees and, dropping his
hands as it were unconsciously about a crucifix, spoke an
edited version of his soliloquy (V.3.178–207) as prayer.
Nothing of Richard's pitiless self-condemnation at this
point was heard.

Cibber's shaping of the play as Richard's tragedy dominated the first half of the twentieth century. Laurence
Olivier's famous interpretation of the role (New
Theatre, 1944; and subsequently released on film in 1955)
retained elements of Irving's tragic pointing, such as
looking on a crucifix (his sword-hilt) as he died. His film
script also cut the 'conscience' speech, and closed the
scene with Richard's cry, 'Have mercy, Jesu!' (V.3.179),
hanging in the air. Like Irving, Olivier reduced the
female figures, cutting Queen Margaret (played in the
1944 production by Sybil Thorndike) and limiting the
contributions of Queen Elizabeth and the Duchess of
York. Richard dominated the action, drawing the audience in to his peep-show world, literally sharing with
them his point of view.

The more that Richard's private story drives the
textual adaptation, however, the more chance there is
that the political motivation for his duplicity disappears.
If his victims become silent dupes, his villainy can seem
disproportionate to any threat they pose. By the turn of
the century, this Richard-centred tradition had so
narrowed the play's dramatic focus that some revivals

came close to one-man melodramas, and the role of Richard – the wicked uncle – a vehicle for 'star' turns.

The consequences of war and revolution in the early years of the twentieth century revived theatrical interest in the historical moment portrayed in Shakespeare's first tetralogy. *Richard III* in particular was seen to mark an equivalent turning point in history, from feudal to Renaissance thought. This gave rise to a wider range of interpretations, and to playing more of Shakespeare's text. In examining the play's historical context, productions increasingly alluded to contemporary issues, with adaptation and interpretative choices shaping the action variously as modern political allegory or secular morality play. Thus the tragedy became that of a community, rather than of a single man.

In politically inflected stagings, the play's structural symmetry is often emphasized. A memorable metaphor for this archetypal rise and fall was the blood-soaked staircase which dominated the stage in Leopold Jessner's production at Berlin's Staatliches Schauspielhaus in 1920; an image later taken up in the writings of Jan Kott (see Introduction, p. lv). A similar concept of political history as a vicious and potentially immutable cycle informed interpretations which teamed *Richard III* with Shakespeare's *Henry VI* plays, either in full or heavily adapted form. More or less detailed systems of doubling traced the recurring figures and situations across the first tetralogy, in productions directed by Jane Howell (BBC television, 1982), Michael Bogdanov (English Shakespeare Company, 1988), Adrian Noble (Royal Shakespeare Company, 1988) and Michael Boyd (RSC, 2001); and Peter Hall staged John Barton's three-play adaptation of the same texts, *The Wars of the Roses* (RSC, 1963), on a single metal set – the great steel cage of war.

Tracing the retributive pattern back into the Roses wars in this way clarifies the discontented past that animates Richard and Margaret. It presents Richard's tyranny as the political legacy of his Yorkist and Lancastrian forbears, mapping the play's moral hinterland, and helping to explain the women's score-chart of dead sons (IV.4.39–78). Placing Richard within chronicle history as last in a line of ambitious politicians, each of the cycle productions underplayed his physical handicaps, while some directors reinforced his place in the clan by casting boyish-looking actors in the role (Ian Holm, RSC, 1963; Ron Cook, BBC, 1982; Anton Lesser, RSC, 1988; and Aidan McArdle, RSC, 2001). Richard's personal magnetism was now supplemented by the intimidatory systems of *realpolitik*, with spies and henchmen – Ratcliffe, Catesby and Lovel – eavesdropping on the citizens (RSC, 1988), silently commanding Richard's stormtroopers (RSC, 1963), assassinating his enemies in secret (ESC, 1988), and always responsive to Buckingham's surreptitious onstage control. The political partnership, and obvious rivalry, between Gloucester and Buckingham reached something of a crisis with Buckingham's vow to woo the London citizens, 'As if the golden fee for which I plead | Were for myself' (III.5.95–6). Noble (RSC, 1988) cut the Scrivener's scene which follows, to leave his uneasy Richard alone onstage awaiting the ambitious Duke's return.

Scenes once regularly cut in performance – those of the Scrivener (III.6) and the citizens (II.3) – now came into their own as voices of the silent but observant commons, bearing the same witness as they do in Shakespeare's sources to the public tragedy. Characterizing these citizens as learned professionals allows productions to imply something of their fearful complicity in Richard's rise: Noble made them lawyers; in 1998 (Elijah Moshinsky,

RSC), they were clerics; and in 2001 (Boyd, RSC), the optimistic Second Citizen was the undercover Catesby himself.

By adding a section of pastiche verse at the end of Act IV, scene 1, John Barton's adaptation (RSC, 1963) matched this public unease with rising discontent at court, as the Bishop of Ely and Lord Stanley began a counter-plot against Richard, with the Queen's consent. It was this establishment of a positive, proto-democratic process, centred on Richmond, that moved Hall's interpretation away from Kott's image of history's destructive mechanism with which the cycle had begun.

Queen Margaret is often made the agent of this cyclical history. Indeed in 1975 (Barry Kyle, RSC) and 1979 (Robert Strurua, Rustaveli Theatre Company), she stage-managed and directed the action. In 2001 (Boyd), she carried the burden of a dead past with her, in the form of a sack containing her son Edward's bones. As in the 1963 production, this Margaret represented an anachronistic feudalism that eventually gave way to trust in the rational structures of good government promised by the new king's reign. But in 1963 the closing moments left some room for doubt, as the departing Richmond dragged his sword across the metal floor. It was a pointed warning that the long-lived peace, for which he had just prayed, might be some time coming. Equally ambiguous have been Margaret's appearances at Bosworth, either distracting Richard from Richmond's deadly blow (Sam Mendes, RSC, 1992), or watching side-stage as Richmond claims victory (Moshinsky). In 1975 (Kyle), she helped 'dead' Buckingham with the costume change that brought him back as Richmond; a doubling hint that the new regime would differ little from the last.

As politician, Richard represents unfettered ambition for power. Other productions, however, have cast him as a victim of the beliefs and expectations of a dysfunctional society, whose failings he exposes and exploits. In this interpretation, Edward's court becomes a troubled world struggling with post-war change: colour-coded costumes denote potentially disturbing factional loyalties (Glen Byam Shaw, Shakespeare Memorial Theatre, 1953), and ostentatious materialism (Terry Hands, RSC, 1980) or excessive icon-worship (Hands, RSC, 1970) bespeak an underlying malaise.

Where political readings frequently minimize Richard's physical handicaps, the secular morality play underlines his obvious non-conformity, and thereby draws attention to society's taboos. In Hands's 1970 production, the court reacted to Richard's first appearance with some horror, running from the stage in fear; in his 1980 version, Richard's body twisted into painful incapacity as his opening words described his physical exclusion from the peacetime court. It was blinkered victimization by those from whom he had learned his perverse view of life that set each of these Richards upon villainy.

Some productions (Hands, 1970 and 1980; Mendes, 1992) extended their examination of the marginal and demonized to include the roles of women in a patriarchal world. The 'honey words' which captivate Anne in IV.1.79 release emotions stifled by public expectations and constraints – the arranged marriage, the young widow's formal grief; a masked life indicated in Richard's exposure of a red dress beneath Anne's mourning black (Hands, 1980). The gradual softening of their exchanges in this production suggested that each had found some temporary consolation in the other; that Richard knew her vulnerabilities because they were his own.

Images of childhood happiness came with the use of children's toys in a nursery setting for Act II, scene 4 (Noble, 1988), and in gifts brought by the women to the Tower in Act IV, scene 1 (Hands, 1980 and Noble, 1988), making the killing of the princes as much an act of jealousy on Richard's part as political expediency. In 1992 (Mendes), Tyrrel brought Richard news of the princes' deaths with the delivery of a parcel containing miniature sets of pyjamas. In a gesture at once perverse and wistful, Richard held up one of the jackets and sniffed it, the long slow intake of breath an attempt to capture something of a childhood he had never known.

Where interpretations portray Richard as the victim of a loveless society, his mother's curse (IV.4.184–96) becomes significant, particularly if the final encounter with Elizabeth (IV.4.197–431) is cut. David Troughton's Richard (Steven Pimlott, RSC, 1995) listened to his mother as he lay, foetus-like, his head in her lap, and his mouth opening into a silent scream at the rejection. It is a curse born of the paradoxical status of women in Edward's patriarchal world; powerless except in bearing children, yet guilty for having wombs that bring forth flawed fruit; widowed onlookers more than players in politics – 'Brief abstract and record of tedious days' (IV.4.28). The restoration of Richard's lengthy dialogue with Elizabeth in the second half of the last century gave voice and force to the woman's point of view: her skilled rhetoric driven by a depth of grief and anger at least equal to his; her deployment of the unexpected – as in the kiss which Frances Tomelty's Elizabeth stole from Antony Sher's shocked Richard (Bill Alexander, RSC, 1984) – leaving him as uncertain about the future as one of his own victims would have been.

Recent years have seen innovative productions stimu-
lated by the play's playfulness. On stage and screen,
directors have welcomed those structural inconsistencies
and interpretative ambiguities which challenge unitary
readings of this play (see Introduction, pp. xxxi–vii).
Robert Strurua's production for the Rustaveli Theatre
Company of Georgia (Edinburgh Festival, 1979) drew
on Brecht and Bakhtin to play up its carnivalesque grotes-
query, with Richard (Ramaz Chikhavadze) as a gargoyle
toad mocking history. *Richard III* has often seemed uneasy
with its subject, showing Richard as a legendary protagonist whose historical identity is always and already out
of his control – the premise of Al Pacino's film, *Looking
for Richard* (1996).

In 1984 (RSC) and 1991 (Royal National Theatre)
respectively, Antony Sher and Ian McKellen played
virtuoso Richards in the Olivier vein. Each manipulated
disability magnificently: Sher's 'bottled spider' figure spun
about the stage on crutches, pinning victims in his pincer-
claws; McKellen, a gentleman-officer with his left torso
paralysed, literally ran his villainous life single-handedly.
But what set these acclaimed performances apart from
the solo tradition discussed earlier, was that the
surrounding productions gave space to the text's historical dimension in an equally self-conscious, and ironically theatrical, way. For example, William Dudley's
design in 1984 put seemingly inconsistent aspects of the
play's dramatic architecture on the stage. The setting
combined the iconographies of history and of myth, with
a pastiche neo-gothic cathedral inhabited by Sher's
diabolic Richard; a Victorian picture-stage reconstruction of medieval history, ironized by the pseudo-morality
figure of the spider-king.

The English Shakespeare Company's modern dress

production (Bogdanov, 1988) staged the Richard/ Richmond battle anachronistically, transforming it into a chivalric conflict between good and evil, with medieval armour, slow motion, and an orchestral score. It was an artful image, on which the media-savvy Richmond's victory press conference (an edited V.5) then cast an ironic light.

In its opening moments, Pimlott's production (1995) hinted at an alternative account of Richard's history. Standing at the stage edge and about to address the audience, Richard was interrupted by the court processing across the balcony behind him. Prompted back, it seemed by this, to the official script, he turned to entertain his onstage audience with the famous opening lines (I.1.1–13), delivered in court jester style. His subsequent anger (confided to the audience in lines 14–40) was aimed as much at this pre-scripted history as against a court which took him for a fool. Here was *Richard III* as play-in-play, a metadramatic framework picked out in Thomas Hoheisel's design, where multiple performance spaces outlined the play's different concepts of time. The Richard/Richmond fight was replaced by their respective battle orations (V.3.315–42; 238–71), the intercut voices competing for public attention on history's stage. Richard did not die as such. Running out of words, the actor (David Troughton) simply stood upright, relaxed the body shape which had defined his Richard, and moved aside, ceding role and stage to his successor. Finally, his slow handclap led the audience's applause.

The play's place in the Richard III legend was recognized in Richard Eyre's production (Royal National Theatre, 1991) – itself the inspiration for Richard Loncraine's 1996 film. Eyre interwove two historicist readings: one which updated the action to 1930s England, portraying Richard as a leading pro-fascist aristocrat; and one in which symbols and images taken from the play's stage and cinematic afterlife underlined its own role in history's myth-making process. Something of this ironic double vision survives in Loncraine's film, which counterpoints the realist Richard/Hitler parallels with allusion to Hollywood's gangster legends.

Inventive, smaller-scale productions have responded to the play's ambiguities by literally giving audiences more than a single point of view: setting the action in the round (Kyle, 1975) or in various transverse stagings (Barrie Rutter, Northern Broadsides, 1992); putting both actors and audience on the stage (Jon Pope, Glasgow Citizens' Theatre, 1988); or playing with, through, and on ropes above the spectators (Boyd, 2001). Each production sought a way to foreground the text's diverse dramatic, literary, historical and theological frames.

Richard III challenges modern actors and directors in the same way that it challenged Colley Cibber three centuries ago: the text is long; it demands vitality, flexibility and stamina in the actor playing Richard; the historical context is unfamiliar to most audiences; and the text itself seems structurally inconsistent, with contrasting linguistic styles and dramatic modes. The play's performance history shows that some directors see these challenges in terms of choices; with the principal choice being either to cast and cut the play as a 'star' vehicle for a virtuoso Richard, and risk the deflationary effect when the history turns against him in the later acts (see Introduction, p. lvi), or to play it as an ensemble piece addressing social issues and risk sacrificing some of Richard's comic force. Refusing such stark choices, a third directorial approach has been to cast theatrically powerful Richards within productions that deliberately draw out the text's structural shifts and inconsistencies, and to reinforce its theatrical and literary self-consciousness in both the staging and design. Not surprisingly, this approach plays best when audiences are familiar with the text.

The rich variety of interpretations outlined here attests to the continuing popularity of this most busy villain, to the enthusiasm of companies to meet the challenges of the play and to the willingness of actors and directors to re-examine theatrical precedent and convention by turning afresh to what remains an intriguing text.

Gillian Day

Further Reading

All editions of *Richard III* have had to come to terms
with the provocative, dismaying and stimulating existence of several states of the text; especially the first
Quarto of 1597 and the 1623 Folio (see An Account of
the Text). Controversy continues to swirl round the
possibility of establishing a 'definitive' text. (*Richard III*
is not, of course, unique in this respect.) Kristian Smidt's
*'The Tragedy of King Richard the Third': Parallel Texts
of the First Quarto and the First Folio with Variants of
the Early Quartos* (1968) lays out the problem in all its
entertaining complexity in one convenient volume. Peter
Davison comprehensively edits *The First Quarto of
'King Richard III'* (1996) in the New Cambridge
Shakespeare in the belief that the differences between
the two original texts can be put down in the case of
the Quarto to a 'very tight recasting for a small number
of players'. Janis Lull's follow-on volume in the New
Cambridge Shakespeare (1999), a synthetic edition of
Richard III, refrains from adopting most of Davison's
well-argued readings from the Quarto; she relies (as has
traditionally been the case) on the Folio. John Jowett's
edition in The Oxford Shakespeare (1999) follows the
example of Davison – relegating the unique Folio
passages to an appendix, for example – in the belief,

persuasively argued, that the Quarto was probably a later text and a more performance-oriented one than the Folio.

Examples of further reading these days should include examples of further viewing. A number of videos and films also offer parallel texts of *Richard III* of varying degrees of iconoclasm. One instructive pairing is Laurence Olivier's film version in 1955 and Ian McKellen's forty years later. Both actors take huge liberties with the text, most notably, and traditionally, focusing on Richard at the expense of the women characters (especially Margaret) thereby playing fast and loose with Shakespeare's grand design. McKellen's film, though, has all the advantages of an extra forty years of technological advances. Set in an England of the late 1930s, its high-gloss, cool impudence makes Olivier's version seem old-fashioned and stagey. The BBC video (1982), directed by Jane Howell, and starring Ron Cook, is closer to Olivier's style than McKellen's (though Cook is no Olivier) and closer also to Shakespeare's text. Michael Bogdanov's English Shakespeare Company's *Richard III* (1988), filmed live at the Grand Theatre, Swansea, is in McKellen country, set in the 1920s, with Andrew Jarvis's Richard a grinning, leering skinhead, incredulously bug-eyed at his own success and others' misconduct. Viewing these highly entertaining, often mischievously wayward interpretations is a rewarding gloss on the profusion of Richards that we find in criticism and textual studies.

And in history. Shakespeare's partisan demolition of Richard's character is highly contestable as we may see, for instance, from Taylor Littleton and Robert R. Rea's anthology *To Prove a Villain: The Case of King Richard III* (1964), which samples the conflicting attempts to solve

the mystery of Richard's character, stretching from
Thomas More's indictment through Shakespeare's to
Josephine Tey's short novel for the defence, *The
Daughter of Time* (1951). As in Shakespeare's play
Richard in history arouses mighty passions, pro and con,
and a couple of them may be enjoyed in Paul Murray
Kendall's edition of More's *History of King Richard III
and Walpole's Historic Doubts* (1965). A more sober re-
assessment of the historical Richard – typical perhaps
of the view of the modern historian – can be found in
Rosemary Horrox's *Richard III: A Study of Service* (1989)
with its dry, sensible, undramatic conclusion: 'Had he
defeated Tudor at Bosworth there is no reason why he
should not have gone on . . . to die in his bed, respected
if not much loved.' The historical texts that Shakespeare
turned to for his version of events can be found most
accessibly in the third volume of Geoffrey Bullough's
Narrative and Dramatic Sources of Shakespeare (1960).
These accounts should not be given the last word, which
belongs to Shakespeare. It almost goes without saying,
then, that the history most pertinent to *Richard III* is in
Shakespeare's *Henry VI, Parts I, II* and *III* which dram-
atize events leading to *Richard III*, involve many of the
same characters, with Richard himself appearing in *Part
II* and becoming a force to be reckoned with in *Part III*.

Not surprisingly, then, Richard III in, outside or
against history is a nagging concern for criticism. What
kind of history though? It used to be the kind exempli-
fied by E. M. W. Tillyard's still highly popular *Shakespeare's History Plays* (1944), written at a time when
reassurance from all quarters (including the literary critical) was a felt need. His Richard III climaxes a tetralogy
whose grand design leads to the divinely ordained establishment of Richmond as Henry VII. Richard III is evil's

last gasp (as it was in Shakespeare's principal sources, More and Hall). Criticism is still circling round this view of things. In *Shakespeare's Arguments with History* (2002) – a revealing, representative title – Ronald Knowles feels obliged to re-encounter Tillyard. Just how providential is a providence, he asks, that includes the deaths of most of the innocents in the play? His book is one in a long revisionist line. Henry Ansgar Kelly's *Divine Providence in the England of Shakespeare's Histories* (1970), for instance, thinks the play's providence is really Tillyard's. In an important book, *The End Crowns All: Closure and Contradiction in Shakespeare's History* (1991), Barbara Hodgdon calls the play 'Shakespeare's pseudo-providentialist history'.

If the history dramatized in *Richard III* is not providential, or even pseudo-providential, what is it? The famous counterview to Tillyard's is Jan Kott's *Shakespeare Our Contemporary* (1964) which took the critical (and theatrical) world by storm. It sees history in Shakespeare's history plays not as providential but as a Grand Mechanism 'that constantly repeats its cruel cycle . . . an elemental force, like hail, storm, or hurricane, birth and death'. But history encounters, one might say, another elemental force in the play, namely Richard himself, who is larger than life, and, some argue, larger than history. Much interesting criticism explores this collision. John W. Blanpied in *Time and the Artist in Shakespeare's English Histories* (1983) thinks of Richard as the artist crushed by time. The play sinks into 'dramatic exhaustion' in which history overwhelms character. Richard '"stays alive" theatrically so long as he does not succumb to that "historical" character that lies waiting for him like a net under an aerialist'. More positively for Graham Holderness in *Shakespeare: The Histories* (1999) by the end of the play the 'delusively untrammelled ego is obliged to acknowledge the network of human and social relations within which its apparently isolated existence is shaped and formed.' For many critics, Richard fights a losing battle against his pre-determined existence. For Linda Charnes in her fascinating, difficult book *Notorious Identity: Materializing the Subject in Shakespeare* (1993), Richard is one of a number of Shakespeare protagonists who inhabit dramatic texts that are 'linguistically saturated with their prior textual histories', who yet 'nevertheless act out a sense that there may still be something undisclosed about themselves ... something that exceeds the containment of their own citationality'. Robert Weimann's essay 'Performance-Game and Representation in *Richard III*', in *Textual and Theatrical Shakespeare: Questions of Evidence*, ed. Edward Pechter (1996), replays the collision as that between 'textually determined representation and performative play-action'. Nicholas Brooke's sparkling essay 'Reflecting Gems and Dead Bones: Tragedy Versus History in *Richard III*', in *Shakespeare's Wide and Universal Stage*, ed. C. B. Cox and D. J. Palmer (1984), widens the discussion to argue that the conflict in the play is really one between genres: tragedy and history. Despite Kott – maybe because of him – Tillyard's position should not be lightly abandoned.

In a well-balanced, generous essay, '*Richard III* Restored', in his *Critical Essays on Shakespeare's 'Richard III'* (1999), H. M. Richmond argues that we can't ignore Tillyard's 'pivotal essay'. And A. P. Rossiter's famous essay, 'Angel with Horns: The Unity of *Richard III*', in *Angel with Horns: Fifteen Lectures on Shakespeare*, ed. Graham Storey (1961), certainly doesn't. Rossiter applies Tillyard's thesis to the play with characteristic wit and deft informality. But there is more to *Richard III* than Richard, and more to its history than Richard's. A rich seam of criticism looks at the play as itself the product of a literary history and as a commentary also on the history of Shakespeare's time. For the former, Wolfgang Clemen's *A Commentary on Shakespeare's 'Richard III'* (1957) is still worth reading for the way in which its scene by scene summary and analysis links Shakespeare's play with what has preceded it. A discussion of the encounter between Anne and Richard, for instance, is followed by a section entitled 'Conversion-Scenes and Wooing-Scenes in Pre-Shakespearian Drama'. And Clemen does the same for the cursing, dream and murder scenes. Harold F. Brooks's '*Richard III*: Historical Amplifications: The Women's Scenes and Seneca', *Modern Language Review* 75 (1980), usefully details the influence of Seneca on the play, while Bernard Spivack's *Shakespeare and the Allegory of Evil* (1958) traces Richard's connection with the Vice figure in the Moralities. He argues that Richard is so moulded by this theatrical tradition that it is difficult to construct a motive for his actions, or at least one that is 'morally intelligible'. *Richard III* is, of course, itself a huge influence on theatrical tradition, as we see in books like Robert Jones's *Engagement with Knavery: Point of View in 'Richard III', 'The Jew of Malta', 'Volpone', and 'The Revenger's Tragedy'* (1986).

Shakespeare's play tells us as much about Shakespeare's time as Richard's. So Phyllis Rackin argues in *Stages of History: Shakespeare's English Chronicles* (1990) as does R. W. Bushnell in *Tragedies of Tyrants: Political Thought and Theatre in the English Renaissance* (1990), which considers the play in 'a period of shifting social classes and capitalist enterprise'. An

interesting essay by Ian Frederick Moulton, '"A Monster
Great Deformed": The Unruly Masculinity of *Richard
III*', *Shakespeare Quarterly* 47 (1996), argues that
'Shakespeare's characterization of *Richard III* functions
as both a critique and an ambivalent celebration of excessive and unruly masculinity and, in so doing, highlights
the incoherence of masculinity as a concept in early
modern English culture'. More narrowly, C. W. R. D.
Moseley's *Shakespeare: 'Richard III'* (1989) suggests that
we need to consider the connection between Richard
and members of Elizabeth's Council; these connections
'make it quite clear that his career and character were
seen as paradigmatic long before Shakespeare wrote his
play'.

If Richard is more than history, the play is more than
Richard. (There are fifty-two speaking parts.) A valuable
strain of criticism counters the critical obsession with
Richard. In 'Bit Parts in *Richard III*', in *Critical Essays
on Shakespeare's 'Richard III'*, M. M. Mahood claims that
the minor characters in this play are not just 'shadows'.
She asks us to consider, for instance, Sir Richard
Ratcliffe's 'aura of physical brutality' or Catesby, who
'is an extension of Richard's intellect, the shadow of his
inventiveness and dissimulation'. Hastings, for Edward
Berry in *Patterns of Decay: Shakespeare's Early Histories*
(1975), is much like Richard 'in his arrogance, his ignorance of his impending downfall, his jovial viciousness'.
On the other hand, as Paola Pugliatti points out in her
fine *Shakespeare the Historian* (1996), the voices of
compassion and pity in *Richard III* are messengers,
murderers, jailers and a scrivener. Donald G. Watson in
*Shakespeare's Early History Plays: Politics at Play on the
Elizabethan Stage* (1990) considers how important faction-
alism is as a cause of events, and he too instances Catesby,

who 'embodies the style of entrapment essential to the intrigue of faction-fighting and sometimes state government'. Much depends on what the actors choose to emphasize in their characters. In '"The plain devil and dissembling looks": Ambivalent Physiognomy and Shakespeare's *Richard III*', *English Literary Renaissance* 30 (2000), Michael Torrey notices how Shakespeare often does not signal what minor characters feel: 'he keeps all the lords silent on the question of Richard's ruse, and consequently the audience can look to nothing other than the lords' appearances in trying to discern what the lords actually think'.

The women in *Richard III* have commanded critical attention especially since the publication in 1980 of *The Woman's Part: Feminist Criticism of Shakespeare*, ed. Carolyn Lenz. In this ground-breaking collection, Madonne Miner's essay, '"Neither mother, wife, nor England's queen": The Roles of Women in *Richard III*' concludes percipiently: 'the argument of *Richard III* moves in two directions. The first insists that women are purely media of exchange and have no value in themselves; the second, overriding the first, insists that even when used as currency, women's value cannot be completely destroyed.' In *Engendering a Nation: A Feminist Account of Shakespeare's English Histories* (1997) Jean Howard and Phyllis Rackin are equally percipient in the way they relate women and tragedy. What we have in *Richard III*, they argue, is the reconstruction of history as tragedy in which the women are ennobled but disempowered; they lose their 'vividly individualized voices and the dangerous theatrical power that made characters like Joan and Margaret potent threats to the masculine project of English history-making'. And Coppélia Kahn's *Man's Estate: Masculine Identity in Shakespeare* (1984) explores the importance of the mother in the formation of masculine identity in Shakespeare's plays – a useful notion for _Richard III_.

However manhandled, _Richard III_ has always been immensely popular on the stage. A number of stage histories attest to this. As Julie Hankey notes in her edition of _Richard III_ in the 'Plays in Performance' series (1981) the play lives because of Richard's role in the theatre. The most ambitious treatment is R. Chris Hassel's _Songs of Death: Performance, Interpretation, and the Text of 'Richard III'_ (1987). Scott Colley's _Richard's Himself Again: A Stage History of 'Richard III'_ (1992) notes that the best interpretations are those that 'have accepted the Greek-like tragic structure of _Richard III_, with its formal rhetoric and its relentless, almost machine-like pattern of retribution'. More narrowly, Gillian Day traces the history of the play in Stratford in her _Shakespeare at Stratford_ volume (2002). And H. M. Richmond in the 'Shakespeare in Performance' series (1989) writes a stern but merited attack on the distortions of the theatrical tradition in its obsession with the 'hypnotically inhuman characterization of Richard', the demon king of pantomime. (He contrasts the more Shakespearian Richards of Marius Goring, Christopher Plummer, Ian Holm and Ron Cook.) At the expense of the women characters and the play's religious context, he argues, too many performances break 'the innate rhythms of the script in order to force it into a false consonance with modern nihilism'. He follows this book with a perspicacious little essay, written in a tone of mild distaste – 'Postmodern Renderings of _Richard III_', in _Critical Essays on Shakespeare's 'Richard III'_ (1999) – taking issue with recent productions of _Richard III_ in which the play is 'once again to be dismantled, redesigned, rebuilt, and reinterpreted in the light of purely modern preferences, concerns, and theories'.

THE TRAGEDY OF
KING RICHARD THE THIRD

The Characters in the Play

KING EDWARD IV
PRINCE EDWARD, of Wales,
   afterwards King Edward V   } sons of King Edward
Richard, Duke of YORK
George, Duke of CLARENCE
RICHARD, Duke of Gloucester, after- } brothers of King
   wards KING RICHARD III   Edward
QUEEN ELIZABETH, wife of King Edward
DUCHESS OF YORK, mother of King Edward and his
   brothers
Lady ANNE, widow of Edward, Prince of Wales, the son
   of King Henry VI; afterwards married to Richard,
   Duke of Gloucester
BOY } Edward Plantagenet and Margaret Plantagenet,
GIRL } children of Clarence
QUEEN MARGARET, widow of King Henry VI
Henry, Earl of RICHMOND, afterwards King Henry VII
CARDINAL BOURCHIER (Thomas Bourchier, Archbishop
   of Canterbury)
ARCHBISHOP (Thomas Rotheram, Archbishop of York)
John Morton, BISHOP OF ELY
Duke of BUCKINGHAM
Duke of NORFOLK
Earl of SURREY, son of Norfolk

Earl of OXFORD

Anthony Woodville, Earl RIVERS, brother of Queen Elizabeth

Marquess of DORSET ⎱ sons of Queen Elizabeth
Lord GREY ⎰

Earl of DERBY (also called Lord Stanley)

Lord HASTINGS

Lord LOVEL

Sir Richard RATCLIFFE

Sir William CATESBY

Sir James TYRREL

Sir Thomas VAUGHAN

Sir James BLUNT

Sir Walter HERBERT

Sir Robert BRAKENBURY, Lieutenant of the Tower

KEEPER in the Tower

Christopher URSWICK, a Priest

John, another PRIEST

Tressel, Berkeley, GENTLEMEN attending on Lady Anne

LORD MAYOR of London

SHERIFF of Wiltshire

GHOSTS of King Henry VI, Edward Prince of Wales, and other victims of Richard

Hastings, a PURSUIVANT

SCRIVENER

PAGE

FIRST MURDERER

SECOND MURDERER

LORDS

MESSENGERS and other attendants

FIRST CITIZEN

SECOND CITIZEN

THIRD CITIZEN

Soldiers, bishops, aldermen

RICHARD
  Now is the winter of our discontent
  Made glorious summer by this sun of York,
  And all the clouds that loured upon our house
  In the deep bosom of the ocean buried.
  Now are our brows bound with victorious wreaths,
  Our bruisèd arms hung up for monuments,
  Our stern alarums changed to merry meetings,
  Our dreadful marches to delightful measures.
  Grim-visaged war hath smoothed his wrinkled front,
  And now, instead of mounting barbèd steeds   10
  To fright the souls of fearful adversaries,
  He capers nimbly in a lady's chamber
  To the lascivious pleasing of a lute.
  But I, that am not shaped for sportive tricks
  Nor made to court an amorous looking-glass;
  I, that am rudely stamped, and want love's majesty
  To strut before a wanton ambling nymph;
  I, that am curtailed of this fair proportion,
  Cheated of feature by dissembling Nature,
  Deformed, unfinished, sent before my time   20
  Into this breathing world, scarce half made up,
  And that so lamely and unfashionable

That dogs bark at me as I halt by them –
Why I, in this weak piping time of peace,
Have no delight to pass away the time,
Unless to spy my shadow in the sun
And descant on mine own deformity.
And therefore, since I cannot prove a lover
To entertain these fair well-spoken days,
I am determined to prove a villain
And hate the idle pleasures of these days.
Plots have I laid, inductions dangerous,
By drunken prophecies, libels, and dreams,
To set my brother Clarence and the King
In deadly hate the one against the other;
And if King Edward be as true and just
As I am subtle, false, and treacherous,
This day should Clarence closely be mewed up
About a prophecy which says that G
Of Edward's heirs the murderer shall be.
Dive, thoughts, down to my soul – here Clarence comes!

Enter Clarence, guarded, and Brakenbury, Lieutenant
of the Tower

Brother, good day. What means this armèd guard
That waits upon your grace?

CLARENCE   His majesty,
Tendering my person's safety, hath appointed
This conduct to convey me to the Tower.

RICHARD
Upon what cause?

CLARENCE   Because my name is George.

RICHARD
Alack, my lord, that fault is none of yours,
He should for that commit your godfathers.
O, belike his majesty hath some intent
That you should be new-christened in the Tower.

But what's the matter, Clarence, may I know?

CLARENCE

Yea, Richard, when I know; for I protest
As yet I do not. But, as I can learn,
He hearkens after prophecies and dreams,
And from the cross-row plucks the letter G,
And says a wizard told him that by G
His issue disinherited should be.
And, for my name of George begins with G,
It follows in his thought that I am he.
These, as I learn, and such-like toys as these   60
Hath moved his highness to commit me now.

RICHARD

Why this it is when men are ruled by women;
'Tis not the King that sends you to the Tower.
My Lady Grey his wife, Clarence, 'tis she
That tempers him to this extremity.
Was it not she, and that good man of worship,
Anthony Woodville, her brother there,
That made him send Lord Hastings to the Tower,
From whence this present day he is delivered?
We are not safe, Clarence, we are not safe.   70

CLARENCE

By heaven, I think there is no man secure
But the Queen's kindred, and night-walking heralds
That trudge betwixt the King and Mistress Shore.
Heard you not what an humble suppliant
Lord Hastings was for his delivery?

RICHARD

Humbly complaining to her deity
Got my Lord Chamberlain his liberty.
I'll tell you what, I think it is our way,
If we will keep in favour with the King,
To be her men and wear her livery.   80

The jealous o'erworn widow and herself,
Since that our brother dubbed them gentlewomen,
Are mighty gossips in this monarchy.

BRAKENBURY

I beseech your graces both to pardon me.
His majesty hath straitly given in charge
That no man shall have private conference,
Of what degree soever, with his brother.

RICHARD

Even so? An't please your worship, Brakenbury,
You may partake of anything we say.
90   We speak no treason, man; we say the King
Is wise and virtuous, and his noble Queen
Well struck in years, fair, and not jealous;
We say that Shore's wife hath a pretty foot,
A cherry lip, a bonny eye, a passing pleasing tongue;
And that the Queen's kindred are made gentlefolks.
How say you, sir? Can you deny all this?

BRAKENBURY

With this, my lord, myself have naught to do.

RICHARD

Naught to do with Mistress Shore? I tell thee, fellow,
He that doth naught with her, excepting one,
100   Were best he do it secretly, alone.

BRAKENBURY

What one, my lord?

RICHARD

Her husband, knave. Wouldst thou betray me?

BRAKENBURY

I do beseech your grace to pardon me, and withal
Forbear your conference with the noble Duke.

CLARENCE

We know thy charge, Brakenbury, and will obey.

RICHARD

We are the Queen's abjects, and must obey.
Brother, farewell. I will unto the King;
And whatsoe'er you will employ me in,
Were it to call King Edward's widow sister,
I will perform it to enfranchise you.   110
Meantime, this deep disgrace in brotherhood
Touches me deeper than you can imagine.

CLARENCE

I know it pleaseth neither of us well.

RICHARD

Well, your imprisonment shall not be long:
I will deliver you, or else lie for you.
Meantime, have patience.

CLARENCE   I must perforce. Farewell.

Exit Clarence with Brakenbury and guard

RICHARD

Go, tread the path that thou shalt ne'er return.
Simple plain Clarence, I do love thee so
That I will shortly send thy soul to heaven,
If heaven will take the present at our hands.   120
But who comes here? The new-delivered Hastings?

Enter Lord Hastings

HASTINGS

Good time of day unto my gracious lord.

RICHARD

As much unto my good Lord Chamberlain.
Well are you welcome to the open air.
How hath your lordship brooked imprisonment?

HASTINGS

With patience, noble lord, as prisoners must;
But I shall live, my lord, to give them thanks
That were the cause of my imprisonment.

RICHARD

　　No doubt, no doubt; and so shall Clarence too,
130　　For they that were your enemies are his,
　　And have prevailed as much on him as you.

HASTINGS

　　More pity that the eagles should be mewed,
　　Whiles kites and buzzards prey at liberty.

RICHARD

　　What news abroad?

HASTINGS

　　No news so bad abroad as this at home:
　　The King is sickly, weak, and melancholy,
　　And his physicians fear him mightily.

RICHARD

　　Now, by Saint John, that news is bad indeed!
　　O, he hath kept an evil diet long
140　　And over-much consumed his royal person.
　　'Tis very grievous to be thought upon.
　　Where is he? In his bed?

HASTINGS

　　He is.

RICHARD

　　Go you before, and I will follow you.　　*Exit Hastings*
　　He cannot live, I hope, and must not die
　　Till George be packed with post-horse up to heaven.
　　I'll in, to urge his hatred more to Clarence
　　With lies well steeled with weighty arguments;
　　And, if I fail not in my deep intent,
150　　Clarence hath not another day to live;
　　Which done, God take King Edward to His mercy
　　And leave the world for me to bustle in!
　　For then I'll marry Warwick's youngest daughter.
　　What though I killed her husband and her father?
　　The readiest way to make the wench amends

Is to become her husband and her father,
The which will I – not all so much for love
As for another secret close intent
By marrying her which I must reach unto.
But yet I run before my horse to market: 160
Clarence still breathes; Edward still lives and reigns;
When they are gone, then must I count my gains. *Exit*

Enter the corse of Henry the Sixth, with halberds to   I.2
guard it; Lady Anne being the mourner, attended by
Tressel and Berkeley

ANNE

Set down, set down your honourable load –
If honour may be shrouded in a hearse –
Whilst I awhile obsequiously lament
Th'untimely fall of virtuous Lancaster.
   The bearers set down the hearse
Poor key-cold figure of a holy king,
Pale ashes of the house of Lancaster,
Thou bloodless remnant of that royal blood,
Be it lawful that I invocate thy ghost
To hear the lamentations of poor Anne,
Wife to thy Edward, to thy slaughtered son   10
Stabbed by the selfsame hand that made these wounds!
Lo, in these windows that let forth thy life
I pour the helpless balm of my poor eyes.
O, cursèd be the hand that made these holes!
Cursèd the heart that had the heart to do it!
Cursèd the blood that let this blood from hence!
More direful hap betide that hated wretch
That makes us wretched by the death of thee
Than I can wish to wolves – to spiders, toads,
Or any creeping venomed thing that lives!   20

If ever he have child, abortive be it,
Prodigious, and untimely brought to light,
Whose ugly and unnatural aspect
May fright the hopeful mother at the view,
And that be heir to his unhappiness!
If ever he have wife, let her be made
More miserable by the life of him
Than I am made by my young lord and thee!
Come now, towards Chertsey with your holy load,
Taken from Paul's to be interrèd there.
 The bearers take up the hearse
And still, as you are weary of this weight,
Rest you, whiles I lament King Henry's corse.
 Enter Richard, Duke of Gloucester

RICHARD
Stay, you that bear the corse, and set it down.

ANNE
What black magician conjures up this fiend
To stop devoted charitable deeds?

RICHARD
Villains, set down the corse, or, by Saint Paul,
I'll make a corse of him that disobeys!

GENTLEMAN
My lord, stand back, and let the coffin pass.

RICHARD
Unmannered dog! Stand thou, when I command!
Advance thy halberd higher than my breast,
Or, by Saint Paul, I'll strike thee to my foot
And spurn upon thee, beggar, for thy boldness.
 The bearers set down the hearse

ANNE
What, do you tremble? Are you all afraid?
Alas, I blame you not, for you are mortal,
And mortal eyes cannot endure the devil.

Avaunt, thou dreadful minister of hell!
Thou hadst but power over his mortal body;
His soul thou canst not have. Therefore, be gone.

RICHARD

Sweet saint, for charity, be not so curst.

ANNE

Foul devil, for God's sake hence, and trouble us not,   50
For thou hast made the happy earth thy hell,
Filled it with cursing cries and deep exclaims.
If thou delight to view thy heinous deeds,
Behold this pattern of thy butcheries.
O gentlemen, see, see! Dead Henry's wounds
Open their congealed mouths and bleed afresh!
Blush, blush, thou lump of foul deformity;
For 'tis thy presence that exhales this blood
From cold and empty veins where no blood dwells.
Thy deeds inhuman and unnatural   60
Provokes this deluge most unnatural.
O God, which this blood mad'st, revenge his death!
O earth, which this blood drink'st, revenge his death!
Either heaven with lightning strike the murderer dead;
Or earth gape open wide and eat him quick,
As thou dost swallow up this good King's blood
Which his hell-governed arm hath butcherèd!

RICHARD

Lady, you know no rules of charity,
Which renders good for bad, blessings for curses.

ANNE

Villain, thou know'st nor law of God nor man: 70
No beast so fierce but knows some touch of pity.

RICHARD

But I know none, and therefore am no beast.

ANNE

O wonderful, when devils tell the truth!

RICHARD
    More wonderful, when angels are so angry.
    Vouchsafe, divine perfection of a woman,
    Of these supposèd crimes to give me leave
    By circumstance but to acquit myself.

ANNE
    Vouchsafe, diffused infection of a man,
    Of these known evils, but to give me leave
80   By circumstance to accuse thy cursèd self.

RICHARD
    Fairer than tongue can name thee, let me have
    Some patient leisure to excuse myself.

ANNE
    Fouler than heart can think thee, thou canst make
    No excuse current but to hang thyself.

RICHARD
    By such despair I should accuse myself.

ANNE
    And by despairing shalt thou stand excused
    For doing worthy vengeance on thyself
    That didst unworthy slaughter upon others.

RICHARD
    Say that I slew them not?

ANNE   Then say they were not slain.
90   But dead they are, and, devilish slave, by thee.

RICHARD
    I did not kill your husband.

ANNE   Why, then he is alive.

RICHARD
    Nay, he is dead, and slain by Edward's hands.

ANNE
    In thy foul throat thou li'st! Queen Margaret saw
    Thy murderous falchion smoking in his blood;
    The which thou once didst bend against her breast,
    But that thy brothers beat aside the point.

RICHARD
    I was provokèd by her slanderous tongue
    That laid their guilt upon my guiltless shoulders.
ANNE
    Thou wast provokèd by thy bloody mind
    That never dream'st on aught but butcheries.   100
    Didst thou not kill this King?
RICHARD   I grant ye — yea.
ANNE
    Dost grant me, hedgehog? Then God grant me too
    Thou mayst be damnèd for that wicked deed!
    O, he was gentle, mild, and virtuous!
RICHARD
    The better for the King of Heaven that hath him.
ANNE
    He is in heaven, where thou shalt never come.
RICHARD
    Let him thank me that holp to send him thither;
    For he was fitter for that place than earth.
ANNE
    And thou unfit for any place, but hell.
RICHARD
    Yes, one place else, if you will hear me name it.   110
ANNE
    Some dungeon.
RICHARD   Your bedchamber.
ANNE
    Ill rest betide the chamber where thou liest!
RICHARD
    So will it, madam, till I lie with you.
ANNE
    I hope so.
RICHARD   I know so. But, gentle Lady Anne,
    To leave this keen encounter of our wits

And fall something into a slower method,
Is not the causer of the timeless deaths
Of these Plantagenets, Henry and Edward,
As blameful as the executioner?

ANNE

120   Thou wast the cause and most accursed effect.

RICHARD

Your beauty was the cause of that effect —
Your beauty, that did haunt me in my sleep
To undertake the death of all the world,
So I might live one hour in your sweet bosom.

ANNE

If I thought that, I tell thee, homicide,
These nails should rent that beauty from my cheeks.

RICHARD

These eyes could not endure that beauty's wrack;
You should not blemish it, if I stood by.
As all the world is cheerèd by the sun,

130   So I by that. It is my day, my life.

ANNE

Black night o'ershade thy day, and death thy life!

RICHARD

Curse not thyself, fair creature — thou art both.

ANNE

I would I were, to be revenged on thee.

RICHARD

It is a quarrel most unnatural
To be revenged on him that loveth thee.

ANNE

It is a quarrel just and reasonable
To be revenged on him that killed my husband.

RICHARD

He that bereft thee, lady, of thy husband
Did it to help thee to a better husband.

ANNE

His better doth not breathe upon the earth.   140

RICHARD

He lives, that loves thee better than he could.

ANNE

Name him.

RICHARD   Plantagenet.

ANNE   Why that was he.

RICHARD

The selfsame name, but one of better nature.

ANNE

Where is he?

RICHARD   Here.

She spits at him

                              Why dost thou spit at me?

ANNE

Would it were mortal poison for thy sake!

RICHARD

Never came poison from so sweet a place.

ANNE

Never hung poison on a fouler toad.

Out of my sight! Thou dost infect mine eyes.

RICHARD

Thine eyes, sweet lady, have infected mine.

ANNE

Would they were basilisks to strike thee dead!   150

RICHARD

I would they were, that I might die at once,

For now they kill me with a living death.

Those eyes of thine from mine have drawn salt tears,

Shamed their aspects with store of childish drops.

These eyes, which never shed remorseful tear –

No, when my father York and Edward wept

To hear the piteous moan that Rutland made

When black-faced Clifford shook his sword at him;
Nor when thy warlike father, like a child,
Told the sad story of my father's death
And twenty times made pause to sob and weep,
That all the standers-by had wet their cheeks
Like trees bedashed with rain – in that sad time
My manly eyes did scorn an humble tear;
And what these sorrows could not thence exhale,
Thy beauty hath, and made them blind with weeping.
I never sued to friend nor enemy;
My tongue could never learn sweet smoothing word;
But, now thy beauty is proposed my fee,
My proud heart sues, and prompts my tongue to speak.
        She looks scornfully at him
Teach not thy lip such scorn; for it was made
For kissing, lady, not for such contempt.
If thy revengeful heart cannot forgive,
Lo, here I lend thee this sharp-pointed sword,
Which if thou please to hide in this true breast
And let the soul forth that adoreth thee,
I lay it naked to the deadly stroke
And humbly beg the death upon my knee.
        He lays his breast open. She offers at it with his sword
Nay, do not pause; for I did kill King Henry –
But 'twas thy beauty that provokèd me.
Nay now, dispatch; 'twas I that stabbed young Edward –
But 'twas thy heavenly face that set me on.
        She falls the sword
Take up the sword again, or take up me.

ANNE
Arise, dissembler; though I wish thy death
I will not be thy executioner.

RICHARD
Then bid me kill myself, and I will do it.

ANNE
  I have already.
RICHARD   That was in thy rage.
  Speak it again, and even with the word
  This hand, which for thy love did kill thy love,
  Shall for thy love kill a far truer love;   190
  To both their deaths shalt thou be accessory.
ANNE
  I would I knew thy heart.
RICHARD
  'Tis figured in my tongue.
ANNE
  I fear me both are false.
RICHARD
  Then never was man true.
ANNE
  Well, well, put up your sword.
RICHARD
  Say then my peace is made.
ANNE
  That shalt thou know hereafter.
RICHARD
  But shall I live in hope?
ANNE
  All men, I hope, live so.   200
RICHARD
  Vouchsafe to wear this ring.
ANNE
  To take is not to give.
    She puts on the ring
RICHARD
  Look how my ring encompasseth thy finger,
  Even so thy breast encloseth my poor heart.
  Wear both of them, for both of them are thine;

And if thy poor devoted servant may
But beg one favour at thy gracious hand,
Thou dost confirm his happiness for ever.

ANNE
    What is it?

RICHARD
210   That it may please you leave these sad designs
    To him that hath more cause to be a mourner,
    And presently repair to Crosby House;
    Where, after I have solemnly interred
    At Chertsey monastery this noble king
    And wet his grave with my repentant tears,
    I will with all expedient duty see you.
    For divers unknown reasons, I beseech you,
    Grant me this boon.

ANNE
    With all my heart; and much it joys me too
220   To see you are become so penitent.
    Tressel and Berkeley, go along with me.

RICHARD
    Bid me farewell.

ANNE   'Tis more than you deserve;
    But since you teach me how to flatter you,
    Imagine I have said farewell already.
                    Exeunt Tressel and Berkeley, with Anne

RICHARD
    Sirs, take up the corse.

GENTLEMAN   Towards Chertsey, noble lord?

RICHARD
    No, to Whitefriars – there attend my coming.
                    Exeunt bearers and guard with corse
    Was ever woman in this humour wooed?
    Was ever woman in this humour won?
    I'll have her, but I will not keep her long.

What? I that killed her husband and his father   230
To take her in her heart's extremest hate,
With curses in her mouth, tears in her eyes,
The bleeding witness of my hatred by,
Having God, her conscience, and these bars against me,
And I no friends to back my suit at all
But the plain devil and dissembling looks?
And yet to win her! All the world to nothing!
Ha!
Hath she forgot already that brave prince,
Edward, her lord, whom I, some three months since,   240
Stabbed in my angry mood at Tewkesbury?
A sweeter and a lovelier gentleman,
Framed in the prodigality of nature,
Young, valiant, wise, and, no doubt, right royal,
The spacious world cannot again afford;
And will she yet abase her eyes on me,
That cropped the golden prime of this sweet prince
And made her widow to a woeful bed?
On me, whose all not equals Edward's moiety?
On me, that halts and am misshapen thus?   250
My dukedom to a beggarly denier
I do mistake my person all this while!
Upon my life, she finds, although I cannot,
Myself to be a marvellous proper man.
I'll be at charges for a looking-glass
And entertain a score or two of tailors
To study fashions to adorn my body;
Since I am crept in favour with myself
I will maintain it with some little cost.
But first I'll turn yon fellow in his grave,   260
And then return lamenting to my love.
Shine out, fair sun, till I have bought a glass,
That I may see my shadow as I pass.   *Exit*

I.3   *Enter Queen Elizabeth, Lord Rivers, Marquess of*
             Dorset, and Lord Grey

RIVERS
    Have patience, madam; there's no doubt his majesty
    Will soon recover his accustomed health.

GREY
    In that you brook it ill, it makes him worse;
    Therefore for God's sake entertain good comfort
    And cheer his grace with quick and merry eyes.

QUEEN ELIZABETH
    If he were dead, what would betide on me?

GREY
    No other harm but loss of such a lord.

QUEEN ELIZABETH
    The loss of such a lord includes all harm.

GREY
    The heavens have blessed you with a goodly son
10 To be your comforter when he is gone.

QUEEN ELIZABETH
    Ah, he is young; and his minority
    Is put unto the trust of Richard Gloucester,
    A man that loves not me, nor none of you.

RIVERS
    Is it concluded he shall be Protector?

QUEEN ELIZABETH
    It is determined, not concluded yet;
    But so it must be, if the King miscarry.
        Enter Buckingham and Derby

GREY
    Here come the lords of Buckingham and Derby.

BUCKINGHAM
    Good time of day unto your royal grace!

DERBY
    God make your majesty joyful, as you have been!

QUEEN ELIZABETH

    The Countess Richmond, good my Lord of Derby,   20

    To your good prayer will scarcely say amen.

    Yet, Derby, notwithstanding she's your wife

    And loves not me, be you, good lord, assured

    I hate not you for her proud arrogance.

DERBY

    I do beseech you, either not believe

    The envious slanders of her false accusers;

    Or, if she be accused on true report,

    Bear with her weakness, which I think proceeds

    From wayward sickness, and no grounded malice.

QUEEN ELIZABETH

    Saw you the King today, my Lord of Derby?   30

DERBY

    But now the Duke of Buckingham and I

    Are come from visiting his majesty.

QUEEN ELIZABETH

    What likelihood of his amendment, lords?

BUCKINGHAM

    Madam, good hope; his grace speaks cheerfully.

QUEEN ELIZABETH

    God grant him health! Did you confer with him?

BUCKINGHAM

    Ay, madam; he desires to make atonement

    Between the Duke of Gloucester and your brothers,

    And between them and my Lord Chamberlain,

    And sent to warn them to his royal presence.

QUEEN ELIZABETH

    Would all were well! But that will never be.   40

    I fear our happiness is at the highest.

      Enter Richard, Duke of Gloucester, and Lord Hastings

RICHARD

    They do me wrong, and I will not endure it!

Who is it that complains unto the King
That I, forsooth, am stern, and love them not?
By holy Paul, they love his grace but lightly
That fill his ears with such dissentious rumours.
Because I cannot flatter and look fair,
Smile in men's faces, smooth, deceive, and cog,
Duck with French nods and apish courtesy,
50   I must be held a rancorous enemy.
Cannot a plain man live and think no harm,
But thus his simple truth must be abused
With silken, sly, insinuating Jacks?

GREY

To whom in all this presence speaks your grace?

RICHARD

To thee, that hast nor honesty nor grace.
When have I injured thee? When done thee wrong?
Or thee? Or thee? Or any of your faction?
A plague upon you all! His royal grace –
Whom God preserve better than you would wish! –
60   Cannot be quiet scarce a breathing while
But you must trouble him with lewd complaints.

QUEEN ELIZABETH

Brother of Gloucester, you mistake the matter.
The King, of his own royal disposition,
And not provoked by any suitor else,
Aiming, belike, at your interior hatred,
That in your outward action shows itself
Against my children, brothers, and myself,
Makes him to send, that he may learn the ground.

RICHARD

I cannot tell; the world is grown so bad
70   That wrens make prey where eagles dare not perch.
Since every Jack became a gentleman
There's many a gentle person made a Jack.

QUEEN ELIZABETH

    Come, come, we know your meaning, brother
        Gloucester:
    You envy my advancement and my friends'.
    God grant we never may have need of you!

RICHARD

    Meantime, God grants that I have need of you.
    Our brother is imprisoned by your means,
    Myself disgraced, and the nobility
    Held in contempt, while great promotions
    Are daily given to ennoble those   80
    That scarce, some two days since, were worth a noble.

QUEEN ELIZABETH

    By Him that raised me to this careful height
    From that contented hap which I enjoyed,
    I never did incense his majesty
    Against the Duke of Clarence, but have been
    An earnest advocate to plead for him.
    My lord, you do me shameful injury
    Falsely to draw me in these vile suspects.

RICHARD

    You may deny that you were not the mean
    Of my Lord Hastings' late imprisonment.   90

RIVERS

    She may, my lord, for –

RICHARD

    She may, Lord Rivers! Why, who knows not so?
    She may do more, sir, than denying that;
    She may help you to many fair preferments,
    And then deny her aiding hand therein
    And lay those honours on your high desert.
    What may she not? She may, yea, marry, may she –

RIVERS

    What, marry, may she?

RICHARD

    What, marry, may she? Marry with a king,
100   A bachelor and a handsome stripling too!
    Iwis your grandam had a worser match.

QUEEN ELIZABETH

    My Lord of Gloucester, I have too long borne
    Your blunt upbraidings and your bitter scoffs.
    By heaven, I will acquaint his majesty
    Of those gross taunts that oft I have endured.
    I had rather be a country servant-maid
    Than a great queen, with this condition,
    To be so baited, scorned, and stormèd at;
       Enter old Queen Margaret, behind
    Small joy have I in being England's Queen.

QUEEN MARGARET (*aside*)

110   And lessened be that small, God I beseech Him!
    Thy honour, state, and seat is due to me.

RICHARD

    What? Threat you me with telling of the King?
    Tell him, and spare not. Look what I have said
    I will avouch't in presence of the King;
    I dare adventure to be sent to the Tower.
    'Tis time to speak, my pains are quite forgot.

QUEEN MARGARET (*aside*)

    Out, devil! I do remember them too well.
    Thou kill'dst my husband Henry in the Tower,
    And Edward, my poor son, at Tewkesbury.

RICHARD

120   Ere you were queen, yea, or your husband king,
    I was a packhorse in his great affairs;
    A weeder-out of his proud adversaries,
    A liberal rewarder of his friends.
    To royalize his blood I spent mine own.

QUEEN MARGARET (*aside*)
    Yea, and much better blood than his or thine.

RICHARD
    In all which time you and your husband Grey
    Were factious for the house of Lancaster;
    And, Rivers, so were you. Was not your husband
    In Margaret's battle at Saint Albans slain?
    Let me put in your minds, if you forget,   130
    What you have been ere this, and what you are;
    Withal, what I have been, and what I am.

QUEEN MARGARET (*aside*)
    A murderous villain, and so still thou art.

RICHARD
    Poor Clarence did forsake his father, Warwick;
    Yea, and forswore himself, which Jesu pardon! –

QUEEN MARGARET (*aside*)
    Which God revenge!

RICHARD
    – To fight on Edward's party for the crown;
    And for his meed, poor lord, he is mewed up.
    I would to God my heart were flint like Edward's,
    Or Edward's soft and pitiful like mine!   140
    I am too childish-foolish for this world.

QUEEN MARGARET (*aside*)
    Hie thee to hell for shame, and leave this world,
    Thou cacodemon! There thy kingdom is.

RIVERS
    My Lord of Gloucester, in those busy days
    Which here you urge to prove us enemies,
    We followed then our lord, our sovereign king;
    So should we you, if you should be our king.

RICHARD
    If I should be? I had rather be a pedlar.
    Far be it from my heart, the thought thereof!

QUEEN ELIZABETH

150 As little joy, my lord, as you suppose
     You should enjoy, were you this country's king,
     As little joy you may suppose in me
     That I enjoy, being the Queen thereof.

QUEEN MARGARET (*aside*)

     As little joy enjoys the Queen thereof;
     For I am she, and altogether joyless.
     I can no longer hold me patient.
          She comes forward
     Hear me, you wrangling pirates, that fall out
     In sharing that which you have pilled from me!
     Which of you trembles not that looks on me?
160 If not, that I am Queen, you bow like subjects,
     Yet that, by you deposed, you quake like rebels?
     Ah, gentle villain, do not turn away!

RICHARD

     Foul wrinkled witch, what mak'st thou in my sight?

QUEEN MARGARET

     But repetition of what thou hast marred,
     That will I make before I let thee go.

RICHARD

     Wert thou not banishèd on pain of death?

QUEEN MARGARET

     I was; but I do find more pain in banishment
     Than death can yield me here by my abode.
     A husband and a son thou ow'st to me –
170 And thou a kingdom – all of you allegiance.
     This sorrow that I have, by right is yours,
     And all the pleasures you usurp are mine.

RICHARD

   ‹ The curse my noble father laid on thee
     When thou didst crown his warlike brows with paper
     And with thy scorns drew'st rivers from his eyes,

And then, to dry them, gav'st the Duke a clout
Steeped in the faultless blood of pretty Rutland –
His curses then, from bitterness of soul
Denounced against thee, are all fallen upon thee;
And God, not we, hath plagued thy bloody deed.   180

QUEEN ELIZABETH
So just is God, to right the innocent.

HASTINGS
O, 'twas the foulest deed to slay that babe,
And the most merciless, that e'er was heard of!

RIVERS
Tyrants themselves wept when it was reported.

DORSET
No man but prophesied revenge for it.

BUCKINGHAM
Northumberland, then present, wept to see it.

QUEEN MARGARET
What! Were you snarling all before I came,
Ready to catch each other by the throat,
And turn you all your hatred now on me?
Did York's dread curse prevail so much with heaven   190
That Henry's death, my lovely Edward's death,
Their kingdom's loss, my woeful banishment,
Should all but answer for that peevish brat?
Can curses pierce the clouds and enter heaven?
Why then, give way, dull clouds, to my quick curses!
Though not by war, by surfeit die your king,
As ours by murder, to make him a king!
Edward thy son, that now is Prince of Wales,
For Edward our son, that was Prince of Wales,
Die in his youth by like untimely violence!   200
Thyself a queen, for me that was a queen,
Outlive thy glory, like my wretched self!
Long mayst thou live to wail thy children's death

And see another, as I see thee now,
Decked in thy rights as thou art stalled in mine!
Long die thy happy days before thy death,
And after many lengthened hours of grief,
Die neither mother, wife, nor England's queen!
Rivers and Dorset, you were standers-by,
And so wast thou, Lord Hastings, when my son
Was stabbed with bloody daggers. God, I pray Him,
That none of you may live his natural age,
But by some unlooked accident cut off!

RICHARD
Have done thy charm, thou hateful withered hag!

QUEEN MARGARET
And leave out thee? Stay, dog, for thou shalt hear me.
If heaven have any grievous plague in store
Exceeding those that I can wish upon thee,
O let them keep it till thy sins be ripe,
And then hurl down their indignation
On thee, the troubler of the poor world's peace!
The worm of conscience still begnaw thy soul!
Thy friends suspect for traitors while thou liv'st,
And take deep traitors for thy dearest friends!
No sleep close up that deadly eye of thine,
Unless it be while some tormenting dream
Affrights thee with a hell of ugly devils!
Thou elvish-marked, abortive, rooting hog!
Thou that wast sealed in thy nativity
The slave of nature and the son of hell!
Thou slander of thy heavy mother's womb!
Thou loathèd issue of thy father's loins!
Thou rag of honour! Thou detested –

RICHARD
Margaret.

QUEEN MARGARET Richard!

RICHARD   Ha?
QUEEN MARGARET   I call thee not.
RICHARD
  I cry thee mercy then; for I did think
  That thou hadst called me all these bitter names.
QUEEN MARGARET
  Why, so I did, but looked for no reply.
  O, let me make the period to my curse!
RICHARD
  'Tis done by me, and ends in 'Margaret'.
QUEEN ELIZABETH
  Thus have you breathed your curse against yourself.
QUEEN MARGARET
  Poor painted queen, vain flourish of my fortune!   240
  Why strew'st thou sugar on that bottled spider
  Whose deadly web ensnareth thee about?
  Fool, fool! Thou whet'st a knife to kill thyself.
  The day will come that thou shalt wish for me
  To help thee curse this poisonous bunch-backed toad.
HASTINGS
  False-boding woman, end thy frantic curse,
  Lest to thy harm thou move our patience.
QUEEN MARGARET
  Foul shame upon you! You have all moved mine.
RIVERS
  Were you well served, you would be taught your duty.
QUEEN MARGARET
  To serve me well, you all should do me duty,   250
  Teach me to be your queen, and you my subjects.
  O, serve me well, and teach yourselves that duty!
DORSET
  Dispute not with her; she is lunatic.
QUEEN MARGARET
  Peace, master Marquess, you are malapert.

Your fire-new stamp of honour is scarce current.
O, that your young nobility could judge
What 'twere to lose it and be miserable!
They that stand high have many blasts to shake them,
And if they fall, they dash themselves to pieces.

RICHARD

260 Good counsel, marry! Learn it, learn it, Marquess.

DORSET

It touches you, my lord, as much as me.

RICHARD

Yea, and much more; but I was born so high.
Our aery buildeth in the cedar's top
And dallies with the wind and scorns the sun.

QUEEN MARGARET

And turns the sun to shade – alas! alas!
Witness my son, now in the shade of death,
Whose bright outshining beams thy cloudy wrath
Hath in eternal darkness folded up.
Your aery buildeth in our aery's nest.

270 O God, that seest it, do not suffer it!
As it is won with blood, lost be it so!

BUCKINGHAM

Peace, peace, for shame, if not for charity.

QUEEN MARGARET

Urge neither charity nor shame to me.
Uncharitably with me have you dealt,
And shamefully my hopes by you are butchered.
My charity is outrage, life my shame,
And in that shame still live my sorrow's rage!

BUCKINGHAM

Have done, have done.

QUEEN MARGARET

O princely Buckingham, I'll kiss thy hand
280 In sign of league and amity with thee.

Now fair befall thee and thy noble house!
Thy garments are not spotted with our blood,
Nor thou within the compass of my curse.

BUCKINGHAM
Nor no one here; for curses never pass
The lips of those that breathe them in the air.

QUEEN MARGARET
I will not think but they ascend the sky
And there awake God's gentle-sleeping peace.
O Buckingham, take heed of yonder dog!
Look when he fawns he bites; and when he bites
His venom tooth will rankle to the death.   290
Have not to do with him, beware of him.
Sin, death, and hell have set their marks on him,
And all their ministers attend on him.

RICHARD
What doth she say, my Lord of Buckingham?

BUCKINGHAM
Nothing that I respect, my gracious lord.

QUEEN MARGARET
What, dost thou scorn me for my gentle counsel?
And soothe the devil that I warn thee from?
O, but remember this another day,
When he shall split thy very heart with sorrow,
And say poor Margaret was a prophetess!   300
Live each of you the subjects to his hate,
And he to yours, and all of you to God's!   *Exit*

BUCKINGHAM
My hair doth stand an end to hear her curses.

RIVERS
And so doth mine. I muse why she's at liberty.

RICHARD
I cannot blame her. By God's holy Mother,
She hath had too much wrong, and I repent

My part thereof that I have done to her.

QUEEN ELIZABETH

I never did her any, to my knowledge.

RICHARD

Yet you have all the vantage of her wrong.
310 – I was too hot to do somebody good
That is too cold in thinking of it now.
Marry, as for Clarence, he is well repaid;
He is franked up to fatting for his pains –
God pardon them that are the cause thereof!

RIVERS

A virtuous and a Christian-like conclusion –
To pray for them that have done scathe to us.

RICHARD

So do I ever – (*aside*) being well advised;
For had I cursed now, I had cursed myself.
        Enter Catesby

CATESBY

Madam, his majesty doth call for you;
320 And for your grace; and yours, my gracious lord.

QUEEN ELIZABETH

Catesby, I come. Lords, will you go with me?

RIVERS

We wait upon your grace.
              Exeunt all but Richard, Duke of Gloucester

RICHARD

I do the wrong, and first begin to brawl.
The secret mischiefs that I set abroach
I lay unto the grievous charge of others.
Clarence, whom I indeed have cast in darkness,
I do beweep to many simple gulls –
Namely, to Derby, Hastings, Buckingham –
And tell them 'tis the Queen and her allies
330 That stir the King against the Duke my brother.

Now they believe it, and withal whet me
To be revenged on Rivers, Dorset, Grey.
But then I sigh, and, with a piece of Scripture,
Tell them that God bids us do good for evil;
And thus I clothe my naked villainy
With odd old ends stolen forth of Holy Writ,
And seem a saint, when most I play the devil.
  Enter two Murderers
But soft! Here come my executioners.
How now, my hardy, stout, resolvèd mates!
Are you now going to dispatch this thing?   340

FIRST MURDERER
We are, my lord, and come to have the warrant,
That we may be admitted where he is.

RICHARD
Well thought upon; I have it here about me.
  He gives the warrant
When you have done, repair to Crosby Place.
But, sirs, be sudden in the execution,
Withal obdurate, do not hear him plead;
For Clarence is well-spoken, and perhaps
May move your hearts to pity if you mark him.

FIRST MURDERER
Tut, tut, my lord! We will not stand to prate;
Talkers are no good doers. Be assured: 350
We go to use our hands, and not our tongues.

RICHARD
Your eyes drop millstones when fools' eyes fall tears.
I like you, lads; about your business straight.
Go, go, dispatch.

FIRST MURDERER We will, my noble lord.   *Exeunt*

I.4   *Enter Clarence and Keeper*

KEEPER
   Why looks your grace so heavily today?

CLARENCE
   O, I have passed a miserable night,
   So full of fearful dreams, of ugly sights,
   That, as I am a Christian faithful man,
   I would not spend another such a night
   Though 'twere to buy a world of happy days,
   So full of dismal terror was the time.

KEEPER
   What was your dream, my lord? I pray you tell me.

CLARENCE
   Methoughts that I had broken from the Tower
10   And was embarked to cross to Burgundy,
   And in my company my brother Gloucester,
   Who from my cabin tempted me to walk
   Upon the hatches; thence we looked toward England
   And cited up a thousand heavy times,
   During the wars of York and Lancaster,
   That had befallen us. As we paced along
   Upon the giddy footing of the hatches,
   Methought that Gloucester stumbled, and in falling
   Struck me, that thought to stay him, overboard
20   Into the tumbling billows of the main.
   O Lord! Methought what pain it was to drown!
   What dreadful noise of waters in mine ears!
   What sights of ugly death within mine eyes!
   Methoughts I saw a thousand fearful wracks;
   A thousand men that fishes gnawed upon;
   Wedges of gold, great anchors, heaps of pearl,
   Inestimable stones, unvalued jewels,
   All scattered in the bottom of the sea.
   Some lay in dead men's skulls, and in the holes

Where eyes did once inhabit, there were crept,   30
As 'twere in scorn of eyes, reflecting gems,
That wooed the slimy bottom of the deep
And mocked the dead bones that lay scattered by.

KEEPER

Had you such leisure in the time of death,
To gaze upon these secrets of the deep?

CLARENCE

Methought I had; and often did I strive
To yield the ghost; but still the envious flood
Stopped in my soul, and would not let it forth
To find the empty, vast, and wandering air,
But smothered it within my panting bulk,   40
Who almost burst to belch it in the sea.

KEEPER

Awaked you not in this sore agony?

CLARENCE

No, no, my dream was lengthened after life.
O then began the tempest to my soul!
I passed, methought, the melancholy flood,
With that sour ferryman which poets write of,
Unto the kingdom of perpetual night.
The first that there did greet my stranger soul
Was my great father-in-law, renownèd Warwick,
Who spake aloud, 'What scourge for perjury   50
Can this dark monarchy afford false Clarence?'
And so he vanished. Then came wandering by
A shadow like an angel, with bright hair
Dabbled in blood, and he shrieked out aloud,
'Clarence is come – false, fleeting, perjured Clarence,
That stabbed me in the field by Tewkesbury.
Seize on him, Furies, take him unto torment!'
With that, methoughts, a legion of foul fiends
Environed me, and howlèd in mine ears

60   Such hideous cries that with the very noise
      I, trembling, waked, and for a season after
      Could not believe but that I was in hell,
      Such terrible impression made my dream.

KEEPER
      No marvel, my lord, though it affrighted you;
      I am afraid, methinks, to hear you tell it.

CLARENCE
      Ah, keeper, keeper, I have done these things,
      That now give evidence against my soul,
      For Edward's sake, and see how he requits me!
      O God! If my deep prayers cannot appease Thee,
70   But Thou wilt be avenged on my misdeeds,
      Yet execute Thy wrath in me alone;
      O, spare my guiltless wife and my poor children!
      Keeper, I pray thee, sit by me awhile.
      My soul is heavy, and I fain would sleep.

KEEPER
      I will, my lord. God give your grace good rest!
          Clarence sleeps
          Enter Brakenbury, the Lieutenant

BRAKENBURY
      Sorrow breaks seasons and reposing hours,
      Makes the night morning and the noontide night.
      Princes have but their titles for their glories,
      An outward honour for an inward toil;
80   And for unfelt imaginations
      They often feel a world of restless cares;
      So that between their titles and low name
      There's nothing differs but the outward fame.
          Enter two Murderers

FIRST MURDERER Ho! Who's here?

BRAKENBURY What wouldst thou, fellow? And how
      cam'st thou hither?

SECOND MURDERER I would speak with Clarence, and I
  came hither on my legs.

BRAKENBURY Yea, so brief?

FIRST MURDERER 'Tis better, sir, than to be tedious.   90
  Let him see our commission, and talk no more.

  Brakenbury reads it

BRAKENBURY
  I am in this commanded to deliver
  The noble Duke of Clarence to your hands.
  I will not reason what is meant hereby,
  Because I will be guiltless from the meaning.
  There lies the Duke asleep, and there the keys.
  I'll to the King, and signify to him
  That thus I have resigned to you my charge.

                    Exit Brakenbury with Keeper

FIRST MURDERER You may, sir; 'tis a point of wisdom.
  Fare you well.   100

SECOND MURDERER What? Shall I stab him as he sleeps?

FIRST MURDERER No. He'll say 'twas done cowardly
  when he wakes.

SECOND MURDERER Why, he shall never wake until the
  great Judgement Day.

FIRST MURDERER Why, then he'll say we stabbed him
  sleeping.

SECOND MURDERER The urging of that word judgement
  hath bred a kind of remorse in me.

FIRST MURDERER What? Art thou afraid?   110

SECOND MURDERER Not to kill him, having a warrant,
  but to be damned for killing him, from the which no
  warrant can defend me.

FIRST MURDERER I thought thou hadst been resolute.

SECOND MURDERER So I am — to let him live.

FIRST MURDERER I'll back to the Duke of Gloucester
  and tell him so.

SECOND MURDERER Nay, I pray thee stay a little. I hope
     this passionate humour of mine will change. It was wont
120 to hold me but while one tells twenty.

FIRST MURDERER How dost thou feel thyself now?

SECOND MURDERER Faith, some certain dregs of con-
     science are yet within me.

FIRST MURDERER Remember our reward when the
     deed's done.

SECOND MURDERER Zounds, he dies! I had forgot the
     reward.

FIRST MURDERER Where's thy conscience now?

SECOND MURDERER O, in the Duke of Gloucester's
130 purse.

FIRST MURDERER When he opens his purse to give us
     our reward, thy conscience flies out.

SECOND MURDERER 'Tis no matter; let it go. There's
     few or none will entertain it.

FIRST MURDERER What if it come to thee again?

SECOND MURDERER I'll not meddle with it; it makes a
     man a coward. A man cannot steal, but it accuseth him;
     a man cannot swear, but it checks him; a man cannot lie
     with his neighbour's wife, but it detects him. 'Tis a
140 blushing shamefaced spirit that mutinies in a man's
     bosom. It fills a man full of obstacles. It made me once
     restore a purse of gold that by chance I found. It beggars
     any man that keeps it. It is turned out of towns and
     cities for a dangerous thing, and every man that means
     to live well endeavours to trust to himself and live with-
     out it.

FIRST MURDERER Zounds, 'tis even now at my elbow,
     persuading me not to kill the Duke.

SECOND MURDERER Take the devil in thy mind – and
150 believe him not. He would insinuate with thee but to
     make thee sigh.

FIRST MURDERER Tut, I am strong-framed; he cannot prevail with me.

SECOND MURDERER Spoke like a tall man that respects thy reputation. Come, shall we fall to work?

FIRST MURDERER Take him on the costard with the hilts of thy sword, and then throw him into the malmsey-butt in the next room.

SECOND MURDERER O excellent device! And make a sop of him.   160

FIRST MURDERER Soft! He wakes.

SECOND MURDERER Strike!

FIRST MURDERER No, we'll reason with him.

CLARENCE
Where art thou, keeper? Give me a cup of wine.

SECOND MURDERER
You shall have wine enough, my lord, anon.

CLARENCE
In God's name, what art thou?

FIRST MURDERER A man, as you are.

CLARENCE But not as I am, royal.

SECOND MURDERER Nor you as we are, loyal.

CLARENCE
Thy voice is thunder, but thy looks are humble.   170

FIRST MURDERER
My voice is now the King's, my looks mine own.

CLARENCE
How darkly and how deadly dost thou speak!
Your eyes do menace me. Why look you pale?
Who sent you hither? Wherefore do you come?

SECOND MURDERER To, to, to —

CLARENCE To murder me?

FIRST and SECOND MURDERER Ay, ay.

CLARENCE
You scarcely have the hearts to tell me so,

And therefore cannot have the hearts to do it.
180 Wherein, my friends, have I offended you?

FIRST MURDERER
Offended us you have not, but the King.

CLARENCE
I shall be reconciled to him again.

SECOND MURDERER
Never, my lord; therefore prepare to die.

CLARENCE
Are you drawn forth among a world of men
To slay the innocent? What is my offence?
Where is the evidence that doth accuse me?
What lawful quest have given their verdict up
Unto the frowning judge? Or who pronounced
The bitter sentence of poor Clarence' death
190 Before I be convict by course of law?
To threaten me with death is most unlawful.
I charge you, as you hope to have redemption
By Christ's dear blood shed for our grievous sins,
That you depart, and lay no hands on me.
The deed you undertake is damnable.

FIRST MURDERER
What we will do, we do upon command.

SECOND MURDERER
And he that hath commanded is our king.

CLARENCE
Erroneous vassals! The great King of kings
Hath in the table of His law commanded
200 That thou shalt do no murder. Will you then
Spurn at His edict, and fulfil a man's?
Take heed; for He holds vengeance in His hand
To hurl upon their heads that break His law.

SECOND MURDERER
And that same vengeance doth He hurl on thee

For false forswearing and for murder too:
Thou didst receive the sacrament to fight
In quarrel of the house of Lancaster.

FIRST MURDERER
And like a traitor to the name of God
Didst break that vow, and with thy treacherous blade
Unrip'st the bowels of thy sovereign's son.   210

SECOND MURDERER
Whom thou wast sworn to cherish and defend.

FIRST MURDERER
How canst thou urge God's dreadful law to us
When thou hast broke it in such dear degree?

CLARENCE
Alas! For whose sake did I that ill deed?
For Edward, for my brother, for his sake.
He sends you not to murder me for this,
For in that sin he is as deep as I.
If God will be avengèd for the deed,
O, know you yet He doth it publicly!
Take not the quarrel from His powerful arm.   220
He needs no indirect or lawless course
To cut off those that have offended Him.

FIRST MURDERER
Who made thee then a bloody minister
When gallant-springing brave Plantagenet,
That princely novice, was struck dead by thee?

CLARENCE
My brother's love, the devil, and my rage.

FIRST MURDERER
Thy brother's love, our duty, and thy fault
Provoke us hither now to slaughter thee.

CLARENCE
If you do love my brother, hate not me;
I am his brother, and I love him well.   230

If you are hired for meed, go back again,
And I will send you to my brother Gloucester,
Who shall reward you better for my life
Than Edward will for tidings of my death.

SECOND MURDERER

You are deceived. Your brother Gloucester hates you.

CLARENCE

O, no, he loves me and he holds me dear!
Go you to him from me.

FIRST MURDERER   Ay, so we will.

CLARENCE

Tell him, when that our princely father York
Blessed his three sons with his victorious arm
240 And charged us from his soul to love each other,
He little thought of this divided friendship;
Bid Gloucester think of this, and he will weep.

FIRST MURDERER

Ay, millstones, as he lessoned us to weep.

CLARENCE

O, do not slander him, for he is kind.

FIRST MURDERER

Right, as snow in harvest. Come, you deceive yourself;
'Tis he that sends us to destroy you here.

CLARENCE

It cannot be, for he bewept my fortune,
And hugged me in his arms, and swore with sobs
That he would labour my delivery.

FIRST MURDERER

250 Why, so he doth, when he delivers you
From this earth's thraldom to the joys of heaven.

SECOND MURDERER

Make peace with God, for you must die, my lord.

CLARENCE

Have you that holy feeling in your souls

To counsel me to make my peace with God,
And are you yet to your own souls so blind
That you will war with God by murdering me?
O, sirs, consider, they that set you on
To do this deed will hate you for the deed.

SECOND MURDERER

What shall we do?

CLARENCE   Relent, and save your souls.
Which of you, if you were a prince's son,   260
Being pent from liberty, as I am now,
If two such murderers as yourselves came to you,
Would not entreat for life? As you would beg
Were you in my distress –

FIRST MURDERER

Relent? No: 'tis cowardly and womanish.

CLARENCE

Not to relent is beastly, savage, devilish!
(*To Second Murderer*)
My friend, I spy some pity in thy looks.
O, if thine eye be not a flatterer,
Come thou on my side, and entreat for me!
A begging prince what beggar pities not?   270

SECOND MURDERER Look behind you, my lord!

FIRST MURDERER

Take that! And that! (*Stabs him*) If all this will not do,
I'll drown you in the malmsey-butt within.
                                    Exit with the body

SECOND MURDERER

A bloody deed, and desperately dispatched!
How fain, like Pilate, would I wash my hands
Of this most grievous murder!
    Enter First Murderer

FIRST MURDERER

How now? What mean'st thou that thou help'st me not?

By heavens, the Duke shall know how slack you have
    been.

SECOND MURDERER

I would he knew that I had saved his brother!

280   Take thou the fee and tell him what I say,

For I repent me that the Duke is slain.   *Exit*

FIRST MURDERER

So do not I. Go, coward as thou art.

Well, I'll go hide the body in some hole

Till that the Duke give order for his burial;

And when I have my meed, I will away,

For this will out, and then I must not stay.   *Exit*

*

II.1   *Flourish. Enter King Edward, sick, the Queen, Lord*
    Marquess Dorset, Grey, Rivers, Hastings, Catesby,
    Buckingham, and attendants

KING EDWARD

Why, so; now have I done a good day's work.

You peers, continue this united league.

I every day expect an embassage

From my Redeemer to redeem me hence;

And more in peace my soul shall part to heaven,

Since I have made my friends at peace on earth.

Hastings and Rivers, take each other's hand;

Dissemble not your hatred, swear your love.

RIVERS

By heaven, my soul is purged from grudging hate,

10   And with my hand I seal my true heart's love.

HASTINGS

So thrive I as I truly swear the like!

KING EDWARD

    Take heed you dally not before your King,

    Lest He that is the supreme King of kings

    Confound your hidden falsehood and award

    Either of you to be the other's end.

HASTINGS

    So prosper I as I swear perfect love!

RIVERS

    And I as I love Hastings with my heart!

KING EDWARD

    Madam, yourself is not exempt from this;

    Nor you, son Dorset; Buckingham, nor you.

    You have been factious one against the other.   20

    Wife, love Lord Hastings, let him kiss your hand,

    And what you do, do it unfeignedly.

QUEEN ELIZABETH

    There, Hastings, I will never more remember

    Our former hatred, so thrive I and mine!

KING EDWARD

    Dorset, embrace him; Hastings, love Lord Marquess.

DORSET

    This interchange of love, I here protest,

    Upon my part shall be inviolable.

HASTINGS

    And so swear I.

KING EDWARD

    Now, princely Buckingham, seal thou this league

    With thy embracements to my wife's allies,   30

    And make me happy in your unity.

BUCKINGHAM (*to the Queen*)

    Whenever Buckingham doth turn his hate

    Upon your grace, but with all duteous love

    Doth cherish you and yours, God punish me

    With hate in those where I expect most love!

When I have most need to employ a friend,
And most assurèd that he is a friend,
Deep, hollow, treacherous, and full of guile
Be he unto me! This do I beg of God,
When I am cold in love to you or yours.
Embrace

KING EDWARD
A pleasing cordial, princely Buckingham,
Is this thy vow unto my sickly heart.
There wanteth now our brother Gloucester here
To make the blessèd period of this peace.

BUCKINGHAM
And, in good time,
Here comes Sir Richard Ratcliffe and the Duke.
Enter Sir Richard Ratcliffe and Richard, Duke of
Gloucester

RICHARD
Good morrow to my sovereign King and Queen;
And, princely peers, a happy time of day!

KING EDWARD
Happy indeed, as we have spent the day.
Gloucester, we have done deeds of charity,
Made peace of enmity, fair love of hate,
Between these swelling, wrong-incensèd peers.

RICHARD
A blessèd labour, my most sovereign lord.
Among this princely heap, if any here
By false intelligence or wrong surmise
Hold me a foe —
If I unwittingly, or in my rage,
Have aught committed that is hardly borne
By any in this presence, I desire
To reconcile me to his friendly peace.
'Tis death to me to be at enmity;

I hate it, and desire all good men's love.
First, madam, I entreat true peace of you,
Which I will purchase with my duteous service;
Of you, my noble cousin Buckingham,
If ever any grudge were lodged between us;
Of you, and you, Lord Rivers, and of Dorset,
That, all without desert, have frowned on me;
Of you, Lord Woodville, and, Lord Scales, of you;
Dukes, earls, lords, gentlemen — indeed, of all.   70
I do not know that Englishman alive
With whom my soul is any jot at odds
More than the infant that is born tonight.
I thank my God for my humility!

QUEEN ELIZABETH
A holy day shall this be kept hereafter;
I would to God all strifes were well compounded.
My sovereign lord, I do beseech your highness
To take our brother Clarence to your grace.

RICHARD
Why, madam, have I offered love for this,
To be so flouted in this royal presence?   80
Who knows not that the gentle Duke is dead?
     They all start
You do him injury to scorn his corse.

KING EDWARD
Who knows not he is dead? Who knows he is?

QUEEN ELIZABETH
All-seeing heaven, what a world is this!

BUCKINGHAM
Look I so pale, Lord Dorset, as the rest?

DORSET
Ay, my good lord; and no man in the presence
But his red colour hath forsook his cheeks.

KING EDWARD

    Is Clarence dead? The order was reversed.

RICHARD

    But he, poor man, by your first order died,
90   And that a wingèd Mercury did bear.
    Some tardy cripple bare the countermand,
    That came too lag to see him buried.
    God grant that some, less noble and less loyal,
    Nearer in bloody thoughts, but not in blood,
    Deserve not worse than wretched Clarence did,
    And yet go current from suspicion!

    Enter the Earl of Derby

DERBY

    A boon, my sovereign, for my service done!

KING EDWARD

    I pray thee peace. My soul is full of sorrow.

DERBY

    I will not rise unless your highness hear me.

KING EDWARD

100   Then say at once what is it thou requests.

DERBY

    The forfeit, sovereign, of my servant's life,
    Who slew today a riotous gentleman
    Lately attendant on the Duke of Norfolk.

KING EDWARD

    Have I a tongue to doom my brother's death,
    And shall that tongue give pardon to a slave?
    My brother killed no man – his fault was thought –
    And yet his punishment was bitter death.
    Who sued to me for him? Who, in my wrath,
    Kneeled at my feet and bid me be advised?
110   Who spoke of brotherhood? Who spoke of love?
    Who told me how the poor soul did forsake
    The mighty Warwick and did fight for me?

Who told me, in the field at Tewkesbury,
When Oxford had me down, he rescued me
And said, 'Dear brother, live, and be a king'?
Who told me, when we both lay in the field
Frozen almost to death, how he did lap me
Even in his garments, and did give himself,
All thin and naked, to the numb-cold night?
All this from my remembrance brutish wrath   120
Sinfully plucked, and not a man of you
Had so much grace to put it in my mind.
But when your carters or your waiting vassals
Have done a drunken slaughter and defaced
The precious image of our dear Redeemer,
You straight are on your knees for pardon, pardon;
And I, unjustly too, must grant it you.
        Derby rises
But for my brother not a man would speak,
Nor I, ungracious, speak unto myself
For him, poor soul! The proudest of you all   130
Have been beholding to him in his life;
Yet none of you would once beg for his life.
O God! I fear thy justice will take hold
On me and you, and mine and yours, for this.
Come, Hastings, help me to my closet. Ah, poor
        Clarence!   *Exeunt some with King and Queen*

RICHARD

This is the fruits of rashness! Marked you not
How that the guilty kindred of the Queen
Looked pale when they did hear of Clarence' death?
O, they did urge it still unto the King!
God will revenge it. Come, lords, will you go   140
To comfort Edward with our company?

BUCKINGHAM

We wait upon your grace.   *Exeunt*

II.2   *Enter the old Duchess of York, with Edward and*
              Margaret Plantagenet (the two children of Clarence)

BOY

    Good grandam, tell us, is our father dead?

DUCHESS OF YORK

    No, boy.

GIRL

    Why do you weep so oft, and beat your breast,
    And cry 'O Clarence, my unhappy son'?

BOY

    Why do you look on us, and shake your head,
    And call us orphans, wretches, castaways,
    If that our noble father were alive?

DUCHESS OF YORK

    My pretty cousins, you mistake me both.
    I do lament the sickness of the King,
10 As loath to lose him, not your father's death;
    It were lost sorrow to wail one that's lost.

BOY

    Then you conclude, my grandam, he is dead?
    The King mine uncle is to blame for it.
    God will revenge it, whom I will importune
    With earnest prayers all to that effect.

GIRL

    And so will I.

DUCHESS OF YORK

    Peace, children, peace! The King doth love you well.
    Incapable and shallow innocents,
    You cannot guess who caused your father's death.

BOY

20 Grandam, we can; for my good uncle Gloucester
    Told me the King, provoked to it by the Queen,
    Devised impeachments to imprison him;
    And when my uncle told me so, he wept,

And pitied me, and kindly kissed my cheek;
Bade me rely on him as on my father,
And he would love me dearly as a child.

DUCHESS OF YORK
Ah, that deceit should steal such gentle shape
And with a virtuous visor hide deep vice!
He is my son – yea, and therein my shame;
Yet from my dugs he drew not this deceit.   30

BOY
Think you my uncle did dissemble, grandam?

DUCHESS OF YORK
Ay, boy.

BOY
I cannot think it. Hark! What noise is this?
    Enter Queen Elizabeth, with her hair about her ears,
    Rivers and Dorset after her

QUEEN ELIZABETH
Ah, who shall hinder me to wail and weep,
To chide my fortune, and torment myself?
I'll join with black despair against my soul
And to myself become an enemy.

DUCHESS OF YORK
What means this scene of rude impatience?

QUEEN ELIZABETH
To make an act of tragic violence.
Edward, my lord, thy son, our King, is dead!   40
Why grow the branches when the root is gone?
Why wither not the leaves that want their sap?
If you will live, lament; if die, be brief,
That our swift-wingèd souls may catch the King's,
Or like obedient subjects follow him
To his new kingdom of ne'er-changing night.

DUCHESS OF YORK
Ah, so much interest have I in thy sorrow

As I had title in thy noble husband.
I have bewept a worthy husband's death,
And lived with looking on his images;
But now two mirrors of his princely semblance
Are cracked in pieces by malignant death,
And I for comfort have but one false glass
That grieves me when I see my shame in him.
Thou art a widow; yet thou art a mother,
And hast the comfort of thy children left;
But death hath snatched my husband from mine arms
And plucked two crutches from my feeble hands,
Clarence and Edward. O, what cause have I,
Thine being but a moiety of my moan,
To overgo thy woes and drown thy cries!

BOY

Ah, aunt! You wept not for our father's death.
How can we aid you with our kindred tears?

GIRL

Our fatherless distress was left unmoaned:
Your widow-dolour likewise be unwept!

QUEEN ELIZABETH

Give me no help in lamentation;
I am not barren to bring forth complaints.
All springs reduce their currents to mine eyes,
That I, being governed by the watery moon,
May send forth plenteous tears to drown the world.
Ah for my husband, for my dear lord Edward!

CHILDREN

Ah for our father, for our dear lord Clarence!

DUCHESS OF YORK

Alas for both, both mine, Edward and Clarence!

QUEEN ELIZABETH

What stay had I but Edward? And he's gone.

CHILDREN
  What stay had we but Clarence? And he's gone.
DUCHESS OF YORK
  What stay had I but they? And they are gone.
QUEEN ELIZABETH
  Was never widow had so dear a loss.
CHILDREN
  Were never orphans had so dear a loss.
DUCHESS OF YORK
  Was never mother had so dear a loss.
  Alas! I am the mother of these griefs;   80
  Their woes are parcelled, mine is general.
  She for an Edward weeps, and so do I;
  I for a Clarence weep, so doth not she;
  These babes for Clarence weep, and so do I;
  I for an Edward weep, so do not they.
  Alas, you three on me, threefold distressed,
  Pour all your tears! I am your sorrow's nurse,
  And I will pamper it with lamentation.

DORSET
  Comfort, dear mother; God is much displeased
  That you take with unthankfulness His doing.   90
  In common worldly things 'tis called ungrateful
  With dull unwillingness to repay a debt
  Which with a bounteous hand was kindly lent;
  Much more to be thus opposite with heaven
  For it requires the royal debt it lent you.

RIVERS
  Madam, bethink you like a careful mother
  Of the young prince, your son. Send straight for him;
  Let him be crowned; in him your comfort lives.
  Drown desperate sorrow in dead Edward's grave
  And plant your joys in living Edward's throne.   100

Enter Richard, Duke of Gloucester, Buckingham,
Derby, Hastings, and Ratcliffe

RICHARD

    Sister, have comfort. All of us have cause
    To wail the dimming of our shining star;
    But none can help our harms by wailing them.
    Madam, my mother, I do cry you mercy;
    I did not see your grace. Humbly on my knee
    I crave your blessing.

DUCHESS OF YORK

    God bless thee, and put meekness in thy breast,
    Love, charity, obedience, and true duty!

RICHARD

    Amen! (*Aside*) And make me die a good old man!
110   That is the butt-end of a mother's blessing;
    I marvel that her grace did leave it out.

BUCKINGHAM

    You cloudy princes and heart-sorrowing peers
    That bear this heavy mutual load of moan,
    Now cheer each other in each other's love.
    Though we have spent our harvest of this king,
    We are to reap the harvest of his son.
    The broken rancour of your high-swollen hearts,
    But lately splintered, knit, and joined together,
    Must gently be preserved, cherished, and kept.
120   Me seemeth good that with some little train
    Forthwith from Ludlow the young Prince be fet
    Hither to London, to be crowned our King.

RIVERS

    Why with some little train, my Lord of Buckingham?

BUCKINGHAM

    Marry, my lord, lest by a multitude
    The new-healed wound of malice should break out,
    Which would be so much the more dangerous

By how much the estate is green and yet ungoverned.
Where every horse bears his commanding rein
And may direct his course as please himself,
As well the fear of harm, as harm apparent,   130
In my opinion, ought to be prevented.

RICHARD

I hope the King made peace with all of us;
And the compact is firm and true in me.

RIVERS

And so in me; and so, I think, in all.
Yet, since it is but green, it should be put
To no apparent likelihood of breach,
Which haply by much company might be urged.
Therefore I say with noble Buckingham
That it is meet so few should fetch the Prince.

HASTINGS

And so say I.   140

RICHARD

Then be it so; and go we to determine
Who they shall be that straight shall post to Ludlow.
Madam, and you, my sister, will you go
To give your censures in this business?

QUEEN ELIZABETH *and* DUCHESS OF YORK

With all our hearts.   *Exeunt*
    Buckingham and Richard remain

BUCKINGHAM

My lord, whoever journeys to the Prince,
For God sake let not us two stay at home;
For by the way I'll sort occasion,
As index to the story we late talked of,
To part the Queen's proud kindred from the Prince.   150

RICHARD

My other self, my counsel's consistory,
My oracle, my prophet, my dear cousin,

I, as a child, will go by thy direction.
Toward Ludlow then, for we'll not stay behind.

Exeunt

II.3   *Enter one Citizen at one door, and another at the*
            other

FIRST CITIZEN
    Good morrow, neighbour. Whither away so fast?

SECOND CITIZEN
    I promise you, I scarcely know myself.
    Hear you the news abroad?

FIRST CITIZEN   Yes, that the King is dead.

SECOND CITIZEN
    Ill news, by 'r Lady – seldom comes the better.
    I fear, I fear 'twill prove a giddy world.

        Enter another Citizen

THIRD CITIZEN
    Neighbours, God speed!

FIRST CITIZEN   Give you good morrow, sir.

THIRD CITIZEN
    Doth the news hold of good King Edward's death?

SECOND CITIZEN
    Ay, sir, it is too true. God help the while!

THIRD CITIZEN
    Then, masters, look to see a troublous world.

FIRST CITIZEN
10 No, no! By God's good grace his son shall reign.

THIRD CITIZEN
    Woe to that land that's governed by a child!

SECOND CITIZEN
    In him there is a hope of government,
    Which, in his nonage, council under him,
    And, in his full and ripened years, himself,

No doubt shall then, and till then, govern well.

FIRST CITIZEN

So stood the state when Henry the Sixth
Was crowned in Paris but at nine months old.

THIRD CITIZEN

Stood the state so? No, no, good friends, God wot!
For then this land was famously enriched
With politic grave counsel; then the King   20
Had virtuous uncles to protect his grace.

FIRST CITIZEN

Why, so hath this, both by his father and mother.

THIRD CITIZEN

Better it were they all came by his father,
Or by his father there were none at all;
For emulation who shall now be nearest
Will touch us all too near, if God prevent not.
O, full of danger is the Duke of Gloucester,
And the Queen's sons and brothers haught and proud;
And were they to be ruled, and not to rule,
This sickly land might solace as before.   30

FIRST CITIZEN

Come, come, we fear the worst. All will be well.

THIRD CITIZEN

When clouds are seen, wise men put on their cloaks;
When great leaves fall, then winter is at hand;
When the sun sets, who doth not look for night?
Untimely storms makes men expect a dearth.
All may be well; but if God sort it so,
'Tis more than we deserve or I expect.

SECOND CITIZEN

Truly, the hearts of men are full of fear;
You cannot reason almost with a man
That looks not heavily and full of dread.   40

THIRD CITIZEN

    Before the days of change, still is it so.

    By a divine instinct men's minds mistrust

    Ensuing danger; as by proof we see

    The water swell before a boisterous storm.

    But leave it all to God. Whither away?

SECOND CITIZEN

    Marry, we were sent for to the justices.

THIRD CITIZEN

    And so was I. I'll bear you company.   *Exeunt*

II.4   *Enter Archbishop of York, the young Duke of York,*
           Queen Elizabeth, and the Duchess of York

ARCHBISHOP

    Last night, I hear, they lay at Stony Stratford,

    And at Northampton they do rest tonight;

    Tomorrow, or next day, they will be here.

DUCHESS OF YORK

    I long with all my heart to see the Prince.

    I hope he is much grown since last I saw him.

QUEEN ELIZABETH

    But I hear no. They say my son of York

    Has almost overta'en him in his growth.

YORK

    Ay, mother; but I would not have it so.

DUCHESS OF YORK

    Why, my young cousin? It is good to grow.

YORK

10   Grandam, one night as we did sit at supper,

    My uncle Rivers talked how I did grow

    More than my brother. 'Ay,' quoth my uncle Gloucester,

    'Small herbs have grace; great weeds do grow apace.'

    And since, methinks, I would not grow so fast,

Because sweet flowers are slow and weeds make haste.

DUCHESS OF YORK

Good faith, good faith, the saying did not hold
In him that did object the same to thee.
He was the wretched'st thing when he was young,
So long a-growing and so leisurely
That, if his rule were true, he should be gracious.   20

ARCHBISHOP

And so no doubt he is, my gracious madam.

DUCHESS OF YORK

I hope he is; but yet let mothers doubt.

YORK

Now, by my troth, if I had been remembered,
I could have given my uncle's grace a flout
To touch his growth nearer than he touched mine.

DUCHESS OF YORK

How, my young York? I pray thee let me hear it.

YORK

Marry, they say my uncle grew so fast
That he could gnaw a crust at two hours old;
'Twas full two years ere I could get a tooth.
Grandam, this would have been a biting jest.   30

DUCHESS OF YORK

I pray thee, pretty York, who told thee this?

YORK

Grandam, his nurse.

DUCHESS OF YORK

His nurse? Why, she was dead ere thou wast born.

YORK

If 'twere not she, I cannot tell who told me.

QUEEN ELIZABETH

A parlous boy! Go to, you are too shrewd.

DUCHESS OF YORK

Good madam, be not angry with the child.

QUEEN ELIZABETH
Pitchers have ears.
Enter a Messenger

ARCHBISHOP
Here comes a messenger. What news?

MESSENGER
Such news, my lord, as grieves me to report.

QUEEN ELIZABETH
40   How doth the Prince?

MESSENGER   Well, madam, and in health.

DUCHESS OF YORK
What is thy news?

MESSENGER
Lord Rivers and Lord Grey are sent to Pomfret,
And with them Sir Thomas Vaughan, prisoners.

DUCHESS OF YORK
Who hath committed them?

MESSENGER   The mighty dukes,
Gloucester and Buckingham.

ARCHBISHOP   For what offence?

MESSENGER
The sum of all I can I have disclosed.
Why or for what the nobles were committed
Is all unknown to me, my gracious lord.

QUEEN ELIZABETH
Ay me! I see the ruin of my house.
50   The tiger now hath seized the gentle hind;
Insulting tyranny begins to jut
Upon the innocent and aweless throne.
Welcome destruction, blood, and massacre!
I see, as in a map, the end of all.

DUCHESS OF YORK
Accursèd and unquiet wrangling days,
How many of you have mine eyes beheld!

My husband lost his life to get the crown,
And often up and down my sons were tossed
For me to joy and weep their gain and loss;
And being seated, and domestic broils   60
Clean overblown, themselves the conquerors
Make war upon themselves, brother to brother,
Blood to blood, self against self. O preposterous
And frantic outrage, end thy damnèd spleen,
Or let me die, to look on death no more!

QUEEN ELIZABETH
Come, come, my boy; we will to sanctuary.
Madam, farewell.

DUCHESS OF YORK Stay, I will go with you.

QUEEN ELIZABETH
You have no cause.

ARCHBISHOP (to the Queen)
                          My gracious lady, go,
And thither bear your treasure and your goods.
For my part, I'll resign unto your grace   70
The seal I keep; and so betide to me
As well I tender you and all of yours!
Go, I'll conduct you to the sanctuary.   Exeunt

                          *

The trumpets sound. Enter young Prince Edward of   III.1
Wales, the Dukes of Gloucester and Buckingham,
Lord Cardinal Bourchier, Catesby, with others

BUCKINGHAM
Welcome, sweet Prince, to London, to your chamber.

RICHARD
Welcome, dear cousin, my thoughts' sovereign!
The weary way hath made you melancholy.

PRINCE EDWARD
   No, uncle; but our crosses on the way
   Have made it tedious, wearisome, and heavy.
   I want more uncles here to welcome me.

RICHARD
   Sweet Prince, the untainted virtue of your years
   Hath not yet dived into the world's deceit;
   Nor more can you distinguish of a man
10   Than of his outward show, which, God He knows,
   Seldom or never jumpeth with the heart.
   Those uncles which you want were dangerous;
   Your grace attended to their sugared words
   But looked not on the poison of their hearts.
   God keep you from them, and from such false friends!

PRINCE EDWARD
   God keep me from false friends! – But they were none.

RICHARD
   My lord, the Mayor of London comes to greet you.
    Enter Lord Mayor and his train

LORD MAYOR
   God bless your grace with health and happy days!

PRINCE EDWARD
   I thank you, good my lord, and thank you all.
    The Lord Mayor and his train stand aside
20   I thought my mother and my brother York
   Would long ere this have met us on the way.
   Fie, what a slug is Hastings that he comes not
   To tell us whether they will come or no!
    Enter Lord Hastings

BUCKINGHAM
   And, in good time, here comes the sweating lord.

PRINCE EDWARD
   Welcome, my lord. What, will our mother come?

HASTINGS

On what occasion God He knows, not I,
The Queen your mother and your brother York
Have taken sanctuary. The tender Prince
Would fain have come with me to meet your grace,
But by his mother was perforce withheld.   30

BUCKINGHAM

Fie, what an indirect and peevish course
Is this of hers! Lord Cardinal, will your grace
Persuade the Queen to send the Duke of York
Unto his princely brother presently?
If she deny, Lord Hastings, go with him
And from her jealous arms pluck him perforce.

CARDINAL BOURCHIER

My Lord of Buckingham, if my weak oratory
Can from his mother win the Duke of York,
Anon expect him here; but if she be obdurate
To mild entreaties, God in heaven forbid   40
We should infringe the holy privilege
Of blessed sanctuary! Not for all this land
Would I be guilty of so deep a sin.

BUCKINGHAM

You are too senseless-obstinate, my lord,
Too ceremonious and traditional.
Weigh it but with the grossness of this age,
You break not sanctuary in seizing him:
The benefit thereof is always granted
To those whose dealings have deserved the place
And those who have the wit to claim the place.   50
This prince hath neither claimed it nor deserved it,
And therefore, in mine opinion, cannot have it.
Then, taking him from thence that is not there,
You break no privilege nor charter there.

Oft have I heard of sanctuary men,
But sanctuary children never till now.

CARDINAL BOURCHIER
My lord, you shall overrule my mind for once.
Come on, Lord Hastings, will you go with me?

HASTINGS
I go, my lord.

PRINCE EDWARD
60   Good lords, make all the speedy haste you may.

Exit Cardinal and Hastings

Say, uncle Gloucester, if our brother come,
Where shall we sojourn till our coronation?

RICHARD
Where it seems best unto your royal self.
If I may counsel you, some day or two
Your highness shall repose you at the Tower;
Then where you please, and shall be thought most fit
For your best health and recreation.

PRINCE EDWARD
I do not like the Tower, of any place.
Did Julius Caesar build that place, my lord?

BUCKINGHAM
70   He did, my gracious lord, begin that place,
Which, since, succeeding ages have re-edified.

PRINCE EDWARD
Is it upon record, or else reported
Successively from age to age, he built it?

BUCKINGHAM
Upon record, my gracious lord.

PRINCE EDWARD
But say, my lord, it were not registered,
Methinks the truth should live from age to age,
As 'twere retailed to all posterity,
Even to the general all-ending day.

RICHARD (*aside*)
　So wise so young, they say, do never live long.
PRINCE EDWARD
　What say you, uncle?   80
RICHARD
　I say, without characters fame lives long.
　(*Aside*) Thus, like the formal Vice, Iniquity,
　I moralize two meanings in one word.
PRINCE EDWARD
　That Julius Caesar was a famous man.
　With what his valour did enrich his wit,
　His wit set down to make his valour live.
　Death makes no conquest of this conqueror,
　For now he lives in fame, though not in life.
　I'll tell you what, my cousin Buckingham –
BUCKINGHAM
　What, my gracious lord?   90
PRINCE EDWARD
　An if I live until I be a man,
　I'll win our ancient right in France again
　Or die a soldier as I lived a king.
RICHARD (*aside*)
　Short summers lightly have a forward spring.
　　Enter the young Duke of York, Hastings, and Cardinal
　　Bourchier
BUCKINGHAM
　Now in good time, here comes the Duke of York.
PRINCE EDWARD
　Richard of York, how fares our loving brother?
YORK
　Well, my dread lord – so must I call you now.
PRINCE EDWARD
　Ay, brother – to our grief, as it is yours.
　Too late he died that might have kept that title,

100   Which by his death hath lost much majesty.

RICHARD
    How fares our cousin, noble Lord of York?

YORK
    I thank you, gentle uncle. O, my lord,
    You said that idle weeds are fast in growth.
    The Prince my brother hath outgrown me far.

RICHARD
    He hath, my lord.

YORK   And therefore is he idle?

RICHARD
    O my fair cousin, I must not say so.

YORK
    Then he is more beholding to you than I.

RICHARD
    He may command me as my sovereign,
    But you have power in me as in a kinsman.

YORK
110   I pray you, uncle, give me this dagger.

RICHARD
    My dagger, little cousin? With all my heart.

PRINCE EDWARD
    A beggar, brother?

YORK
    Of my kind uncle, that I know will give,
    And being but a toy, which is no grief to give.

RICHARD
    A greater gift than that I'll give my cousin.

YORK
    A greater gift? O, that's the sword to it.

RICHARD
    Ay, gentle cousin, were it light enough.

YORK
    O, then I see you will part but with light gifts!

In weightier things you'll say a beggar nay.

RICHARD

It is too heavy for your grace to wear.   120

YORK

I weigh it lightly, were it heavier.

RICHARD

What, would you have my weapon, little lord?

YORK

I would, that I might thank you as you call me.

RICHARD How?

YORK Little.

PRINCE EDWARD

My Lord of York will still be cross in talk.
Uncle, your grace knows how to bear with him.

YORK

You mean, to bear me, not to bear with me.
Uncle, my brother mocks both you and me.
Because that I am little, like an ape,   130
He thinks that you should bear me on your shoulders.

BUCKINGHAM (*aside to Hastings*)

With what a sharp-provided wit he reasons!
To mitigate the scorn he gives his uncle
He prettily and aptly taunts himself.
So cunning, and so young, is wonderful.

RICHARD

My lord, will't please you pass along?
Myself and my good cousin Buckingham
Will to your mother, to entreat of her
To meet you at the Tower and welcome you.

YORK

What, will you go unto the Tower, my lord?   140

PRINCE EDWARD

My Lord Protector needs will have it so.

YORK

    I shall not sleep in quiet at the Tower.

RICHARD

    Why, what should you fear?

YORK

    Marry, my uncle Clarence' angry ghost –

    My grandam told me he was murdered there.

PRINCE EDWARD

    I fear no uncles dead.

RICHARD

    Nor none that live, I hope.

PRINCE EDWARD

    An if they live, I hope I need not fear.

    But come, my lord; and with a heavy heart,

150   Thinking on them, go I unto the Tower.

        A sennet. Exeunt Prince Edward, York, Hastings,

                  Cardinal Bourchier, and others

       Richard, Buckingham, and Catesby remain

BUCKINGHAM

    Think you, my lord, this little prating York

    Was not incensèd by his subtle mother

    To taunt and scorn you thus opprobriously?

RICHARD

    No doubt, no doubt. O, 'tis a parlous boy,

    Bold, quick, ingenious, forward, capable.

    He is all the mother's, from the top to toe.

BUCKINGHAM

    Well, let them rest. Come hither, Catesby. Thou art sworn

    As deeply to effect what we intend

    As closely to conceal what we impart.

160   Thou know'st our reasons urged upon the way.

    What think'st thou? Is it not an easy matter

    To make William Lord Hastings of our mind

    For the instalment of this noble Duke

In the seat royal of this famous isle?

CATESBY

He for his father's sake so loves the Prince
That he will not be won to aught against him.

BUCKINGHAM

What think'st thou then of Stanley? Will not he?

CATESBY

He will do all in all as Hastings doth.

BUCKINGHAM

Well then, no more but this: go, gentle Catesby,
And, as it were afar off, sound thou Lord Hastings   170
How he doth stand affected to our purpose,
And summon him tomorrow to the Tower
To sit about the coronation.
If thou dost find him tractable to us,
Encourage him, and tell him all our reasons;
If he be leaden, icy, cold, unwilling,
Be thou so too, and so break off the talk,
And give us notice of his inclination;
For we tomorrow hold divided councils,
Wherein thyself shalt highly be employed.   180

RICHARD

Commend me to Lord William. Tell him, Catesby,
His ancient knot of dangerous adversaries
Tomorrow are let blood at Pomfret Castle,
And bid my lord, for joy of this good news,
Give Mistress Shore one gentle kiss the more.

BUCKINGHAM

Good Catesby, go, effect this business soundly.

CATESBY

My good lords both, with all the heed I can.

RICHARD

Shall we hear from you, Catesby, ere we sleep?

CATESBY

    You shall, my lord.

RICHARD

190   At Crosby House, there shall you find us both.

                               Exit Catesby

BUCKINGHAM

    Now, my lord, what shall we do if we perceive

    Lord Hastings will not yield to our complots?

RICHARD

    Chop off his head! Something we will determine.

    And look when I am King, claim thou of me

    The earldom of Hereford and all the movables

    Whereof the King my brother was possessed.

BUCKINGHAM

    I'll claim that promise at your grace's hand.

RICHARD

    And look to have it yielded with all kindness.

    Come, let us sup betimes, that afterwards

200   We may digest our complots in some form.   *Exeunt*

III.2   *Enter a Messenger to the door of Hastings*

MESSENGER My lord! My lord!

HASTINGS (*within*) Who knocks?

MESSENGER One from the Lord Stanley.

       Enter Lord Hastings

HASTINGS What is't a clock?

MESSENGER Upon the stroke of four.

HASTINGS

    Cannot my Lord Stanley sleep these tedious nights?

MESSENGER

    So it appears by that I have to say:

    First, he commends him to your noble self.

HASTINGS
    What then?
MESSENGER
    Then certifies your lordship that this night   10
    He dreamt the boar had razèd off his helm.
    Besides, he says there are two councils kept;
    And that may be determined at the one
    Which may make you and him to rue at th'other.
    Therefore he sends to know your lordship's pleasure,
    If you will presently take horse with him
    And with all speed post with him toward the north
    To shun the danger that his soul divines.
HASTINGS
    Go, fellow, go, return unto thy lord;
    Bid him not fear the separated council.   20
    His honour and myself are at the one,
    And at the other is my good friend Catesby;
    Where nothing can proceed that toucheth us
    Whereof I shall not have intelligence.
    Tell him his fears are shallow, without instance;
    And for his dreams, I wonder he's so simple
    To trust the mockery of unquiet slumbers.
    To fly the boar before the boar pursues
    Were to incense the boar to follow us,
    And make pursuit where he did mean no chase.   30
    Go, bid thy master rise and come to me,
    And we will both together to the Tower,
    Where he shall see the boar will use us kindly.
MESSENGER
    I'll go, my lord, and tell him what you say.   *Exit*
        Enter Catesby
CATESBY
    Many good morrows to my noble lord!

HASTINGS

   Good morrow, Catesby; you are early stirring.
   What news, what news, in this our tottering state?

CATESBY

   It is a reeling world indeed, my lord,
   And I believe will never stand upright
40   Till Richard wear the garland of the realm.

HASTINGS

   How! Wear the garland! Dost thou mean the
     crown?

CATESBY

   Ay, my good lord.

HASTINGS

   I'll have this crown of mine cut from my shoulders
   Before I'll see the crown so foul misplaced.
   But canst thou guess that he doth aim at it?

CATESBY

   Ay, on my life, and hopes to find you forward
   Upon his party for the gain thereof;
   And thereupon he sends you this good news,
   That this same very day your enemies,
50   The kindred of the Queen, must die at Pomfret.

HASTINGS

   Indeed I am no mourner for that news,
   Because they have been still my adversaries;
   But that I'll give my voice on Richard's side
   To bar my master's heirs in true descent –
   God knows I will not do it, to the death!

CATESBY

   God keep your lordship in that gracious mind!

HASTINGS

   But I shall laugh at this a twelvemonth hence,
   That they which brought me in my master's hate,
   I live to look upon their tragedy.

Well, Catesby, ere a fortnight make me older,   60
I'll send some packing that yet think not on't.

CATESBY

'Tis a vile thing to die, my gracious lord,
When men are unprepared and look not for it.

HASTINGS

O monstrous, monstrous! And so falls it out
With Rivers, Vaughan, Grey; and so 'twill do
With some men else, that think themselves as safe
As thou and I, who as thou know'st are dear
To princely Richard and to Buckingham.

CATESBY

The princes both make high account of you –
(*Aside*) For they account his head upon the Bridge.   70

HASTINGS

I know they do, and I have well deserved it.
    Enter Earl of Derby
Come on, come on! Where is your boar-spear, man?
Fear you the boar, and go so unprovided?

DERBY

My lord, good morrow. Good morrow, Catesby.
You may jest on, but, by the Holy Rood,
I do not like these several councils, I.

HASTINGS

My lord, I hold my life as dear as you do yours,
And never in my days, I do protest,
Was it so precious to me as 'tis now.
Think you, but that I know our state secure,   80
I would be so triumphant as I am?

DERBY

The lords at Pomfret, when they rode from London,
Were jocund and supposed their states were sure,
And they indeed had no cause to mistrust;
But yet you see how soon the day o'ercast.

This sudden stab of rancour I misdoubt.
Pray God, I say, I prove a needless coward!
What, shall we toward the Tower? The day is spent.

HASTINGS
Come, come, have with you. Wot you what, my lord?
90   Today the lords you talked of are beheaded.

DERBY
They, for their truth, might better wear their heads
Than some that have accused them wear their hats.
But come, my lord, let us away.
      Enter a Pursuivant also named Hastings

HASTINGS
Go on before. I'll talk with this good fellow.
                        Exeunt Earl of Derby and Catesby
How now, Hastings! How goes the world with thee?

PURSUIVANT
The better that your lordship please to ask.

HASTINGS
I tell thee, man, 'tis better with me now
Than when I met thee last where now we meet.
Then was I going prisoner to the Tower
100   By the suggestion of the Queen's allies;
But now I tell thee – keep it to thyself –
This day those enemies are put to death,
And I in better state than e'er I was.

PURSUIVANT
God hold it, to your honour's good content!

HASTINGS
Gramercy, Hastings. There, drink that for me.
      Throws him his purse

PURSUIVANT
I thank your honour.   *Exit Pursuivant*
      Enter a Priest

PRIEST
    Well met, my lord. I am glad to see your honour.
HASTINGS
    I thank thee, good Sir John, with all my heart.
    I am in your debt for your last exercise;
    Come the next Sabbath, and I will content you.   110
        He whispers in his ear
PRIEST
    I'll wait upon your lordship.
        Enter Buckingham
BUCKINGHAM
    What, talking with a priest, Lord Chamberlain?
    Your friends at Pomfret, they do need the priest;
    Your honour hath no shriving work in hand.
HASTINGS
    Good faith, and when I met this holy man,
    The men you talk of came into my mind.
    What, go you toward the Tower?
BUCKINGHAM
    I do, my lord, but long I cannot stay there.
    I shall return before your lordship thence.
HASTINGS
    Nay, like enough, for I stay dinner there.   120
BUCKINGHAM (*aside*)
    And supper too, although thou know'st it not.
    – Come, will you go?
HASTINGS   I'll wait upon your lordship.
                                        Exeunt

III.3   *Enter Sir Richard Ratcliffe, with halberds, carrying*
             Rivers, Grey, and Vaughan to death at Pomfret

RIVERS
    Sir Richard Ratcliffe, let me tell thee this:
    Today shalt thou behold a subject die
    For truth, for duty, and for loyalty.

GREY
    God bless the Prince from all the pack of you!
    A knot you are of damnèd bloodsuckers.

VAUGHAN
    You live that shall cry woe for this hereafter.

RATCLIFFE
    Dispatch! The limit of your lives is out.

RIVERS
    O Pomfret, Pomfret! O thou bloody prison,
    Fatal and ominous to noble peers!
10 Within the guilty closure of thy walls
    Richard the Second here was hacked to death;
    And, for more slander to thy dismal seat,
    We give to thee our guiltless blood to drink.

GREY
    Now Margaret's curse is fallen upon our heads,
    When she exclaimed on Hastings, you, and I,
    For standing by when Richard stabbed her son.

RIVERS
    Then cursed she Richard, then cursed she Buckingham,
    Then cursed she Hastings. O, remember, God,
    To hear her prayer for them, as now for us!
20 And for my sister and her princely sons,
    Be satisfied, dear God, with our true blood,
    Which, as Thou know'st, unjustly must be spilt.

RATCLIFFE
    Make haste. The hour of death is expiate.

RIVERS

    Come, Grey; come, Vaughan; let us here embrace.

    Farewell, until we meet again in heaven.   *Exeunt*

    Enter Buckingham, Derby, Hastings, Bishop of Ely,   III.4
    Norfolk, Ratcliffe, Lovel, with others, at a table

HASTINGS

    Now, noble peers, the cause why we are met

    Is to determine of the coronation.

    In God's name, speak. When is the royal day?

BUCKINGHAM

    Is all things ready for the royal time?

DERBY

    It is, and wants but nomination.

BISHOP OF ELY

    Tomorrow then I judge a happy day.

BUCKINGHAM

    Who knows the Lord Protector's mind herein?

    Who is most inward with the noble Duke?

BISHOP OF ELY

    Your grace, we think, should soonest know his mind.

BUCKINGHAM

    We know each other's faces; for our hearts,   10

    He knows no more of mine than I of yours;

    Or I of his, my lord, than you of mine.

    Lord Hastings, you and he are near in love.

HASTINGS

    I thank his grace, I know he loves me well;

    But, for his purpose in the coronation,

    I have not sounded him, nor he delivered

    His gracious pleasure any way therein;

    But you, my honourable lords, may name the time,

And in the Duke's behalf I'll give my voice,
20   Which, I presume, he'll take in gentle part.

Enter Richard, Duke of Gloucester

BISHOP OF ELY

In happy time, here comes the Duke himself.

RICHARD

My noble lords and cousins all, good morrow.
I have been long a sleeper; but I trust
My absence doth neglect no great design
Which by my presence might have been concluded.

BUCKINGHAM

Had you not come upon your cue, my lord,
William Lord Hastings had pronounced your part –
I mean, your voice for crowning of the King.

RICHARD

Than my Lord Hastings no man might be bolder.
30   His lordship knows me well, and loves me well.
My Lord of Ely, when I was last in Holborn
I saw good strawberries in your garden there.
I do beseech you send for some of them.

BISHOP OF ELY

Marry and will, my lord, with all my heart.

Exit Bishop

RICHARD

Cousin of Buckingham, a word with you.

Takes him aside

Catesby hath sounded Hastings in our business
And finds the testy gentleman so hot
That he will lose his head ere give consent
His master's child, as worshipfully he terms it,
40   Shall lose the royalty of England's throne.

BUCKINGHAM

Withdraw yourself awhile. I'll go with you.

Exeunt Richard and Buckingham

DERBY

    We have not yet set down this day of triumph.

    Tomorrow, in my judgement, is too sudden;

    For I myself am not so well provided

    As else I would be, were the day prolonged.

      Enter the Bishop of Ely

BISHOP OF ELY

    Where is my lord the Duke of Gloucester?

    I have sent for these strawberries.

HASTINGS

    His grace looks cheerfully and smooth this morning;

    There's some conceit or other likes him well

    When that he bids good morrow with such spirit.   50

    I think there's never a man in Christendom

    Can lesser hide his love or hate than he,

    For by his face straight shall you know his heart.

DERBY

    What of his heart perceive you in his face

    By any livelihood he showed today?

HASTINGS

    Marry, that with no man here he is offended;

    For were he, he had shown it in his looks.

DERBY

    I pray God he be not, I say.

      Enter Richard and Buckingham

RICHARD

    I pray you all, tell me what they deserve

    That do conspire my death with devilish plots   60

    Of damnèd witchcraft, and that have prevailed

    Upon my body with their hellish charms.

HASTINGS

    The tender love I bear your grace, my lord,

    Makes me most forward in this princely presence

    To doom th'offenders: whatsoever they be,

I say, my lord, they have deservèd death.

RICHARD

Then be your eyes the witness of their evil.
See how I am bewitched: behold, mine arm
Is like a blasted sapling, withered up;
70 And this is Edward's wife, that monstrous witch,
Consorted with that harlot, strumpet Shore,
That by their witchcraft thus have markèd me.

HASTINGS

If they have done this deed, my noble lord –

RICHARD

If? Thou protector of this damnèd strumpet,
Talk'st thou to me of ifs? Thou art a traitor.
Off with his head! Now by Saint Paul I swear
I will not dine until I see the same!
Lovel and Ratcliffe, look that it be done.
The rest that love me, rise and follow me.   *Exeunt*
    Lovel and Ratcliffe remain, with Lord Hastings

HASTINGS

80 Woe, woe for England, not a whit for me!
For I, too fond, might have prevented this.
Stanley did dream the boar did raze our helms,
And I did scorn it and disdain to fly.
Three times today my footcloth horse did stumble,
And started when he looked upon the Tower,
As loath to bear me to the slaughterhouse.
O, now I need the priest that spake to me!
I now repent I told the pursuivant,
As too triumphing, how mine enemies
90 Today at Pomfret bloodily were butchered,
And I myself secure, in grace and favour.
O Margaret, Margaret, now thy heavy curse
Is lighted on poor Hastings' wretched head!

RATCLIFFE

   Come, come, dispatch! The Duke would be at dinner.
   Make a short shrift; he longs to see your head.

HASTINGS

   O momentary grace of mortal men,
   Which we more hunt for than the grace of God!
   Who builds his hope in air of your good looks
   Lives like a drunken sailor on a mast,
   Ready with every nod to tumble down   100
   Into the fatal bowels of the deep.

LOVEL

   Come, come, dispatch! 'Tis bootless to exclaim.

HASTINGS

   O bloody Richard! Miserable England!
   I prophesy the fearfull'st time to thee
   That ever wretched age hath looked upon.
   Come, lead me to the block; bear him my head.
   They smile at me who shortly shall be dead.   *Exeunt*

   Enter Richard, Duke of Gloucester, and Buckingham,   III.5
     in rotten armour, marvellous ill-favoured

RICHARD

   Come, cousin, canst thou quake and change thy colour,
   Murder thy breath in middle of a word,
   And then again begin, and stop again,
   As if thou wert distraught and mad with terror?

BUCKINGHAM

   Tut, I can counterfeit the deep tragedian,
   Speak and look back, and pry on every side,
   Tremble and start at wagging of a straw;
   Intending deep suspicion, ghastly looks
   Are at my service, like enforcèd smiles;

10   And both are ready in their offices,
At any time to grace my stratagems.
But what, is Catesby gone?

RICHARD

    He is; and see, he brings the Mayor along.

    Enter the Lord Mayor and Catesby

BUCKINGHAM Lord Mayor –

RICHARD Look to the drawbridge there!

BUCKINGHAM Hark! A drum.

RICHARD Catesby, o'erlook the walls.

BUCKINGHAM Lord Mayor, the reason we have sent –

RICHARD

    Look back! Defend thee! Here are enemies!

BUCKINGHAM

20   God and our innocence defend and guard us!

    Enter Lovel and Ratcliffe, with Hastings' head

RICHARD

    Be patient, they are friends, Ratcliffe and Lovel.

LOVEL

    Here is the head of that ignoble traitor,
The dangerous and unsuspected Hastings.

RICHARD

    So dear I loved the man that I must weep.
I took him for the plainest harmless creature
That breathed upon the earth a Christian;
Made him my book, wherein my soul recorded
The history of all her secret thoughts.
So smooth he daubed his vice with show of virtue

30   That, his apparent open guilt omitted –
I mean, his conversation with Shore's wife –
He lived from all attainder of suspects.

BUCKINGHAM

    Well, well, he was the covert'st sheltered traitor.
Would you imagine, or almost believe,

Were't not that by great preservation
We live to tell it, that the subtle traitor
This day had plotted, in the Council House,
To murder me and my good Lord of Gloucester?

LORD MAYOR

Had he done so?

RICHARD

What? Think you we are Turks or infidels?   40
Or that we would, against the form of law,
Proceed thus rashly in the villain's death
But that the extreme peril of the case,
The peace of England, and our persons' safety
Enforced us to this execution?

LORD MAYOR

Now fair befall you! He deserved his death,
And your good graces both have well proceeded
To warn false traitors from the like attempts.

BUCKINGHAM

I never looked for better at his hands
After he once fell in with Mistress Shore.   50
Yet had we not determined he should die
Until your lordship came to see his end,
Which now the loving haste of these our friends,
Something against our meaning, have prevented;
Because, my lord, I would have had you heard
The traitor speak, and timorously confess
The manner and the purpose of his treason,
That you might well have signified the same
Unto the citizens, who haply may
Misconster us in him and wail his death.   60

LORD MAYOR

But, my good lord, your grace's word shall serve,
As well as I had seen, and heard him speak;
And do not doubt, right noble princes both,

But I'll acquaint our duteous citizens
With all your just proceedings in this cause.

RICHARD

And to that end we wished your lordship here,
T'avoid the censures of the carping world.

BUCKINGHAM

Which since you come too late of our intent,
Yet witness what you hear we did intend.
70   And so, my good Lord Mayor, we bid farewell.

Exit Lord Mayor

RICHARD

Go after, after, cousin Buckingham.
The Mayor towards Guildhall hies him in all post;
There, at your meet'st advantage of the time,
Infer the bastardy of Edward's children.
Tell them how Edward put to death a citizen
Only for saying he would make his son
Heir to the Crown, meaning indeed his house,
Which by the sign thereof was termèd so.
Moreover, urge his hateful luxury
80   And bestial appetite in change of lust,
Which stretched unto their servants, daughters, wives,
Even where his raging eye or savage heart,
Without control, listed to make a prey.
Nay, for a need, thus far come near my person:
Tell them, when that my mother went with child
Of that insatiate Edward, noble York,
My princely father, then had wars in France,
And by true computation of the time
Found that the issue was not his begot;
90   Which well appearèd in his lineaments,
Being nothing like the noble duke my father.
Yet touch this sparingly, as 'twere far off,
Because, my lord, you know my mother lives.

BUCKINGHAM

    Doubt not, my lord, I'll play the orator
    As if the golden fee for which I plead
    Were for myself; and so, my lord, adieu.

RICHARD

    If you thrive well, bring them to Baynard's Castle,
    Where you shall find me well accompanied
    With reverend fathers and well-learnèd bishops.

BUCKINGHAM

    I go; and towards three or four a clock   100
    Look for the news that the Guildhall affords.

                       Exit Buckingham

RICHARD

    Go, Lovel, with all speed to Doctor Shaw;
    (*To Catesby*) Go thou to Friar Penker. Bid them both
    Meet me within this hour at Baynard's Castle.

            Exeunt Lovel, Catesby, and Ratcliffe

    Now will I go to take some privy order
    To draw the brats of Clarence out of sight,
    And to give notice that no manner of person
    Have any time recourse unto the princes.   *Exit*

    Enter a Scrivener, with a paper in his hand   III.6

SCRIVENER

    Here is the indictment of the good Lord Hastings,
    Which in a set hand fairly is engrossed
    That it may be today read o'er in Paul's.
    And mark how well the sequel hangs together.
    Eleven hours I have spent to write it over,
    For yesternight by Catesby was it sent me;
    The precedent was full as long a-doing;
    And yet within these five hours Hastings lived,
    Untainted, unexamined, free, at liberty.

10   Here's a good world the while! Who is so gross
      That cannot see this palpable device?
      Yet who's so bold but says he sees it not?
      Bad is the world, and all will come to naught
      When such ill dealing must be seen in thought.   *Exit*

III.7   *Enter Richard, Duke of Gloucester, and Buckingham*
         at several doors

RICHARD
      How now, how now? What say the citizens?
BUCKINGHAM
      Now, by the holy Mother of our Lord,
      The citizens are mum, say not a word.
RICHARD
      Touched you the bastardy of Edward's children?
BUCKINGHAM
      I did, with his contract with Lady Lucy
      And his contract by deputy in France;
      Th'unsatiate greediness of his desire
      And his enforcement of the city wives;
      His tyranny for trifles; his own bastardy,
10   As being got, your father then in France,
      And his resemblance, being not like the Duke.
      Withal I did infer your lineaments,
      Being the right idea of your father
      Both in your form and nobleness of mind;
      Laid open all your victories in Scotland,
      Your discipline in war, wisdom in peace,
      Your bounty, virtue, fair humility;
      Indeed, left nothing fitting for your purpose
      Untouched, or slightly handled in discourse;
20   And when mine oratory drew toward end
      I bid them that did love their country's good

Cry, 'God save Richard, England's royal King!'

RICHARD

And did they so?

BUCKINGHAM

No, so God help me, they spake not a word,
But, like dumb statuas or breathing stones,
Stared each on other, and looked deadly pale.
Which when I saw, I reprehended them
And asked the Mayor what meant this wilful silence.
His answer was, the people were not used
To be spoke to but by the Recorder.   30
Then he was urged to tell my tale again:
'Thus saith the Duke, thus hath the Duke inferred' –
But nothing spoke in warrant from himself.
When he had done, some followers of mine own,
At the lower end of the hall, hurled up their caps,
And some ten voices cried, 'God save King Richard!'
And thus I took the vantage of those few:
'Thanks, gentle citizens and friends,' quoth I.
'This general applause and cheerful shout
Argues your wisdoms and your love to Richard' –   40
And even here brake off and came away.

RICHARD

What tongueless blocks were they! Would they not
     speak?
Will not the Mayor then and his brethren come?

BUCKINGHAM

The Mayor is here at hand. Intend some fear;
Be not you spoke with but by mighty suit;
And look you get a prayer-book in your hand
And stand between two churchmen, good my lord,
For on that ground I'll make a holy descant;
And be not easily won to our requests.
Play the maid's part: still answer nay, and take it.   50

RICHARD

    I go; and if you plead as well for them
    As I can say nay to thee for myself,
    No doubt we'll bring it to a happy issue.

BUCKINGHAM

    Go, go, up to the leads! The Lord Mayor knocks.

Exit Richard

    Enter the Lord Mayor, aldermen, and citizens
    Welcome, my lord. I dance attendance here;
    I think the Duke will not be spoke withal.

    Enter Catesby

    Now, Catesby, what says your lord to my request?

CATESBY

    He doth entreat your grace, my noble lord,
    To visit him tomorrow or next day.
60   He is within, with two right reverend fathers,
    Divinely bent to meditation,
    And in no worldly suits would he be moved
    To draw him from his holy exercise.

BUCKINGHAM

    Return, good Catesby, to the gracious Duke.
    Tell him, myself, the Mayor and Aldermen,
    In deep designs, in matter of great moment,
    No less importing than our general good,
    Are come to have some conference with his grace.

CATESBY

    I'll signify so much unto him straight   *Exit*

BUCKINGHAM

70   Ah ha, my lord! This prince is not an Edward.
    He is not lulling on a lewd love-bed,
    But on his knees at meditation;
    Not dallying with a brace of courtesans,
    But meditating with two deep divines;
    Not sleeping, to engross his idle body,

But praying, to enrich his watchful soul.
Happy were England would this virtuous prince
Take on his grace the sovereignty thereof;
But sure I fear we shall not win him to it.

LORD MAYOR

Marry, God defend his grace should say us nay!   80

BUCKINGHAM

I fear he will. Here Catesby comes again.
    Enter Catesby
Now, Catesby, what says his grace?

CATESBY   My lord,
He wonders to what end you have assembled
Such troops of citizens to come to him,
His grace not being warned thereof before.
He fears, my lord, you mean no good to him.

BUCKINGHAM

Sorry I am my noble cousin should
Suspect me that I mean no good to him.
By heaven, we come to him in perfect love;
And so once more return and tell his grace.   90
                            Exit Catesby
When holy and devout religious men
Are at their beads, 'tis much to draw them thence,
So sweet is zealous contemplation.
    Enter Richard aloft, between two bishops, and
    Catesby

LORD MAYOR

See where his grace stands, 'tween two clergymen.

BUCKINGHAM

Two props of virtue for a Christian prince,
To stay him from the fall of vanity;
And see, a book of prayer in his hand –
True ornaments to know a holy man.
Famous Plantagenet, most gracious prince,

100 Lend favourable ear to our request,
And pardon us the interruption
Of thy devotion and right Christian zeal.

RICHARD
My lord, there needs no such apology.
I do beseech your grace to pardon me,
Who, earnest in the service of my God,
Deferred the visitation of my friends.
But, leaving this, what is your grace's pleasure?

BUCKINGHAM
Even that, I hope, which pleaseth God above
And all good men of this ungoverned isle.

RICHARD
110 I do suspect I have done some offence
That seems disgracious in the city's eye,
And that you come to reprehend my ignorance.

BUCKINGHAM
You have, my lord. Would it might please your grace,
On our entreaties, to amend your fault!

RICHARD
Else wherefore breathe I in a Christian land?

BUCKINGHAM
Know then it is your fault that you resign
The supreme seat, the throne majestical,
The sceptred office of your ancestors,
Your state of fortune and your due of birth,
120 The lineal glory of your royal house,
To the corruption of a blemished stock;
Whiles, in the mildness of your sleepy thoughts,
Which here we waken to our country's good,
The noble isle doth want her proper limbs;
Her face defaced with scars of infamy,
Her royal stock graft with ignoble plants,
And almost shouldered in the swallowing gulf

Of dark forgetfulness and deep oblivion.
Which to recure, we heartily solicit
Your gracious self to take on you the charge   130
And kingly government of this your land;
Not as Protector, steward, substitute,
Or lowly factor for another's gain;
But as successively, from blood to blood,
Your right of birth, your empery, you own.
For this, consorted with the citizens,
Your very worshipful and loving friends,
And by their vehement instigation,
In this just cause come I to move your grace.

RICHARD

I cannot tell if to depart in silence   140
Or bitterly to speak in your reproof
Best fitteth my degree or your condition.
If not to answer, you might haply think
Tongue-tied ambition, not replying, yielded
To bear the golden yoke of sovereignty
Which fondly you would here impose on me.
If to reprove you for this suit of yours,
So seasoned with your faithful love to me,
Then, on the other side, I checked my friends.
Therefore – to speak, and to avoid the first,   150
And then, in speaking, not to incur the last –
Definitively thus I answer you.
Your love deserves my thanks, but my desert
Unmeritable shuns your high request.
First, if all obstacles were cut away,
And that my path were even to the crown
As the ripe revenue and due of birth,
Yet so much is my poverty of spirit,
So mighty and so many my defects,
That I would rather hide me from my greatness,   160

Being a bark to brook no mighty sea,
Than in my greatness covet to be hid
And in the vapour of my glory smothered.
But, God be thanked, there is no need of me,
And much I need to help you, were there need.
The royal tree hath left us royal fruit,
Which, mellowed by the stealing hours of time,
Will well become the seat of majesty
And make, no doubt, us happy by his reign.
170   On him I lay that you would lay on me,
The right and fortune of his happy stars,
Which God defend that I should wring from him!

BUCKINGHAM
My lord, this argues conscience in your grace.
But the respects thereof are nice and trivial,
All circumstances well consider è d.
You say that Edward is your brother's son.
So say we too, but not by Edward's wife;
For first was he contract to Lady Lucy —
Your mother lives a witness to his vow —
180   And afterward by substitute betrothed
To Bona, sister to the King of France.
These both put off, a poor petitioner,
A care-crazed mother to a many sons,
A beauty-waning and distressèd widow,
Even in the afternoon of her best days,
Made prize and purchase of his wanton eye,
Seduced the pitch and height of his degree
To base declension and loathed bigamy.
By her, in his unlawful bed, he got
190   This Edward, whom our manners call the Prince.
More bitterly could I expostulate,
Save that, for reverence to some alive,
I give a sparing limit to my tongue.

Then, good my lord, take to your royal self
This proffered benefit of dignity;
If not to bless us and the land withal,
Yet to draw forth your noble ancestry
From the corruption of abusing times
Unto a lineal, true-derivèd course.

LORD MAYOR

Do, good my lord; your citizens entreat you.   200

BUCKINGHAM

Refuse not, mighty lord, this proffered love.

CATESBY

O, make them joyful, grant their lawful suit!

RICHARD

Alas, why would you heap this care on me?
I am unfit for state and majesty.
I do beseech you take it not amiss,
I cannot nor I will not yield to you.

BUCKINGHAM

If you refuse it – as, in love and zeal,
Loath to depose the child, your brother's son;
As well we know your tenderness of heart
And gentle, kind, effeminate remorse,   210
Which we have noted in you to your kindred
And egally indeed to all estates –
Yet know, whe'er you accept our suit or no,
Your brother's son shall never reign our king,
But we will plant some other in the throne
To the disgrace and downfall of your house;
And in this resolution here we leave you.
Come, citizens. Zounds! I'll entreat no more!

RICHARD

O, do not swear, my lord of Buckingham.
                    Exeunt Buckingham, Lord Mayor,
                        aldermen, and citizens

CATESBY

220   Call him again, sweet prince, accept their suit:
       If you deny them, all the land will rue it.

RICHARD

       Will you enforce me to a world of cares?
       Call them again. I am not made of stone,
       But penetrable to your kind entreaties,
       Albeit against my conscience and my soul.
           Enter Buckingham and the rest
       Cousin of Buckingham, and sage grave men,
       Since you will buckle fortune on my back,
       To bear her burden, whe'er I will or no,
       I must have patience to endure the load;

230   But if black scandal or foul-faced reproach
       Attend the sequel of your imposition,
       Your mere enforcement shall acquittance me
       From all the impure blots and stains thereof;
       For God doth know, and you may partly see,
       How far I am from the desire of this.

LORD MAYOR

       God bless your grace! We see it, and will say it.

RICHARD

       In saying so you shall but say the truth.

BUCKINGHAM

       Then I salute you with this royal title –
       Long live King Richard, England's worthy king!

ALL

240   Amen.

BUCKINGHAM

       Tomorrow may it please you to be crowned?

RICHARD

       Even when you please, for you will have it so.

BUCKINGHAM

       Tomorrow then we will attend your grace,

And so most joyfully we take our leave.
RICHARD (*to the bishops*)
  Come, let us to our holy work again.
  – Farewell, my cousin; farewell, gentle friends.   *Exeunt*

*

Enter Queen Elizabeth, the Duchess of York, and   IV.1
Marquess of Dorset at one door; Anne, Duchess of
Gloucester, and Lady Margaret Plantagenet,
Clarence's young daughter, at another door

DUCHESS OF YORK
  Who meets us here? My niece Plantagenet,
  Led in the hand of her kind aunt of Gloucester?
  Now, for my life, she's wandering to the Tower
  On pure heart's love, to greet the tender Prince.
  Daughter, well met.
ANNE   God give your graces both
  A happy and a joyful time of day!
QUEEN ELIZABETH
  As much to you, good sister. Whither away?
ANNE
  No farther than the Tower, and, as I guess,
  Upon the like devotion as yourselves,
  To gratulate the gentle princes there.   10
QUEEN ELIZABETH
  Kind sister, thanks. We'll enter all together.
    Enter Brakenbury, the Lieutenant
  And in good time, here the Lieutenant comes.
  Master Lieutenant, pray you, by your leave,
  How doth the Prince, and my young son of York?
BRAKENBURY
  Right well, dear madam. By your patience,

I may not suffer you to visit them;
The King hath strictly charged the contrary.

QUEEN ELIZABETH
The King? Who's that?

BRAKENBURY   I mean the Lord Protector.

QUEEN ELIZABETH
The Lord protect him from that kingly title!
20   Hath he set bounds between their love and me?
I am their mother; who shall bar me from them?

DUCHESS OF YORK
I am their father's mother; I will see them.

ANNE
Their aunt I am in law, in love their mother;
Then bring me to their sights. I'll bear thy blame
And take thy office from thee on my peril.

BRAKENBURY
No, madam, no! I may not leave it so:
I am bound by oath, and therefore pardon me.

                                        Exit Brakenbury

        Enter the Earl of Derby

DERBY
Let me but meet you, ladies, one hour hence,
And I'll salute your grace of York as mother
30   And reverend looker-on of two fair queens.
(*To Anne*)
Come, madam, you must straight to Westminster,
There to be crownèd Richard's royal Queen.

QUEEN ELIZABETH
Ah, cut my lace asunder,
That my pent heart may have some scope to beat,
Or else I swoon with this dead-killing news!

ANNE
Despiteful tidings! O unpleasing news!

DORSET
   Be of good cheer. Mother, how fares your grace?

QUEEN ELIZABETH
   O Dorset, speak not to me, get thee gone!
   Death and destruction dogs thee at thy heels;
   Thy mother's name is ominous to children.   40
   If thou wilt outstrip death, go cross the seas,
   And live with Richmond, from the reach of hell.
   Go hie thee, hie thee from this slaughterhouse,
   Lest thou increase the number of the dead
   And make me die the thrall of Margaret's curse,
   Nor mother, wife, nor England's counted Queen.

DERBY
   Full of wise care is this your counsel, madam.
   (*To Dorset*) Take all the swift advantage of the hours.
   You shall have letters from me to my son
   In your behalf, to meet you on the way.   50
   Be not ta'en tardy by unwise delay.

DUCHESS OF YORK
   O ill-dispersing wind of misery!
   O my accursèd womb, the bed of death!
   A cockatrice hast thou hatched to the world,
   Whose unavoided eye is murderous.

DERBY
   Come, madam, come! I in all haste was sent.

ANNE
   And I with all unwillingness will go.
   O, would to God that the inclusive verge
   Of golden metal that must round my brow
   Were red-hot steel, to sear me to the brains!   60
   Anointed let me be with deadly venom
   And die ere men can say, 'God save the Queen!'

QUEEN ELIZABETH
   Go, go, poor soul! I envy not thy glory.

To feed my humour wish thyself no harm.

ANNE

No? Why? When he that is my husband now
Came to me as I followed Henry's corse,
When scarce the blood was well washed from his hands
Which issued from my other angel husband
And that dear saint which then I weeping followed –
70   O, when, I say, I looked on Richard's face,
This was my wish: 'Be thou,' quoth I, 'accursed
For making me, so young, so old a widow!
And when thou wed'st, let sorrow haunt thy bed;
And be thy wife, if any be so mad,
More miserable by the life of thee
Than thou hast made me by my dear lord's death!'
Lo, ere I can repeat this curse again,
Within so small a time, my woman's heart
Grossly grew captive to his honey words
80   And proved the subject of mine own soul's curse,
Which hitherto hath held mine eyes from rest;
For never yet one hour in his bed
Did I enjoy the golden dew of sleep,
But with his timorous dreams was still awaked.
Besides, he hates me for my father Warwick,
And will, no doubt, shortly be rid of me.

QUEEN ELIZABETH

Poor heart, adieu! I pity thy complaining.

ANNE

No more than with my soul I mourn for yours.

DORSET

Farewell, thou woeful welcomer of glory.

ANNE

90   Adieu, poor soul, that tak'st thy leave of it.

DUCHESS OF YORK (to Dorset)

Go thou to Richmond, and good fortune guide thee!

(*To Anne*)
Go thou to Richard, and good angels tend thee!
(*To Queen Elizabeth*)
Go thou to sanctuary, and good thoughts possess thee!
I to my grave, where peace and rest lie with me!
Eighty odd years of sorrow have I seen,
And each hour's joy wracked with a week of teen.

QUEEN ELIZABETH
Stay, yet look back with me unto the Tower.
Pity, you ancient stones, those tender babes
Whom envy hath immured within your walls –
Rough cradle for such little pretty ones!   100
Rude ragged nurse, old sullen playfellow
For tender princes – use my babies well!
So foolish sorrow bids your stones farewell.   *Exeunt*

Sound a sennet. Enter Richard as King, in pomp,   IV.2
*Buckingham, Catesby, Ratcliffe, Lovel, a Page, and
attendants*

KING RICHARD
Stand all apart. Cousin of Buckingham –

BUCKINGHAM
My gracious sovereign?

KING RICHARD
Give me thy hand.
    Sound
    Here he ascendeth the throne
                    Thus high, by thy advice
And thy assistance, is King Richard seated.
But shall we wear these glories for a day?
Or shall they last, and we rejoice in them?

BUCKINGHAM
Still live they, and for ever let them last!

KING RICHARD

Ah, Buckingham, now do I play the touch,
To try if thou be current gold indeed.
Young Edward lives. Think now what I would speak.

BUCKINGHAM

Say on, my loving lord.

KING RICHARD

Why, Buckingham, I say I would be king.

BUCKINGHAM

Why, so you are, my thrice-renownèd lord.

KING RICHARD

Ha! Am I king? 'Tis so. But Edward lives.

BUCKINGHAM

True, noble prince.

KING RICHARD   O bitter consequence
That Edward still should live true noble prince!
Cousin, thou wast not wont to be so dull.
Shall I be plain? I wish the bastards dead,
And I would have it suddenly performed.
What sayst thou now? Speak suddenly, be brief.

BUCKINGHAM

Your grace may do your pleasure.

KING RICHARD

Tut, tut, thou art all ice; thy kindness freezes.
Say, have I thy consent that they shall die?

BUCKINGHAM

Give me some little breath, some pause, dear lord,
Before I positively speak in this.
I will resolve you herein presently.   *Exit Buckingham*

CATESBY (*aside*)

The King is angry. See, he gnaws his lip.

KING RICHARD

I will converse with iron-witted fools
And unrespective boys. None are for me

That look into me with considerate eyes.   30
High-reaching Buckingham grows circumspect.
Boy!

PAGE
My lord?

KING RICHARD
Know'st thou not any whom corrupting gold
Will tempt unto a close exploit of death?

PAGE
I know a discontented gentleman
Whose humble means match not his haughty spirit.
Gold were as good as twenty orators,
And will, no doubt, tempt him to anything.

KING RICHARD
What is his name?

PAGE   His name, my lord, is Tyrrel.   40

KING RICHARD
I partly know the man. Go call him hither, boy.
                                        Exit Page
The deep-revolving witty Buckingham
No more shall be the neighbour to my counsels.
Hath he so long held out with me, untired,
And stops he now for breath? Well, be it so.
    Enter the Earl of Derby
How now, Lord Stanley? What's the news?

DERBY   Know, my loving lord,
The Marquess Dorset, as I hear, is fled
To Richmond in the parts where he abides.
    Derby stands aside

KING RICHARD
Come hither, Catesby. Rumour it abroad
That Anne my wife is very grievous sick.   50
I will take order for her keeping close.
Inquire me out some mean poor gentleman,

Whom I will marry straight to Clarence' daughter.
The boy is foolish, and I fear not him.
Look how thou dream'st! I say again, give out
That Anne, my Queen, is sick and like to die.
About it! For it stands me much upon
To stop all hopes whose growth may damage me.

                                              Exit Catesby

I must be married to my brother's daughter,
Or else my kingdom stands on brittle glass.
Murder her brothers, and then marry her —
Uncertain way of gain! But I am in
So far in blood that sin will pluck on sin.
Tear-falling pity dwells not in this eye.

      Enter Page, with Tyrrel

Is thy name Tyrrel?

TYRREL

James Tyrrel, and your most obedient subject.

KING RICHARD

Art thou indeed?

TYRREL   Prove me, my gracious lord.

KING RICHARD

Dar'st thou resolve to kill a friend of mine?

TYRREL

Please you;
But I had rather kill two enemies.

KING RICHARD

Why, there thou hast it! Two deep enemies,
Foes to my rest and my sweet sleep's disturbers,
Are they that I would have thee deal upon.
Tyrrel, I mean those bastards in the Tower.

TYRREL

Let me have open means to come to them,
And soon I'll rid you from the fear of them.

KING RICHARD

Thou sing'st sweet music. Hark, come hither, Tyrrel.
Go by this token. Rise, and lend thine ear.
    Whispers
There is no more but so; say it is done,
And I will love thee and prefer thee for it.   80

TYRREL

I will dispatch it straight.   *Exit*
    Enter Buckingham

BUCKINGHAM

My lord, I have considered in my mind
The late request that you did sound me in.

KING RICHARD

Well, let that rest. Dorset is fled to Richmond.

BUCKINGHAM

I hear the news, my lord.

KING RICHARD

Stanley, he is your wife's son. Well, look unto it.

BUCKINGHAM

My lord, I claim the gift, my due by promise,
For which your honour and your faith is pawned,
Th'earldom of Hereford and the movables
Which you have promisèd I shall possess.   90

KING RICHARD

Stanley, look to your wife; if she convey
Letters to Richmond, you shall answer it.

BUCKINGHAM

What says your highness to my just request?

KING RICHARD

I do remember me Henry the Sixth
Did prophesy that Richmond should be king
When Richmond was a little peevish boy.
A king! – Perhaps! –

BUCKINGHAM
  My lord —
KING RICHARD
  How chance the prophet could not at that time
  Have told me, I being by, that I should kill him?
BUCKINGHAM
  My lord, your promise for the earldom!
KING RICHARD
  Richmond! When last I was at Exeter,
  The Mayor in courtesy showed me the castle,
  And called it Rouge-mount; at which name I started,
  Because a bard of Ireland told me once
  I should not live long after I saw Richmond.
BUCKINGHAM
  My lord —
KING RICHARD
  Ay, what's a clock?
BUCKINGHAM
  I am thus bold to put your grace in mind
  Of what you promised me.
KING RICHARD   Well, but what's a clock?
BUCKINGHAM
  Upon the stroke of ten.
KING RICHARD   Well, let it strike.
BUCKINGHAM
  Why let it strike?
KING RICHARD
  Because that like a Jack thou keep'st the stroke
  Betwixt thy begging and my meditation.
  I am not in the giving vein today.
BUCKINGHAM
  May it please you to resolve me in my suit?

KING RICHARD
Thou troublest me; I am not in the vein.
                              Exeunt all but Buckingham

BUCKINGHAM
And is it thus? Repays he my deep service
With such contempt? Made I him king for this?
O, let me think on Hastings, and be gone   120
To Brecknock while my fearful head is on!   *Exit*

            Enter Tyrrel   IV.3
TYRREL
The tyrannous and bloody act is done,
The most arch deed of piteous massacre
That ever yet this land was guilty of.
Dighton and Forrest, whom I did suborn
To do this piece of ruthless butchery,
Albeit they were fleshed villains, bloody dogs,
Melting with tenderness and mild compassion,
Wept like to children in their death's sad story.
'O, thus,' quoth Dighton, 'lay the gentle babes.'
'Thus, thus,' quoth Forrest, 'girdling one another   10
Within their alablaster innocent arms.
Their lips were four red roses on a stalk,
Which in their summer beauty kissed each other.
A book of prayers on their pillow lay,
Which once,' quoth Forrest, 'almost changed my mind;
But O! The devil' – there the villain stopped;
When Dighton thus told on – 'We smotherèd
The most replenishèd sweet work of nature
That from the prime creation e'er she framed.'
Hence both are gone with conscience and remorse.   20
They could not speak; and so I left them both,
To bear this tidings to the bloody King.

Enter King Richard

And here he comes. All health, my sovereign lord!

KING RICHARD

Kind Tyrrel, am I happy in thy news?

TYRREL

If to have done the thing you gave in charge
Beget your happiness, be happy then,
For it is done.

KING RICHARD   But didst thou see them dead?

TYRREL

I did, my lord.

KING RICHARD   And buried, gentle Tyrrel?

TYRREL

The chaplain of the Tower hath buried them;
30   But where, to say the truth, I do not know.

KING RICHARD

Come to me, Tyrrel, soon at after-supper,
When thou shalt tell the process of their death.
Meantime, but think how I may do thee good,
And be inheritor of thy desire.
Farewell till then.

TYRREL   I humbly take my leave.   *Exit*

KING RICHARD

The son of Clarence have I pent up close,
His daughter meanly have I matched in marriage,
The sons of Edward sleep in Abraham's bosom,
And Anne my wife hath bid this world good night.
40   Now, for I know the Britain Richmond aims
At young Elizabeth, my brother's daughter,
And by that knot looks proudly on the crown,
To her go I, a jolly thriving wooer.

Enter Ratcliffe

RATCLIFFE

My lord –

KING RICHARD
  Good or bad news, that thou com'st in so bluntly?
RATCLIFFE
  Bad news, my lord. Morton is fled to Richmond,
  And Buckingham, backed with the hardy Welshmen,
  Is in the field, and still his power increaseth.
KING RICHARD
  Ely with Richmond troubles me more near
  Than Buckingham and his rash-levied strength.   50
  Come! I have learned that fearful commenting
  Is leaden servitor to dull delay;
  Delay leads impotent and snail-paced beggary.
  Then fiery expedition be my wing,
  Jove's Mercury, and herald for a king!
  Go, muster men. My counsel is my shield;
  We must be brief when traitors brave the field. *Exeunt*

        Enter old Queen Margaret   IV.4
QUEEN MARGARET
  So now prosperity begins to mellow
  And drop into the rotten mouth of death.
  Here in these confines slyly have I lurked
  To watch the waning of mine enemies.
  A dire induction am I witness to,
  And will to France, hoping the consequence
  Will prove as bitter, black, and tragical.
  Withdraw thee, wretched Margaret! Who comes here?
        Queen Margaret retires
        Enter Duchess of York and Queen Elizabeth
QUEEN ELIZABETH
  Ah, my poor princes! Ah, my tender babes!
  My unblown flowers, new-appearing sweets!   10
  If yet your gentle souls fly in the air

And be not fixed in doom perpetual,
Hover about me with your airy wings
And hear your mother's lamentation!

QUEEN MARGARET (*aside*)

Hover about her. Say that right for right
Hath dimmed your infant morn to agèd night.

DUCHESS OF YORK

So many miseries have crazed my voice
That my woe-wearied tongue is still and mute.
Edward Plantagenet, why art thou dead?

QUEEN MARGARET (*aside*)

20   Plantagenet doth quit Plantagenet;
Edward for Edward pays a dying debt.

QUEEN ELIZABETH

Wilt Thou, O God, fly from such gentle lambs
And throw them in the entrails of the wolf?
When didst Thou sleep when such a deed was done?

QUEEN MARGARET (*aside*)

When holy Harry died, and my sweet son.

DUCHESS OF YORK

Dead life, blind sight, poor mortal-living ghost,
Woe's scene, world's shame, grave's due by life usurped,
Brief abstract and record of tedious days,
Rest thy unrest on England's lawful earth,
        Sits down
30   Unlawfully made drunk with innocents' blood!

QUEEN ELIZABETH

Ah, that thou wouldst as soon afford a grave
As thou canst yield a melancholy seat!
Then would I hide my bones, not rest them here.
Ah, who hath any cause to mourn but we?
        Sits down by her

QUEEN MARGARET (*comes forward*)

If ancient sorrow be most reverend,

Give mine the benefit of seniory
And let my griefs frown on the upper hand.
If sorrow can admit society,
 Sits down with them
Tell over your woes again by viewing mine.
I had an Edward, till a Richard killed him;   40
I had a Harry, till a Richard killed him:
Thou hadst an Edward, till a Richard killed him;
Thou hadst a Richard, till a Richard killed him.

DUCHESS OF YORK
I had a Richard too, and thou didst kill him;
I had a Rutland too, thou holp'st to kill him.

QUEEN MARGARET
Thou hadst a Clarence too, and Richard killed him.
From forth the kennel of thy womb hath crept
A hellhound that doth hunt us all to death.
That dog, that had his teeth before his eyes,
To worry lambs and lap their gentle blood,   50
That foul defacer of God's handiwork
That reigns in gallèd eyes of weeping souls,
That excellent grand tyrant of the earth
Thy womb let loose to chase us to our graves.
O upright, just, and true-disposing God,
How do I thank Thee that this carnal cur
Preys on the issue of his mother's body
And makes her pew-fellow with others' moan!

DUCHESS OF YORK
O Harry's wife, triumph not in my woes!
God witness with me I have wept for thine.   60

QUEEN MARGARET
Bear with me! I am hungry for revenge,
And now I cloy me with beholding it.
Thy Edward he is dead, that killed my Edward;
Thy other Edward dead, to quit my Edward;

Young York he is but boot, because both they
Matched not the high perfection of my loss.
Thy Clarence he is dead that stabbed my Edward,
And the beholders of this frantic play,
Th'adulterate Hastings, Rivers, Vaughan, Grey,
70   Untimely smothered in their dusky graves.
Richard yet lives, hell's black intelligencer;
Only reserved their factor to buy souls
And send them thither. But at hand, at hand,
Ensues his piteous and unpitied end.
Earth gapes, hell burns, fiends roar, saints pray,
To have him suddenly conveyed from hence.
Cancel his bond of life, dear God, I pray,
That I may live and say, 'The dog is dead.'

QUEEN ELIZABETH
O, thou didst prophesy the time would come
80   That I should wish for thee to help me curse
That bottled spider, that foul bunch-backed toad!

QUEEN MARGARET
I called thee then vain flourish of my fortune;
I called thee then poor shadow, painted queen,
The presentation of but what I was,
The flattering index of a direful pageant,
One heaved a-high to be hurled down below,
A mother only mocked with two fair babes,
A dream of what thou wast, a garish flag
To be the aim of every dangerous shot;
90   A sign of dignity, a breath, a bubble,
A queen in jest, only to fill the scene.
Where is thy husband now? Where be thy brothers?
Where are thy two sons? Wherein dost thou joy?
Who sues and kneels and says, 'God save the Queen'?
Where be the bending peers that flattered thee?
Where be the thronging troops that followed thee?

Decline all this, and see what now thou art:
For happy wife, a most distressèd widow;
For joyful mother, one that wails the name;
For one being sued to, one that humbly sues;   100
For queen, a very caitiff crowned with care;
For she that scorned at me, now scorned of me;
For she being feared of all, now fearing one;
For she commanding all, obeyed of none.
Thus hath the course of justice wheeled about
And left thee but a very prey to time,
Having no more but thought of what thou wast,
To torture thee the more, being what thou art.
Thou didst usurp my place, and dost thou not
Usurp the just proportion of my sorrow?   110
Now thy proud neck bears half my burdened yoke,
From which even here I slip my weary head
And leave the burden of it all on thee.
Farewell, York's wife, and Queen of sad mischance!
These English woes shall make me smile in France.

QUEEN ELIZABETH
O thou well skilled in curses, stay awhile
And teach me how to curse mine enemies!

QUEEN MARGARET
Forbear to sleep the nights, and fast the days;
Compare dead happiness with living woe;
Think that thy babes were sweeter than they were   120
And he that slew them fouler than he is.
Bettering thy loss makes the bad causer worse;
Revolving this will teach thee how to curse.

QUEEN ELIZABETH
My words are dull. O, quicken them with thine!

QUEEN MARGARET
Thy woes will make them sharp and pierce like mine.
                                        Exit Queen Margaret

DUCHESS OF YORK
    Why should calamity be full of words?
QUEEN ELIZABETH
    Windy attorneys to their client's woes,
    Airy succeeders of intestate joys,
    Poor breathing orators of miseries,
130 Let them have scope! Though what they will impart
    Help nothing else, yet do they ease the heart.
DUCHESS OF YORK
    If so, then be not tongue-tied: go with me,
    And in the breath of bitter words let's smother
    My damnèd son that thy two sweet sons smothered.
    The trumpet sounds. Be copious in exclaims.
        Enter King Richard and his train, marching, with drums
        and trumpets
KING RICHARD
    Who intercepts me in my expedition?
DUCHESS OF YORK
    O, she that might have intercepted thee,
    By strangling thee in her accursèd womb,
    From all the slaughters, wretch, that thou hast done!
QUEEN ELIZABETH
140 Hid'st thou that forehead with a golden crown
    Where should be branded, if that right were right,
    The slaughter of the prince that owed that crown
    And the dire death of my poor sons and brothers?
    Tell me, thou villain-slave, where are my children?
DUCHESS OF YORK
    Thou toad, thou toad, where is thy brother Clarence?
    And little Ned Plantagenet, his son?
QUEEN ELIZABETH
    Where is the gentle Rivers, Vaughan, Grey?
DUCHESS OF YORK
    Where is kind Hastings?

KING RICHARD

A flourish, trumpets! Strike alarum, drums!
Let not the heavens hear these tell-tale women   150
Rail on the Lord's anointed. Strike, I say!
    Flourish. Alarums
Either be patient and entreat me fair,
Or with the clamorous report of war
Thus will I drown your exclamations.

DUCHESS OF YORK

Art thou my son?

KING RICHARD

Ay, I thank God, my father, and yourself.

DUCHESS OF YORK

Then patiently hear my impatience.

KING RICHARD

Madam, I have a touch of your condition
That cannot brook the accent of reproof.

DUCHESS OF YORK

O, let me speak!

KING RICHARD   Do then, but I'll not hear.   160

DUCHESS OF YORK

I will be mild and gentle in my words.

KING RICHARD

And brief, good mother, for I am in haste.

DUCHESS OF YORK

Art thou so hasty? I have stayed for thee,
God knows, in torment and in agony.

KING RICHARD

And came I not at last to comfort you?

DUCHESS OF YORK

No, by the Holy Rood, thou know'st it well,
Thou cam'st on earth to make the earth my hell.
A grievous burden was thy birth to me;
Tetchy and wayward was thy infancy;

170   Thy schooldays frightful, desperate, wild, and furious;
Thy prime of manhood daring, bold, and venturous;
Thy age confirmed, proud, subtle, sly, and bloody,
More mild, but yet more harmful – kind in hatred.
What comfortable hour canst thou name
That ever graced me with thy company?

KING RICHARD
Faith, none, but Humphrey Hour, that called your grace
To breakfast once, forth of my company.
If I be so disgracious in your eye,
Let me march on and not offend you, madam.
180   Strike up the drum.

DUCHESS OF YORK   I prithee hear me speak.

KING RICHARD
You speak too bitterly.

DUCHESS OF YORK   Hear me a word
For I shall never speak to thee again.

KING RICHARD
So.

DUCHESS OF YORK
Either thou wilt die by God's just ordinance
Ere from this war thou turn a conqueror,
Or I with grief and extreme age shall perish
And never more behold thy face again.
Therefore take with thee my most grievous curse,
Which in the day of battle tire thee more
190   Than all the complete armour that thou wearest!
My prayers on the adverse party fight,
And there the little souls of Edward's children
Whisper the spirits of thine enemies
And promise them success and victory!
Bloody thou art, bloody will be thy end;
Shame serves thy life and doth thy death attend. *Exit*

QUEEN ELIZABETH
Though far more cause, yet much less spirit to curse
Abides in me. I say amen to her.

KING RICHARD
Stay, madam; I must talk a word with you.

QUEEN ELIZABETH
I have no more sons of the royal blood   200
For thee to slaughter. For my daughters, Richard,
They shall be praying nuns, not weeping queens;
And therefore level not to hit their lives.

KING RICHARD
You have a daughter called Elizabeth
Virtuous and fair, royal and gracious.

QUEEN ELIZABETH
And must she die for this? O, let her live,
And I'll corrupt her manners, stain her beauty,
Slander myself as false to Edward's bed,
Throw over her the veil of infamy.
So she may live unscarred of bleeding slaughter,   210
I will confess she was not Edward's daughter.

KING RICHARD
Wrong not her birth; she is a royal princess.

QUEEN ELIZABETH
To save her life, I'll say she is not so.

KING RICHARD
Her life is safest only in her birth.

QUEEN ELIZABETH
And only in that safety died her brothers.

KING RICHARD
Lo, at their births good stars were opposite.

QUEEN ELIZABETH
No, to their lives ill friends were contrary.

KING RICHARD
All unavoided is the doom of destiny.

QUEEN ELIZABETH

    True, when avoided grace makes destiny.

220   My babes were destined to a fairer death

    If grace had blessed thee with a fairer life.

KING RICHARD

    You speak as if that I had slain my cousins!

QUEEN ELIZABETH

    Cousins indeed, and by their uncle cozened

    Of comfort, kingdom, kindred, freedom, life.

    Whose hand soever lanched their tender hearts,

    Thy head, all indirectly, gave direction.

    No doubt the murderous knife was dull and blunt

    Till it was whetted on thy stone-hard heart

    To revel in the entrails of my lambs.

230   But that still use of grief makes wild grief tame,

    My tongue should to thy ears not name my boys

    Till that my nails were anchored in thine eyes;

    And I, in such a desperate bay of death,

    Like a poor bark of sails and tackling reft,

    Rush all to pieces on thy rocky bosom.

KING RICHARD

    Madam, so thrive I in my enterprise

    And dangerous success of bloody wars

    As I intend more good to you and yours

    Than ever you or yours by me were harmed!

QUEEN ELIZABETH

240   What good is covered with the face of heaven,

    To be discovered, that can do me good?

KING RICHARD

    Th'advancement of your children, gentle lady.

QUEEN ELIZABETH

    Up to some scaffold, there to lose their heads!

KING RICHARD

    Unto the dignity and height of fortune,

The high imperial type of this earth's glory.

QUEEN ELIZABETH

Flatter my sorrow with report of it.
Tell me, what state, what dignity, what honour
Canst thou demise to any child of mine?

KING RICHARD

Even all I have – yea, and myself and all –
Will I withal endow a child of thine,   250
So in the Lethe of thy angry soul
Thou drown the sad remembrance of those wrongs
Which thou supposest I have done to thee.

QUEEN ELIZABETH

Be brief, lest that the process of thy kindness
Last longer telling than thy kindness' date.

KING RICHARD

Then know that from my soul I love thy daughter.

QUEEN ELIZABETH

My daughter's mother thinks it with her soul.

KING RICHARD

What do you think?

QUEEN ELIZABETH

That thou dost love my daughter from thy soul.
So from thy soul's love didst thou love her brothers,   260
And from my heart's love I do thank thee for it.

KING RICHARD

Be not so hasty to confound my meaning.
I mean that with my soul I love thy daughter
And do intend to make her Queen of England.

QUEEN ELIZABETH

Well then, who dost thou mean shall be her king?

KING RICHARD

Even he that makes her queen. Who else should be?

QUEEN ELIZABETH

What, thou?

KING RICHARD
                    Even so. How think you of it?
QUEEN ELIZABETH
    How canst thou woo her?
KING RICHARD   That would I learn of you,
    As one being best acquainted with her humour.
QUEEN ELIZABETH
270   And wilt thou learn of me?
KING RICHARD   Madam, with all my heart.
QUEEN ELIZABETH
    Send to her by the man that slew her brothers
    A pair of bleeding hearts; thereon engrave
    'Edward' and 'York'; then haply will she weep.
    Therefore present to her – as sometimes Margaret
    Did to thy father, steeped in Rutland's blood –
    A handkerchief, which say to her did drain
    The purple sap from her sweet brother's body,
    And bid her wipe her weeping eyes withal.
    If this inducement move her not to love,
280   Send her a letter of thy noble deeds:
    Tell her thou mad'st away her uncle Clarence,
    Her uncle Rivers; yea, and for her sake,
    Mad'st quick conveyance with her good aunt Anne!
KING RICHARD
    You mock me, madam; this is not the way
    To win your daughter.
QUEEN ELIZABETH   There is no other way,
    Unless thou couldst put on some other shape,
    And not be Richard that hath done all this.
KING RICHARD
    Say that I did all this for love of her.
QUEEN ELIZABETH
    Nay, then indeed she cannot choose but hate thee,
290   Having bought love with such a bloody spoil.

KING RICHARD
Look what is done cannot be now amended.
Men shall deal unadvisedly sometimes,
Which after-hours gives leisure to repent.
If I did take the kingdom from your sons,
To make amends I'll give it to your daughter;
If I have killed the issue of your womb,
To quicken your increase I will beget
Mine issue of your blood upon your daughter.
A grandam's name is little less in love
Than is the doting title of a mother;   300
They are as children but one step below,
Even of your metal, of your very blood,
Of all one pain, save for a night of groans
Endured of her for whom you bid like sorrow.
Your children were vexation to your youth
But mine shall be a comfort to your age.
The loss you have is but a son being king,
And by that loss your daughter is made queen.
I cannot make you what amends I would;
Therefore accept such kindness as I can.   310
Dorset your son, that with a fearful soul
Leads discontented steps in foreign soil,
This fair alliance quickly shall call home
To high promotions and great dignity.
The King, that calls your beauteous daughter wife,
Familiarly shall call thy Dorset brother.
Again shall you be mother to a king,
And all the ruins of distressful times
Repaired with double riches of content.
What! We have many goodly days to see: 320
The liquid drops of tears that you have shed
Shall come again, transformed to orient pearl,
Advantaging their love with interest

Of ten times double gain of happiness.
Go then, my mother; to thy daughter go;
Make bold her bashful years with your experience;
Prepare her ears to hear a wooer's tale;
Put in her tender heart th'aspiring flame
Of golden sovereignty; acquaint the Princess
330   With the sweet silent hours of marriage joys;
And when this arm of mine hath chastisèd
The petty rebel, dull-brained Buckingham,
Bound with triumphant garlands will I come
And lead thy daughter to a conqueror's bed;
To whom I will retail my conquest won,
And she shall be sole victoress, Caesar's Caesar.

QUEEN ELIZABETH
What were I best to say? Her father's brother
Would be her lord? Or shall I say her uncle?
Or he that slew her brothers and her uncles?
340   Under what title shall I woo for thee
That God, the law, my honour, and her love
Can make seem pleasing to her tender years?

KING RICHARD
Infer fair England's peace by this alliance.

QUEEN ELIZABETH
Which she shall purchase with still-lasting war.

KING RICHARD
Tell her the King, that may command, entreats.

QUEEN ELIZABETH
That at her hands which the King's king forbids.

KING RICHARD
Say she shall be a high and mighty queen.

QUEEN ELIZABETH
To vail the title, as her mother doth.

KING RICHARD
Say I will love her everlastingly.

QUEEN ELIZABETH
  But how long shall that title 'ever' last?   350
KING RICHARD
  Sweetly in force unto her fair life's end.
QUEEN ELIZABETH
  But how long fairly shall her sweet life last?
KING RICHARD
  As long as heaven and nature lengthens it.
QUEEN ELIZABETH
  As long as hell and Richard likes of it.
KING RICHARD
  Say I, her sovereign, am her subject love.
QUEEN ELIZABETH
  But she, your subject, loathes such sovereignty.
KING RICHARD
  Be eloquent in my behalf to her.
QUEEN ELIZABETH
  An honest tale speeds best being plainly told.
KING RICHARD
  Then plainly to her tell my loving tale.
QUEEN ELIZABETH
  Plain and not honest is too harsh a style.   360
KING RICHARD
  Your reasons are too shallow and too quick.
QUEEN ELIZABETH
  O no, my reasons are too deep and dead –
  Too deep and dead, poor infants, in their graves.
KING RICHARD
  Harp not on that string, madam; that is past.
QUEEN ELIZABETH
  Harp on it still shall I till heartstrings break.
KING RICHARD
  Now, by my George, my Garter, and my crown –

QUEEN ELIZABETH
  Profaned, dishonoured, and the third usurped.

KING RICHARD
  I swear —

QUEEN ELIZABETH
         By nothing, for this is no oath.
  Thy George, profaned, hath lost his lordly honour;
370 Thy Garter, blemished, pawned his knightly virtue;
  Thy crown, usurped, disgraced his kingly glory.
  If something thou wouldst swear to be believed,
  Swear then by something that thou hast not wronged.

KING RICHARD
  Then by myself —

QUEEN ELIZABETH
             Thyself is self-misused.

KING RICHARD
  Now by the world —

QUEEN ELIZABETH   'Tis full of thy foul wrongs.

KING RICHARD
  My father's death —

QUEEN ELIZABETH   Thy life hath it dishonoured.

KING RICHARD
  Why then, by God —

QUEEN ELIZABETH   God's wrong is most of all.
  If thou didst fear to break an oath with Him,
  The unity the King my husband made
380 Thou hadst not broken, nor my brothers died.
  If thou hadst feared to break an oath by Him,
  Th'imperial metal, circling now thy head,
  Had graced the tender temples of my child,
  And both the princes had been breathing here,
  Which now, two tender bedfellows for dust,
  Thy broken faith hath made the prey for worms.

What canst thou swear by now?

KING RICHARD   The time to come.

QUEEN ELIZABETH
That thou hast wrongèd in the time o'er-past;
For I myself have many tears to wash
Hereafter time, for time past wronged by thee.   390
The children live whose fathers thou hast slaughtered,
Ungoverned youth, to wail it in their age;
The parents live whose children thou hast butchered,
Old barren plants, to wail it with their age.
Swear not by time to come, for that thou hast
Misused ere used, by times ill-used o'erpast.

KING RICHARD
As I intend to prosper and repent,
So thrive I in my dangerous affairs
Of hostile arms! Myself myself confound!
Heaven and fortune bar me happy hours!   400
Day, yield me not thy light, nor, night, thy rest!
Be opposite all planets of good luck
To my proceeding if, with dear heart's love,
Immaculate devotion, holy thoughts,
I tender not thy beauteous princely daughter!
In her consists my happiness and thine;
Without her, follows to myself and thee,
Herself, the land, and many a Christian soul,
Death, desolation, ruin, and decay.
It cannot be avoided but by this;   410
It will not be avoided but by this.
Therefore, dear mother – I must call you so –
Be the attorney of my love to her:
Plead what I will be, not what I have been –
Not my deserts, but what I will deserve;
Urge the necessity and state of times,

And be not peevish-fond in great designs.

KING RICHARD

QUEEN ELIZABETH

Shall I be tempted of the devil thus?

KING RICHARD

Ay, if the devil tempt you to do good.

QUEEN ELIZABETH

420 Shall I forget myself to be myself?

KING RICHARD

Ay, if yourself's remembrance wrong yourself.

QUEEN ELIZABETH

Yet thou didst kill my children.

KING RICHARD

But in your daughter's womb I bury them,
Where, in that nest of spicery, they will breed
Selves of themselves, to your recomforture.

QUEEN ELIZABETH

Shall I go win my daughter to thy will?

KING RICHARD

And be a happy mother by the deed.

QUEEN ELIZABETH

I go. Write to me very shortly,
And you shall understand from me her mind.

KING RICHARD

430 Bear her my true love's kiss; and so farewell —

Exit Queen Elizabeth

Relenting fool, and shallow, changing woman!

Enter Ratcliffe, Catesby following

How now? What news?

RATCLIFFE

Most mighty sovereign, on the western coast
Rideth a puissant navy; to our shores
Throng many doubtful, hollow-hearted friends,
Unarmed, and unresolved to beat them back.
'Tis thought that Richmond is their admiral;

And there they hull, expecting but the aid
Of Buckingham to welcome them ashore.

KING RICHARD
Some light-foot friend post to the Duke of Norfolk: 440
Ratcliffe, thyself – or Catesby – where is he?

CATESBY
Here, my good lord.

KING RICHARD   Catesby, fly to the Duke.

CATESBY
I will, my lord, with all convenient haste.

KING RICHARD
Ratcliffe, come hither. Post to Salisbury.
When thou com'st thither – (*To Catesby*) Dull unmindful
    villain,
Why stay'st thou here and go'st not to the Duke?

CATESBY
First, mighty liege, tell me your highness' pleasure,
What from your grace I shall deliver to him.

KING RICHARD
O, true, good Catesby; bid him levy straight
The greatest strength and power that he can make   450
And meet me suddenly at Salisbury.

CATESBY
I go.   *Exit*

RATCLIFFE
What, may it please you, shall I do at Salisbury?

KING RICHARD
Why, what wouldst thou do there before I go?

RATCLIFFE
Your highness told me I should post before.

KING RICHARD
My mind is changed.
        Enter Earl of Derby
                    Stanley, what news with you?

DERBY
  None good, my liege, to please you with the hearing,
  Nor none so bad but well may be reported.

KING RICHARD
  Hoyday, a riddle! Neither good nor bad!
460 What need'st thou run so many miles about,
  When thou mayst tell thy tale the nearest way?
  Once more, what news?

DERBY   Richmond is on the seas.

KING RICHARD
  There let him sink, and be the seas on him!
  White-livered runagate, what doth he there?

DERBY
  I know not, mighty sovereign, but by guess.

KING RICHARD
  Well, as you guess?

DERBY
  Stirred up by Dorset, Buckingham, and Morton,
  He makes for England, here to claim the crown.

KING RICHARD
  Is the chair empty? Is the sword unswayed?
470 Is the King dead? The empire unpossessed?
  What heir of York is there alive but we?
  And who is England's king but great York's heir?
  Then tell me, what makes he upon the seas?

DERBY
  Unless for that, my liege, I cannot guess.

KING RICHARD
  Unless for that he comes to be your liege,
  You cannot guess wherefore the Welshman comes.
  Thou wilt revolt and fly to him, I fear.

DERBY
  No, my good lord; therefore mistrust me not.

KING RICHARD

  Where is thy power then to beat him back?
  Where be thy tenants and thy followers?   480
  Are they not now upon the western shore,
  Safe-conducting the rebels from their ships?

DERBY

  No, my good lord, my friends are in the north.

KING RICHARD

  Cold friends to me! What do they in the north
  When they should serve their sovereign in the west?

DERBY

  They have not been commanded, mighty king.
  Pleaseth your majesty to give me leave,
  I'll muster up my friends and meet your grace
  Where and what time your majesty shall please.

KING RICHARD

  Ay, thou wouldst be gone to join with Richmond;   490
  But I'll not trust thee.

DERBY   Most mighty sovereign,
  You have no cause to hold my friendship doubtful.
  I never was nor never will be false.

KING RICHARD

  Go then, and muster men. But leave behind
  Your son, George Stanley. Look your heart be firm,
  Or else his head's assurance is but frail.

DERBY

  So deal with him as I prove true to you.   *Exit*
    Enter a Messenger

FIRST MESSENGER

  My gracious sovereign, now in Devonshire,
  As I by friends am well advertisèd,
  Sir Edward Courtney and the haughty prelate,   500
  Bishop of Exeter, his elder brother,
  With many more confederates, are in arms.

Enter another Messenger

SECOND MESSENGER

  In Kent, my liege, the Guildfords are in arms,

  And every hour more competitors

  Flock to the rebels, and their power grows strong.

    Enter another Messenger

THIRD MESSENGER

  My lord, the army of great Buckingham –

KING RICHARD

  Out on you, owls! Nothing but songs of death?

    He striketh him

  There, take thou that, till thou bring better news.

THIRD MESSENGER

  The news I have to tell your majesty

510 Is that by sudden flood and fall of water

  Buckingham's army is dispersed and scattered,

  And he himself wandered away alone,

  No man knows whither.

KING RICHARD   I cry thee mercy.

  There is my purse to cure that blow of thine.

  Hath any well-advisèd friend proclaimed

  Reward to him that brings the traitor in?

THIRD MESSENGER

  Such proclamation hath been made, my lord.

    Enter another Messenger

FOURTH MESSENGER

  Sir Thomas Lovel and Lord Marquess Dorset,

  'Tis said, my liege, in Yorkshire are in arms.

520 But this good comfort bring I to your highness:

  The Britain navy is dispersed by tempest;

  Richmond in Dorsetshire sent out a boat

  Unto the shore to ask those on the banks

  If they were his assistants, yea or no;

  Who answered him they came from Buckingham,

Upon his party. He, mistrusting them,
Hoised sail, and made his course again for Britain.

KING RICHARD
March on, march on, since we are up in arms;
If not to fight with foreign enemies,
Yet to beat down these rebels here at home.   530

Enter Catesby

CATESBY
My liege, the Duke of Buckingham is taken.
That is the best news. That the Earl of Richmond
Is with a mighty power landed at Milford
Is colder tidings, but yet they must be told.

KING RICHARD
Away towards Salisbury! While we reason here,
A royal battle might be won and lost.
Someone take order Buckingham be brought
To Salisbury; the rest march on with me.

Flourish. Exeunt

Enter Earl of Derby, and Sir Christopher Urswick,   IV.5
a Priest

DERBY
Sir Christopher, tell Richmond this from me:
That in the sty of the most deadly boar
My son George Stanley is franked up in hold;
If I revolt, off goes young George's head;
The fear of that holds off my present aid.
So, get thee gone; commend me to thy lord.
Withal say that the Queen hath heartily consented
He should espouse Elizabeth her daughter.
But tell me, where is princely Richmond now?

URSWICK
At Pembroke, or at Ha'rfordwest in Wales.   10

DERBY

What men of name resort to him?

URSWICK

Sir Walter Herbert, a renownèd soldier,
Sir Gilbert Talbot, Sir William Stanley,
Oxford, redoubted Pembroke, Sir James Blunt,
And Rice ap Thomas, with a valiant crew,
And many other of great name and worth;
And towards London do they bend their power,
If by the way they be not fought withal.

DERBY

Well, hie thee to thy lord. I kiss his hand;
20   My letter will resolve him of my mind.
        Gives letter
Farewell.

*

V.1   *Enter Buckingham with halberds and the Sheriff, led
           to execution*

BUCKINGHAM

Will not King Richard let me speak with him?

SHERIFF

No, my good lord; therefore be patient.

BUCKINGHAM

Hastings, and Edward's children, Grey and Rivers,
Holy King Henry and thy fair son Edward,
Vaughan, and all that have miscarrièd
By underhand corrupted foul injustice,
If that your moody discontented souls
Do through the clouds behold this present hour,
Even for revenge mock my destruction!
10   This is All Souls' Day, fellow, is it not?

SHERIFF
  It is.
BUCKINGHAM
  Why, then All Souls' Day is my body's doomsday.
  This is the day which in King Edward's time
  I wished might fall on me when I was found
  False to his children and his wife's allies;
  This is the day wherein I wished to fall
  By the false faith of him whom most I trusted;
  This, this All Souls' Day to my fearful soul
  Is the determined respite of my wrongs.
  That high All-seer which I dallied with   20
  Hath turned my feignèd prayer on my head
  And given in earnest what I begged in jest.
  Thus doth He force the swords of wicked men
  To turn their own points in their masters' bosoms;
  Thus Margaret's curse falls heavy on my neck:
  'When he,' quoth she, 'shall split thy heart with sorrow,
  Remember Margaret was a prophetess.'
  – Come lead me, officers, to the block of shame.
  Wrong hath but wrong, and blame the due of blame.
                              Exeunt Buckingham with officers

  Enter Richmond, Oxford, Sir James Blunt, Sir   **V.2**
    Walter Herbert, and others, with drum and colours
RICHMOND
  Fellows in arms, and my most loving friends
  Bruised underneath the yoke of tyranny,
  Thus far into the bowels of the land
  Have we marched on without impediment;
  And here receive we from our father Stanley
  Lines of fair comfort and encouragement.
  The wretched, bloody, and usurping boar,

That spoiled your summer fields and fruitful vines,
Swills your warm blood like wash, and makes his trough
10 In your embowelled bosoms – this foul swine
Is now even in the centre of this isle,
Near to the town of Leicester, as we learn;
From Tamworth thither is but one day's march.
In God's name cheerly on, courageous friends,
To reap the harvest of perpetual peace
By this one bloody trial of sharp war.

OXFORD
Every man's conscience is a thousand men,
To fight against this guilty homicide.

HERBERT
I doubt not but his friends will turn to us.

BLUNT
20 He hath no friends but what are friends for fear,
Which in his dearest need will fly from him.

RICHMOND
All for our vantage. Then in God's name march!
True hope is swift and flies with swallow's wings;
Kings it makes gods, and meaner creatures kings.

                                                    Exeunt

V.3   *Enter King Richard in arms, with Norfolk, Ratcliffe,*
           and the Earl of Surrey, and soldiers

KING RICHARD
Here pitch our tent, even here in Bosworth field.
My Lord of Surrey, why look you so sad?

SURREY
My heart is ten times lighter than my looks.

KING RICHARD
My Lord of Norfolk –

NORFOLK   Here, most gracious liege.

KING RICHARD

 Norfolk, we must have knocks. Ha! Must we not?

NORFOLK

 We must both give and take, my loving lord.

KING RICHARD

 Up with my tent! Here will I lie tonight.
  Soldiers begin to set up the King's tent
 But where tomorrow? Well, all's one for that.
 Who hath descried the number of the traitors?

NORFOLK

 Six or seven thousand is their utmost power.   10

KING RICHARD

 Why, our battalia trebles that account;
 Besides, the King's name is a tower of strength,
 Which they upon the adverse faction want.
 Up with the tent! Come, noble gentlemen,
 Let us survey the vantage of the ground.
 Call for some men of sound direction.
 Let's lack no discipline, make no delay,
 For, lords, tomorrow is a busy day.   *Exeunt*
  Enter Richmond, Sir William Brandon, Oxford,
  Dorset, Herbert, and Blunt. Some of the soldiers
  pitch Richmond's tent

RICHMOND

 The weary sun hath made a golden set
 And by the bright tract of his fiery car   20
 Gives token of a goodly day tomorrow.
 Sir William Brandon, you shall bear my standard.
 Give me some ink and paper in my tent:
 I'll draw the form and model of our battle,
 Limit each leader to his several charge,
 And part in just proportion our small power.
 My Lord of Oxford – you, Sir William Brandon –
 And you, Sir Walter Herbert – stay with me.

The Earl of Pembroke keeps his regiment;
30   Good Captain Blunt, bear my good-night to him,
And by the second hour in the morning
Desire the Earl to see me in my tent.
Yet one thing more, good captain, do for me –
Where is Lord Stanley quartered, do you know?

BLUNT

Unless I have mista'en his colours much,
Which well I am assured I have not done,
His regiment lies half a mile at least
South from the mighty power of the King.

RICHMOND

If without peril it be possible,
40   Sweet Blunt, make some good means to speak with him
And give him from me this most needful note.

BLUNT

Upon my life, my lord, I'll undertake it;
And so God give you quiet rest tonight!

RICHMOND

Good night, good Captain Blunt.   *Exit Blunt*
                        Come, gentlemen,
Let us consult upon tomorrow's business.
Into my tent; the dew is raw and cold.
    They withdraw into the tent
    Enter, to his tent, King Richard, Ratcliffe, Norfolk,
    and Catesby

KING RICHARD

What is't a clock?

CATESBY   It's supper time, my lord;
It's nine a clock.

KING RICHARD   I will not sup tonight.
Give me some ink and paper.
50   What, is my beaver easier than it was?
And all my armour laid into my tent?

CATESBY

   It is, my liege; and all things are in readiness.

KING RICHARD

   Good Norfolk, hie thee to thy charge;

   Use careful watch, choose trusty sentinels.

NORFOLK I go, my lord.

KING RICHARD

   Stir with the lark tomorrow, gentle Norfolk.

NORFOLK I warrant you, my lord.   *Exit*

KING RICHARD Catesby!

CATESBY

   My lord?

KING RICHARD

       Send out a pursuivant-at-arms

   To Stanley's regiment; bid him bring his power   60

   Before sunrising, lest his son George fall

   Into the blind cave of eternal night.   *Exit Catesby*

   Fill me a bowl of wine. Give me a watch.

   Saddle white Surrey for the field tomorrow.

   Look that my staves be sound and not too heavy.

   Ratcliffe!

RATCLIFFE

   My lord?

KING RICHARD

   Saw'st thou the melancholy Lord Northumberland?

RATCLIFFE

   Thomas the Earl of Surrey and himself,

   Much about cockshut time, from troop to troop   70

   Went through the army, cheering up the soldiers.

KING RICHARD

   So, I am satisfied. Give me a bowl of wine.

   I have not that alacrity of spirit

   Nor cheer of mind that I was wont to have.

     A bowl of wine is brought

Set it down. Is ink and paper ready?

RATCLIFFE

It is, my lord.

KING RICHARD

Bid my guard watch. Leave me. Ratcliffe,
About the mid of night come to my tent
And help to arm me. Leave me, I say.

Exit Ratcliffe with others
King Richard withdraws into his tent, and sleeps
Enter Earl of Derby to Richmond in his tent, Lords
and others attending

DERBY

80   Fortune and victory sit on thy helm!

RICHMOND

All comfort that the dark night can afford
Be to thy person, noble father-in-law!
Tell me, how fares our loving mother?

DERBY

I, by attorney, bless thee from thy mother,
Who prays continually for Richmond's good.
So much for that. The silent hours steal on
And flaky darkness breaks within the east.
In brief, for so the season bids us be,
Prepare thy battle early in the morning
90   And put thy fortune to th'arbitrement
Of bloody strokes and mortal-staring war.
I, as I may – that which I would I cannot –
With best advantage will deceive the time
And aid thee in this doubtful shock of arms.
But on thy side I may not be too forward,
Lest, being seen, thy brother, tender George,
Be executed in his father's sight.
Farewell. The leisure and the fearful time
Cuts off the ceremonious vows of love

And ample interchange of sweet discourse   100
Which so long sundered friends should dwell upon.
God give us leisure for these rites of love!
Once more adieu. Be valiant, and speed well!

RICHMOND

Good lords, conduct him to his regiment.
I'll strive with troubled thoughts to take a nap,
Lest leaden slumber peise me down tomorrow,
When I should mount with wings of victory.
Once more, good night, kind lords and gentlemen.

Exeunt

Richmond remains

O Thou, whose captain I account myself,
Look on my forces with a gracious eye;   110
Put in their hands Thy bruising irons of wrath,
That they may crush down with a heavy fall
Th'usurping helmets of our adversaries;
Make us Thy ministers of chastisement,
That we may praise Thee in the victory.
To Thee I do commend my watchful soul
Ere I let fall the windows of mine eyes.
Sleeping and waking, O defend me still!

Sleeps
Enter the Ghost of Prince Edward, son to Henry the Sixth

GHOST (*to Richard*)

Let me sit heavy on thy soul tomorrow!
Think how thou stab'st me in my prime of youth   120
At Tewkesbury; despair therefore, and die!
(*To Richmond*)
Be cheerful, Richmond; for the wrongèd souls
Of butchered princes fight in thy behalf.
King Henry's issue, Richmond, comforts thee   *Exit*
Enter the Ghost of Henry the Sixth

GHOST (*to Richard*)

    When I was mortal, my anointed body

    By thee was punchèd full of deadly holes.

    Think on the Tower, and me; despair, and die!

    Harry the Sixth bids thee despair, and die!

    (*To Richmond*) Virtuous and holy, be thou conqueror!

130   Harry, that prophesied thou shouldst be king,

    Doth comfort thee in thy sleep; live, and flourish!

                                     Exit

     Enter the Ghost of Clarence

GHOST (*to Richard*)

    Let me sit heavy in thy soul tomorrow –

    I that was washed to death with fulsome wine,

    Poor Clarence, by thy guile betrayed to death!

    Tomorrow in the battle think on me,

    And fall thy edgeless sword; despair and die!

    (*To Richmond*) Thou offspring of the house of Lancaster,

    The wrongèd heirs of York do pray for thee;

    Good angels guard thy battle! Live, and flourish!

                                       Exit

     Enter the Ghosts of Rivers, Grey, and Vaughan

RIVERS (*to Richard*)

140   Let me sit heavy in thy soul tomorrow,

    Rivers, that died at Pomfret; despair, and die!

GREY

    Think upon Grey, and let thy soul despair!

VAUGHAN

    Think upon Vaughan and with guilty fear

    Let fall thy lance; despair, and die!

ALL (*to Richmond*)

    Awake, and think our wrongs in Richard's bosom

    Will conquer him! Awake, and win the day!

                                  Exeunt Ghosts

     Enter the Ghost of Lord Hastings

GHOST (*to Richard*)

Bloody and guilty, guiltily awake

And in a bloody battle end thy days!

Think on Lord Hastings; despair, and die!

(*To Richmond*) Quiet untroubled soul, awake, awake!   150

Arm, fight, and conquer, for fair England's sake!

Exit

Enter the Ghosts of the two young Princes

GHOSTS (*to Richard*)

Dream on thy cousins smothered in the Tower.

Let us be lead within thy bosom, Richard,

And weigh thee down to ruin, shame, and death!

Thy nephews' souls bid thee despair, and die!

(*To Richmond*)

Sleep, Richmond, sleep in peace and wake in joy.

Good angels guard thee from the boar's annoy!

Live, and beget a happy race of kings!

Edward's unhappy sons do bid thee flourish.   *Exeunt*

Enter the Ghost of Anne, his wife

GHOST (*to Richard*)

Richard, thy wife, that wretched Anne thy wife,   160

That never slept a quiet hour with thee,

Now fills thy sleep with perturbations.

Tomorrow in the battle think on me,

And fall thy edgeless sword; despair, and die!

(*To Richmond*) Thou quiet soul, sleep thou a quiet sleep.

Dream of success and happy victory!

Thy adversary's wife doth pray for thee.   *Exit*

Enter the Ghost of Buckingham

GHOST (*to Richard*)

The first was I that helped thee to the crown;

The last was I that felt thy tyranny.

O, in the battle think on Buckingham,   170

And die in terror of thy guiltiness!

Dream on, dream on, of bloody deeds and death.
Fainting, despair; despairing, yield thy breath!
(*To Richmond*) I died for hope ere I could lend thee aid,
But cheer thy heart and be thou not dismayed;
God and good angels fight on Richmond's side,
And Richard falls in height of all his pride!   *Exit*
    Richard starts out of his dream

KING RICHARD

Give me another horse! Bind up my wounds!
Have mercy, Jesu! – Soft! I did but dream.
180 O coward conscience, how dost thou afflict me!
The lights burn blue. It is now dead midnight.
Cold fearful drops stand on my trembling flesh.
What do I fear? Myself? There's none else by.
Richard loves Richard: that is, I am I.
Is there a murderer here? No. Yes, I am.
Then fly. What, from myself? Great reason why –
Lest I revenge. Myself upon myself?
Alack, I love myself. Wherefore? For any good
That I myself have done unto myself?
190 O no! Alas, I rather hate myself
For hateful deeds committed by myself.
I am a villain. Yet I lie, I am not.
Fool, of thyself speak well. Fool, do not flatter.
My conscience hath a thousand several tongues,
And every tongue brings in a several tale,
And every tale condemns me for a villain.
Perjury, perjury, in the highest degree.
Murder, stern murder, in the direst degree,
All several sins, all used in each degree,
200 Throng to the bar, crying all 'Guilty! Guilty!'
I shall despair. There is no creature loves me;
And if I die, no soul will pity me.
Nay, wherefore should they, since that I myself

Find in myself no pity to myself?
Methought the souls of all that I had murdered
Came to my tent, and every one did threat
Tomorrow's vengeance on the head of Richard.
    Enter Ratcliffe

RATCLIFFE My lord!

KING RICHARD Zounds, who is there?

RATCLIFFE
    Ratcliffe, my lord, 'tis I. The early village cock   210
    Hath twice done salutation to the morn;
    Your friends are up and buckle on their armour.

KING RICHARD
    O Ratcliffe, I have dreamed a fearful dream!
    What thinkest thou? Will our friends prove all true?

RATCLIFFE
    No doubt, my lord.

KING RICHARD   Ratcliffe, I fear, I fear!

RATCLIFFE
    Nay, good my lord, be not afraid of shadows.

KING RICHARD
    By the apostle Paul, shadows tonight
    Have struck more terror to the soul of Richard
    Than can the substance of ten thousand soldiers
    Armèd in proof and led by shallow Richmond.   220
    'Tis not yet near day. Come, go with me.
    Under our tents I'll play the eavesdropper,
    To see if any mean to shrink from me.
                          Exeunt Richard and Ratcliffe
          Enter the Lords to Richmond sitting in his tent

LORDS
    Good morrow, Richmond.

RICHMOND
    Cry mercy, lords and watchful gentlemen,
    That you have ta'en a tardy sluggard here.

LORDS

How have you slept, my lord?

RICHMOND

The sweetest sleep, and fairest-boding dreams
That ever entered in a drowsy head
230   Have I since your departure had, my lords.
Methought their souls whose bodies Richard murdered
Came to my tent and cried on victory.
I promise you my heart is very jocund
In the remembrance of so fair a dream.
How far into the morning is it, lords?

LORDS

Upon the stroke of four.

RICHMOND

Why, then 'tis time to arm and give direction.
His oration to his soldiers
More than I have said, loving countrymen,
The leisure and enforcement of the time
240   Forbids to dwell upon. Yet remember this:
God and our good cause fight upon our side;
The prayers of holy saints and wrongèd souls,
Like high-reared bulwarks, stand before our faces.
Richard except, those whom we fight against
Had rather have us win than him they follow.
For what is he they follow? Truly, gentlemen,
A bloody tyrant and a homicide;
One raised in blood and one in blood established;
One that made means to come by what he hath,
250   And slaughtered those that were the means to help him;
A base foul stone, made precious by the foil
Of England's chair, where he is falsely set;
One that hath ever been God's enemy.
Then if you fight against God's enemy,
God will in justice ward you as his soldiers;

If you do sweat to put a tyrant down,
You sleep in peace, the tyrant being slain;
If you do fight against your country's foes,
Your country's fat shall pay your pains the hire;
If you do fight in safeguard of your wives,   260
Your wives shall welcome home the conquerors;
If you do free your children from the sword,
Your children's children quits it in your age.
Then in the name of God and all these rights,
Advance your standards, draw your willing swords.
For me, the ransom of my bold attempt
Shall be this cold corpse on the earth's cold face;
But if I thrive, the gain of my attempt
The least of you shall share his part thereof.
Sound drums and trumpets boldly and cheerfully: 270
God and Saint George! Richmond and victory!

Exeunt

Enter King Richard, Ratcliffe, and soldiers

KING RICHARD
What said Northumberland as touching Richmond?

RATCLIFFE
That he was never trainèd up in arms.

KING RICHARD
He said the truth. And what said Surrey then?

RATCLIFFE
He smiled and said, 'The better for our purpose.'

KING RICHARD
He was in the right, and so indeed it is.

Clock strikes

Tell the clock there. Give me a calendar.
Who saw the sun today?

RATCLIFFE   Not I, my lord.

KING RICHARD
Then he disdains to shine; for by the book

280   He should have braved the east an hour ago.
      A black day will it be to somebody.
      Ratcliffe!

RATCLIFFE
      My lord?

KING RICHARD
            The sun will not be seen today;
      The sky doth frown and lour upon our army.
      I would these dewy tears were from the ground.
      Not shine today? Why, what is that to me
      More than to Richmond? For the selfsame heaven
      That frowns on me looks sadly upon him.
            Enter Norfolk

NORFOLK
      Arm, arm, my lord; the foe vaunts in the field.

KING RICHARD
290   Come, bustle, bustle! Caparison my horse!
      Call up Lord Stanley, bid him bring his power.
      I will lead forth my soldiers to the plain,
      And thus my battle shall be ordered:
      My foreward shall be drawn out all in length,
      Consisting equally of horse and foot;
      Our archers shall be placèd in the midst;
      John Duke of Norfolk, Thomas Earl of Surrey,
      Shall have the leading of this foot and horse.
      They thus directed, we will follow
300   In the main battle, whose puissance on either side
      Shall be well wingèd with our chiefest horse.
      This, and Saint George to boot! What think'st thou,
            Norfolk?

NORFOLK
      A good direction, warlike sovereign.
      This found I on my tent this morning.
            He showeth him a paper

KING RICHARD (*reads*)
 '*Jockey of Norfolk, be not so bold,*
 For Dickon thy master is bought and sold.'
 A thing devisèd by the enemy.
 Go, gentlemen, every man unto his charge.
 (*Aside*) Let not our babbling dreams affright our souls;
 Conscience is but a word that cowards use,   310
 Devised at first to keep the strong in awe.
 Our strong arms be our conscience, swords our law!
 (*To them*) March on, join bravely, let us to't pell-mell,
 If not to heaven, then hand in hand to hell.
  His oration to his army
 What shall I say more than I have inferred?
 Remember whom you are to cope withal –
 A sort of vagabonds, rascals, and runaways,
 A scum of Britains and base lackey peasants,
 Whom their o'ercloyèd country vomits forth
 To desperate adventures and assured destruction. 320
 You sleeping safe, they bring to you unrest;
 You having lands, and blessed with beauteous wives,
 They would distrain the one, distain the other.
 And who doth lead them but a paltry fellow,
 Long kept in Britain at our mother's cost,
 A milksop, one that never in his life
 Felt so much cold as over shoes in snow?
 Let's whip these stragglers o'er the seas again,
 Lash hence these overweening rags of France,
 These famished beggars, weary of their lives, 330
 Who, but for dreaming on this fond exploit,
 For want of means, poor rats, had hanged themselves.
 If we be conquered, let men conquer us,
 And not these bastard Britains, whom our fathers
 Have in their own land beaten, bobbed, and thumped,
 And, in record, left them the heirs of shame.

Shall these enjoy our lands? Lie with our wives?
Ravish our daughters? (*Drum afar off*) Hark! I hear
    their drum.
Fight, gentlemen of England! Fight, bold yeomen!
340   Draw, archers, draw your arrows to the head!
Spur your proud horses hard, and ride in blood!
Amaze the welkin with your broken staves!
    Enter a Messenger
What says Lord Stanley? Will he bring his power?

MESSENGER
My lord, he doth deny to come.

KING RICHARD
Off with his son George's head!

NORFOLK
My lord, the enemy is past the marsh.
After the battle let George Stanley die.

KING RICHARD
A thousand hearts are great within my bosom!
Advance our standards, set upon our foes.
350   Our ancient word of courage, fair Saint George,
Inspire us with the spleen of fiery dragons!
Upon them! Victory sits on our helms.   *Exeunt*

V.4   *Alarm; excursions. Enter Catesby*
CATESBY
Rescue, my Lord of Norfolk, rescue, rescue!
The King enacts more wonders than a man,
Daring an opposite to every danger.
His horse is slain, and all on foot he fights,
Seeking for Richmond in the throat of death.
Rescue, fair lord, or else the day is lost!
    Alarums. Enter King Richard

KING RICHARD

   A horse! A horse! My kingdom for a horse!

CATESBY

   Withdraw, my lord. I'll help you to a horse.

KING RICHARD

   Slave, I have set my life upon a cast,

   And I will stand the hazard of the die.   10

   I think there be six Richmonds in the field;

   Five have I slain today instead of him.

   A horse! A horse! My kingdom for a horse!   *Exeunt*

   Alarum. Enter King Richard and Richmond; they   **V.5**
   fight; Richard is slain
   Retreat and flourish. Enter Richmond, the Earl of
   Derby bearing the crown, with divers other lords

RICHMOND

   God and your arms be praised, victorious friends!

   The day is ours; the bloody dog is dead.

DERBY

   Courageous Richmond, well hast thou acquit thee.

   Lo, here this long usurpèd royalty

   From the dead temples of this bloody wretch

   Have I plucked off, to grace thy brows withal.

   Wear it, enjoy it, and make much of it.

RICHMOND

   Great God of heaven, say amen to all!

   But tell me, is young George Stanley living?

DERBY

   He is, my lord, and safe in Leicester town,   10

   Whither, if it please you, we may now withdraw us.

RICHMOND

   What men of name are slain on either side?

DERBY

> John Duke of Norfolk, Walter Lord Ferrers,
> Sir Robert Brakenbury, and Sir William Brandon.

RICHMOND

> Inter their bodies as becomes their births.
> Proclaim a pardon to the soldiers fled
> That in submission will return to us;
> And then, as we have ta'en the sacrament,
> We will unite the White Rose and the Red.
> Smile, heaven, upon this fair conjunction,
> That long have frowned upon their enmity!
> What traitor hears me, and says not amen?
> England hath long been mad and scarred herself,
> The brother blindly shed the brother's blood,
> The father rashly slaughtered his own son,
> The son, compelled, been butcher to the sire:
> All this divided York and Lancaster,
> Divided in their dire division;
> O, now let Richmond and Elizabeth,
> The true succeeders of each royal house,
> By God's fair ordinance conjoin together!
> And let their heirs, God, if Thy will be so,
> Enrich the time to come with smooth-faced peace,
> With smiling plenty, and fair prosperous days!
> Abate the edge of traitors, gracious Lord,
> That would reduce these bloody days again
> And make poor England weep in streams of blood!
> Let them not live to taste this land's increase
> That would with treason wound this fair land's peace!
> Now civil wounds are stopped, peace lives again;
> That she may long live here, God say amen! *Exeunt*

An Account of the Text

For the editor of *Richard III* two early editions are of paramount importance. Unfortunately neither the Quarto (Q or Q1: published in 1597) nor the Folio (F: published in 1623) was authorized by Shakespeare: neither can be regarded as reliable, and therefore editors prepare a synthetic text based on Q and later Quartos (Q2 Q3, etc.) published before F, and on F.

The Quarto, the shorter of the two by about two hundred lines, appears to suffer from memorial errors, such as synonym substitution, verbal transposition and omission. For example, II.2.12–16 run as follows (line 16 has disappeared from Q):

> *Boy.* Then Granam you conclude that he is dead,
> The King my Vnckle is too blame for this:
> God will reuenge it, whom I will importune
> With daily praiers, all to that effect.

Most editors now agree that the Q text was reconstructed from memory by Shakespeare's company, presumably to replace a lost prompt book. The reconstructed text seems to have been cut, perhaps for provincial performance: several speeches, and some minor characters, were eliminated, not surprisingly since the play is long and needs a large cast. (Shorter omissions doubtless resulted from inadvertence.) Single words or phrases added unnecessarily at the beginning and the end of a speech, such as 'O', 'Well', 'my lord', are also most simply explained as actors' interpolations. Of the Quarto, which differs in hundreds of readings from the Folio text, one can say with certainty that it contains a very large number of errors.

Many, but by no means all, of the Quarto's errors and omissions were corrected in the Folio. This text, though also disfigured by omissions, is thought to be based on Shakespeare's own papers – but not as directly as one would wish. For prior to 1623 five reprints had followed the Quarto (Q2–Q6), each of which added a new stratum of error: the Folio compositors set their text from one or more of these derivative Quartos, into which an editor had written corrections from Shakespeare's manuscript.

Some think that the copy for the Folio consisted of a corrected Q6, with two passages (III.1.1–164, V.3.47–5.41) based on virtually uncorrected Q3; others, that the copy was Q3 throughout; others, that it was Q6, Q3, and also Q1, unevenly corrected; one editor, Gary Taylor (in *William Shakespeare: A Textual Companion*, 1987), argues that Q3 and Q6 were both extensively used 'in an alternating pattern', based on Q and F page-breaks, 'and on the need to interleave major insertions from the manuscript'. Whichever of these theories turns out to be right, the Folio text clearly incorporates many readings from the Quartos that should have been changed but were overlooked by the editor. Manifest errors originating in one of the derivative Quartos (Q2–Q6) found their way into the Folio (for example, 'as as' in Q3 and F, III.1.123); a great many other non-manifest corruptions, introduced in the derivative Quartos in the process of reprinting, also survive in the Folio (III.1.43: 'so *deepe* a sinne', Q1, Q2; '*great*', Q3–Q6, F) – and so we are driven to conclude that many unauthorized Q1 readings were also left uncorrected by the Folio editor. To make confusion worse, one of the Folio compositors worked most carelessly, introducing a new set of corrupt but often plausible variants.

The Folio manuscript is today held by scholars to have been Shakespeare's original draft (or 'foul papers') of the play, whereas the Quarto probably represents a later version, as the play was performed. The later version *may* derive from an authorial fair copy, for some of its alternative readings impress editors as improvements on the Folio. But, taking into account the memorial transmission of Q, many Q variants could be either authorial substitutions (if so, we should adopt them) or memorial corruptions (if so, we should reject them). How unfortunate that authorial substitutions and memorial corruptions are not always easily distinguished!

What, then, is the modern editor to do? Recognizing the textual superiority of the Folio, he will prefer its readings whenever they seem better than, or as good as, Quarto alternatives, except for the two passages where Q3 served as Folio copy in III.1 and V.3–5. On the other hand, a Folio variant that has been anticipated by a derivative Quarto, especially Q3 or Q6, must be rejected – being, in all probability, a mere hangover from derivative copy – with the proviso that if the equivalent Q1 reading is corrupt the Folio's alternative, though again probably derivative, may be reluctantly adopted. Another exception must be made in the case of oaths and profanity, which were deleted or toned down in this as in other Folio texts: the modern editor consequently has to trust Q, though he may sometimes hesitate to do so when the dialogue has been patently vulgarized, as in I.4.

Accepting this policy in outline, I differ slightly from other editors in interpreting its implications. Because of the demonstrable corruptness of Q and F, the two primary texts, some editors have emended very freely. I agree that both Q and F are corrupt *in general*, but not that we should take it upon ourselves to emend every *particular* reading that seems awkward or difficult. We must allow for the possibility that Shakespeare wrote awkwardly at times, and thus avoid altering the text more than is absolutely necessary. Again, I feel less pessimistic than other editors about the memorial contamination of Q, and more uneasy about the reliability of F: accordingly my text reverts to Q in a few dozen readings that were not preserved in other modern editions.

COLLATIONS

1

The following readings are adopted from Q in preference to F. (The alternative version comes from F. I have excluded F's manifest misprints and F readings copied from, or influenced by, Q2–Q6.)

I.1

         26 spy] see
         52 for] but
         83 this] our
         87 his] your
        100 he] to
        133 prey] play

I.2

         39 Stand] Stand'st
         78 a man] man
        201 RICHARD (F *continues speech as Anne's*)
        211 more] most

I.3

          8 harm] harmes
         41 highest] height
         54 whom] who
         63 of] on
         97 (and 120, 125, 135, 262) yea] I
        308 QUEEN ELIZABETH] *Mar.*
        326 whom] who

I.4

         64 my] *not in* F
         73 (and 118) pray thee] prythee
         89 Yea] What
        122 Faith] *not in* F
        126 Zounds] Come
        147 Zounds] *not in* F
        152 Tut] *not in* F
        227 fault] Faults

II.1

    5 in] to
  39 God] heauen
  57 unwittingly] vnwillingly
  59 By] To
  94 but] and
  98 pray thee] prethee
 109 at] and

II.2

  29 yea] I
  47 I] *not in* F
  83 weep] weepes
 117 hearts] hates
 142 (and 154) Ludlow] London

II.3

  43 Ensuing] Pursuing

II.4

   9 young] good
  26 (and 31) pray thee] prythee
  65 death] earth

III.1

   9 Nor] No
  40 in heaven] *not in* F
  56 never] ne're
  57 overrule] o're-rule
 170 afar] farre

III.2

  77 you do] *not in* F
  93 let us] let's
  95 Hastings] Sirrha
  98 I met thee] thou met'st me
 105 Hastings] fellow

III.4

  65 whatsoever] whosoe're
  68 See] Looke
  82 raze] rowse

III.5

   4 wert] were
  54 meaning] meanings

            57 treason] Treasons
            61 word] words
            65 cause] case (ease Q6)
            83 listed] lusted
           107 notice] order
III.7
            35 At the] At
            53 we 'll] we
            82 My lord] *not in* F
           100 request] requests
           125 Her] His
           218 Zounds! I'll] we will
           246 cousin] Cousins
IV.2
            71 there] then
IV.3
             4 whom] who
             7 Melting] Melted
            13 Which] And
            15 once] one
            31 at] and
IV.4
            10 unblown] vnblowed
            30 innocents'] innocent
            64 Thy] The
           105 wheeled] whirl'd
           128 intestate] intestine
           216 births] Birth
           249 (and 282) yea] I
           355 love] low
         364–5 KING . . . break] F *prints the two lines in reverse order*
           377 God . . . God's] Heauen . . . Heauens
           396 o'erpast] repast
           417 peevish-fond] peeuish found
           510 flood . . . water] Floods . . . Waters
V.2
            11 centre] Centry

V.3

    68 thou] *not in* F
   105 thoughts] noise
   131 thy] *not in* F
   155 souls bid] soule bids
   177 falls] fall
   209 Zounds, who is] Who's
   308 unto] to

V.5

   11 if . . . withdraw] (if you please) we may withdraw

2

A selection of interesting Q variants rejected in this edition. (The
alternative version comes from Q.)

I.1

   138 Saint John] Saint Paul

I.2

   19 wolves – to spiders] adders, spiders
   105 better] fitter
   124 live] rest
   187 That] Tush that
   206 servant] suppliant
   212 House] place

I.3

   67 brothers] brother
   68 that he may learn the ground] that thereby he may
      gather | The ground of your ill will and to remoue it
   232 detested] detested, &c.

I.4

   0 (and 1–75) *Keeper*] Brokenbury
   66 keeper, keeper] Brokenbury
   73 Keeper . . . awhile] I pray thee gentle keeper stay by
      me
   76 BRAKENBURY] *speech continued*

II.1

    83 KING EDWARD] *Ryu.*

II.4

    37 *a Messenger*] Dorset. *The Messenger's speeches are then assigned to Dorset.*

    38 *a . . . news?*] your sonne, Lo: M. Dorset. | What newes Lo: Marques?

III.1

    190 House] place

III.3

    0 *a line not in* F] Ratl. [*sic*] Come bring foorth the prisoners

III.4

    97 God] heauen

III.5

    11–21 Q *rearranges and rephrases; line* 14 *is* Let me alone to entertaine him. Lo: Maior,

    49 BUCKINGHAM] *speech continues as Lord Mayor's*

III.7

    42 speak?] speake? *Buc.* No by my troth my Lo: | *Glo.*

IV.2

    81 *after this line* Q *inserts two not in* F, *probably echoing* III.1.188–9: *King* Shal we heare from thee *Tirrel* ere we sleep? | *Tir.* Ye shall my lord.

    97 Perhaps!] perhaps, perhaps.

    117 Thou] Tut, tut, thou

IV.4

    266 Who else should be?] Who should be else?

V.1

    11 It is] It is my Lord

3

The following passages, which are not in Q, are first found in F. (The list excludes passages transferred to another context in Q, and F additions to the murderers' prose dialogue in I.4, where Q improvises most irresponsibly.)

I.2
     16 Cursèd . . . hence
     25 And . . . unhappiness
 155–66 These . . . weeping
I.3
    115 I . . . Tower
 166–8 RICHARD . . . abode
I.4
   9–10 Methoughts . . . Burgundy (Q: Me thoughts I was
          imbarkt for Burgundy)
     28 All . . . sea
   36–7 and . . . ghost
  69–72 O . . . children
     84 FIRST . . . here
 114–15 FIRST . . . live
    133 'Tis no matter
    173 Your . . . pale
    219 O . . . publicly
 260–64 Which . . . distress
    271 SECOND . . . lord
II.1
     25 KING . . . Marquess
     46 Sir . . . the (Q: the noble)
     69 Of . . . of you
    142 BUCKINGHAM . . . grace
II.2
     16 GIRL . . . I
  89–100 DORSET . . . throne
 123–40 RIVERS . . . I
II.3
      6 FIRST . . . sir
II.4
     67 Madam, farewell
III.1
 172–3 And . . . coronation
III.2
    111 PRIEST . . . lordship

III.3
    6–7 VAUGHAN . . . out
     15 When . . . I
III.4
   102–5 LOVEL . . . upon
III.5
      7 Tremble . . . straw
   102–4 Go . . . Castle
III.7
    5–6 his . . . France
      8 And . . . wives
     11 And . . . Duke
     24 they . . . word
     37 And . . . few
   97–8 And . . . man
    119 Your . . . birth
    126 Her . . . plants
  143–52 If . . . you
    201 BUCKINGHAM . . . love
    244 And . . . leave
IV.1
    2–6 Led . . . day
     36 ANNE . . . news
  97–103 QUEEN . . . farewell
IV.2
      2 BUCKINGHAM . . . sovereign
     45 Well . . . so
IV.3
     35 TYRREL . . . leave
IV.4
   20–21 QUEEN . . . debt
     28 Brief . . . days
    52–3 That . . . earth
    103 For . . . one
    160 DUCHESS . . . hear
    173 More . . . hatred
  222–35 KING . . . bosom
   276–7 which . . . body
  288–342 KING . . . years

387 What . . . now
400 Heaven . . . hours
429 And . . . mind
432 How . . . news
452 CATESBY I go
521 by tempest

V.3
27–8 My . . . me
43 And . . . tonight

4

The following passages, not found in F, are reprinted from Q.

I.2
202 ANNE . . . give
225 RICHARD . . . corse
I.3
113 Tell . . . said
I.4
192–3 to . . . sins (F: for any goodnesse)
240 And . . . other
II.2
84–5 and . . . Edward weep
145 QUEEN . . . hearts (Q: *Ans.* With all our hearts)
III.4
58 DERBY . . . say
III.7
219 RICHARD . . . Buckingham
IV.2
98–115 BUCKINGHAM . . . today
IV.4
39 Tell . . . mine
V.3
213–15 KING . . . lord

5

The following readings were first printed in Q2–Q6 or in other
derivative editions. (Some found their way into F from Q2–Q6.)
The list of The Characters in the Play (first printed in the eighteenth century) and stage directions and speech-prefixes are not
included.

I.1

    40 murderer] Q3; murtherers Q1
    75 for his] to her for his Q; for her F

I.2

    27 life] death Q, F
    80 accuse] curse Q, F
    101 ye – yea] yea Q; ye F

I.3

    154 As] A Q, F

I.4

    22 (and 23) mine] Q2; my Q1

II.1

    7 Hastings and Rivers] Riuers and Hastings Q; Dorset
      and Riuers F

III.4

    6 BISHOP OF ELY] Q3; *Ryu.* Q1

III.5

    33 traitor] traitor | That euer liu'd Q, F

III.7

    25 statuas] statues Q, F
    126 Her] His F; *line omitted* Q
    223 stone] stones Q, F

IV.1

    81 mine] Q6; my Q1
    103 sorrow bids] Sorrowes bids F; *omitted* Q

IV.2

    89 Hereford] Herford Q; Hertford F

IV.3

    5 piece of ruthless] ruthles peece of Q; peece of
      ruthfull F
   25 gave] Q3; give Q1

IV.4

   41 Harry] Richard Q; Husband F
   45 holp'st] hopst Q, F
  411 by] Q2; *omitted* Q1
  444 Ratcliffe] *omitted* Q; Catesby F
  448 to him] Q3; them Q1

V.3

   59 CATESBY] Rat. Q, F
  184 I am I] Q2; I and I Q1
  187 Myself] What my selfe Q; What? my Selfe F
  215 Ratcliffe] O Ratcliffe Q, F
  302 boot] Q3; bootes Q1
  323 distrain] restraine Q, F

V.5

   13 Ferrers] Ferris Q, F
   15 becomes] become Q, F

6

The stage directions of both Q and F are incomplete. In this
edition the words of Q and F are retained wherever possible, but
titles are sometimes added, names are normalized, Latin words
are generally translated, and many new directions have been
inserted. The following are some of the more interesting Q and
F readings.

I.2

    0 *Enter the Coarse of Henrie the sixt with Halberds to guard*
      it, Lady Anne being the Mourner (F)
  144 *Shee spitteth at him* (Q); *Spits at him* (F)
  170 *She lookes scornfully at him* (F)

178 *He layes his brest open, she offers at with his sword* (F)
182 *She fals the Sword* (F)

I.3

108 *Enter old Queene Margaret* (F)
317 *Speakes to himself* (F)

I.4

0 *Enter Clarence, Brokenbury* (Q); *Enter Clarence and Keeper* (F)
75 *Enter Brakenbury the Lieutenant* (F)
272 *He stabs him* (Q); *Stabs him* (F)

II.1

0 *Flourish. Enter the King sicke, the Queene, Lord Marquesse Dorset, Riuers, Hastings, Catesby, Buckingham, Wooduill* (F)
40 *Embrace* (F)
81 *They all start* (F)
135 *Exeunt some with K. & Queen* (F)

II.2

33 *Enter the Queene with her haire about her ears, Riuers & Dorset after her* (F)

II.4

37 *Enter Dorset* (Q); *Enter a Messenger* (F)

III.2

0 *Enter a Messenger to the Doore of Hastings* (F)
93 *Enter Hastin. a Purssuant* (Q); *Enter a Pursuiuant* (F)
105 *He giues him his purse* (Q); *Throwes him his Purse* (F)
110 *He whispers in his eare* (Q)

III.3

0 *Enter Sir Richard Ratcliffe, with Halberds, carrying the Nobles to death at Pomfret* (F)

III.5

0 *Enter Richard, and Buckingham, in rotten Armour, maruellous ill-fauoured* (F); *. . . in armour* (Q)

III.6

0 *Enter a Scriuener with a paper in his hand* (Q)

III.7

93 *Enter Rich. with two bishops a loste* (Q); *Enter Richard aloft, betweene two Bishops* (F)

IV.1

    o *Enter Quee. mother, Duchesse of Yorke, Marques Dorset, at one doore, Duchesse of Glocest. at another doore* (Q)

IV.2

    o *Sound a Sennet. Enter Richard in pompe, Buckingham, Catesby, Ratcliffe, Louel* (F); *The trumpets sound, Enter Richard crownd, . . .* (Q)

    3 *Here he ascendeth the throne* (Q); *Sound* (F)

IV.4

  135 *Enter K. Richard marching with Drummes and Trumpets* (Q); *Enter King Richard, and his Traine* (F)

  151 *Flourish. Alarums* (F)

  507 *He striketh him* (Q, F)

V.1

    o *Enter Buckingham with Halberds, led to Execution* (F)

V.2

    o *Enter Richmond with drums and trumpets* (Q); *Enter Richmond, Oxford, Blunt, Herbert, and others, with drum and colours* (F)

V.3

  46 *They withdraw into the Tent* (F)

  79 *Enter Darby to Richmond in his tent* (Q, F)

 118 *Enter the Ghost of Prince Edward, Sonne to Henry the sixt* (F; so Q)

 177 *Richard starteth vp out of a dreame* (Q); *Richard starts out of his dreame* (F)

 223 *Enter the Lords to Richmond sitting in his Tent* (F)

 237 *His oration to his souldiers* (Q, F)

 276 *The clocke striketh* (Q); *Clocke strikes* (F)

 304 *he sheweth him a paper* (Q)

 314 *His Oration to his army* (Q)

 338 *Drum afarre off* (F)

V.5

    o *Alarum, Enter Richard and Richmond, they fight, Richard is slaine. Retreat, and Flourish. Enter Richmond, Derby bearing the Crowne, with diuers other Lords* (F; so Q)

Genealogical Tables

Table 1: Descendants of Edward III

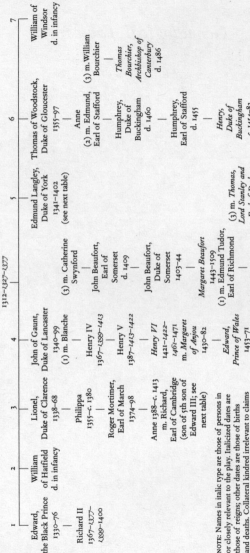

Edward III
1312–1327–1377

1	2	3	4	5	6	7

1 Edward, the Black Prince 1330–76 — Richard II *1377–1399*–1400

2 William of Hatfield d. in infancy

3 Lionel, Duke of Clarence 1338–68 — Philippa 1355–c. 1380 — Roger Mortimer, Earl of March 1374–98 — Anne 1388–c. 1413 m. Richard, Earl of Cambridge (son of 5th son of Edward III; see next table)

4 John of Gaunt, Duke of Lancaster 1340–99
(1) m. Blanche — Henry IV 1367–*1399–1413* — Henry V 1387–*1413–1422* — *Henry VI* 1421–*1422–1461*–1471 m. *Margaret of Anjou* 1430–82 — *Edward, Prince of Wales* 1453–71 m. *Anne Neville*
(3) m. Catherine Swynford — John Beaufort, Earl of Somerset d. 1409 — John Beaufort, Duke of Somerset 1403–44 — *Margaret Beaufort* 1443–1509 (1) m. Edmund Tudor, Earl of Richmond — *Henry VII (Richmond)* 1457–*1485–1509*
(3) m. *Thomas, Lord Stanley and Earl of Derby*

5 Edmund Langley, Duke of York 1341–1402 (see next table)

6 Thomas of Woodstock, Duke of Gloucester 1355–97 — Anne (2) m. Edmund, Earl of Stafford — Humphrey, Duke of Buckingham d. 1460 — Humphrey, Earl of Stafford d. 1455 — *Henry, Duke of Buckingham* c. 1454–83
(3) m. William Bourchier — *Thomas Bourchier, Archbishop of Canterbury* d. 1486

7 William of Windsor d. in infancy

NOTE: Names in italic type are those of persons in or closely relevant to the play. Italicised dates are those of reigns; other dates are those of births and deaths. Collateral kindred irrelevant to claims under lines 4 and 5 have been omitted. The contest arose from the fact that Richard II should have been succeeded not by the Lancastrian Henry IV (line 4) but by the descent from line 3 through the marriage of Anne Mortimer and Richard, Earl of Cambridge.

Table 2: The House of York

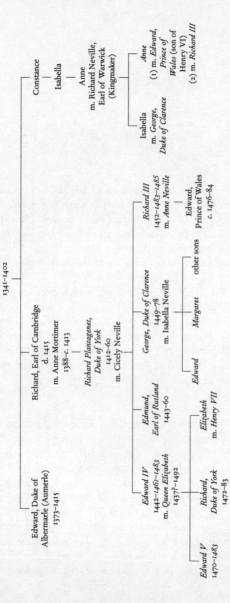

NOTE: Names in italic type are those of persons in or closely relevant to the play. Italicized dates are those of reigns; other dates are those of births and deaths. Collateral kindred irrelevant to the claims of Richard III and Henry VII to the English crown have been omitted.

Commentary

The act and scene divisions are those of the Folio (1623; referred to as F), except for certain scenes that were not divided in the Folio (III.4–7, IV.2–3, V.2–5), where I have followed later editors. The first Quarto (1597) is referred to as Q or Q1, the other five Quartos published before 1623 as Q2, Q3, etc. Biblical quotations are taken from the Bishops' Bible (1568, etc.), the official English translation of Elizabeth's reign.

In II.4, F's stage direction and speech-prefixes name an *Archbishop*, who corresponds to Holinshed's Thomas Rotheram, Archbishop of York; in III.1, F names a *Lord Cardinal*, now usually identified as Thomas Bourchier, Archbishop of Canterbury. In Q a *Cardinal* figures in both scenes: perhaps, then, misled by confusions in Holinshed, Shakespeare thought of the cardinal and archbishop as one person.

I.1

The Elizabethan stage used little scenery, and dramatists often left the location of a scene unspecified. In this Commentary the first note on every scene will indicate whatever location may be inferred from the dialogue. Modern producers who wish to give some visual aid might have a back-drop of the Tower for I.1 (cf. 45, 50, 63, etc., and 124), and for I.2, II.3, III.1 and 2, IV.1. The Tower is an ominous presence throughout the first four acts, and three scenes actually take place inside it (I.4, III.4 and 5).

2 *sun*: (1) Sun (the Yorkist badge); (2) son (King Edward

being the Duke of York's son). York had claimed the crown, but he fell at the Battle of Wakefield (1460); his son, Edward IV, continued the Yorkist struggle against the House of Lancaster, and became King in 1461.

3 *loured*: Looked dark and threatening.

6 *monuments*: Memorials.

7 *alarums*: 'Alar(u)m' can mean either (1) call to arms or (2) sudden attack.

8 *measures*: Stately dances.

9 *wrinkled front*: Frowning forehead or face.

10 *barbèd*: With armed flanks and breast.

12 *He*: The warrior, or war – line 9 – personified; perhaps alluding to King Edward.

13 *lascivious pleasing*: Pleasingly lascivious music.

16 *rudely stamped*: Marked with a rough ('rude') stamp or appearance.

17 *ambling*: Walking affectedly.
    nymph: Beautiful young woman (cant).

18 *curtailed*: Cut short (with quibble on being made a 'curtal', an animal that has lost its tail).

19 *feature*: Bodily shape.
    dissembling: Because my deformity disguises my real qualities.

20 *sent before my time*: Cf. II.4.16–30, IV.4.163–5.

21 *breathing*: Living; briskly exercising.
    made up: Finished (with a quibble on the tailoring sense).

22 *lamely*: Imperfectly; haltingly.

23 *halt*: Limp.

24 *piping*: (1) characterized by the music of peaceful, pastoral pipes; (2) piping like the shrill voices of women and children.

27 *descant*: Comment.

29 *entertain*: Provide occupation for.
    well-spoken: Eloquent.

30 *am determined*: Have decided; or perhaps fore-ordained. Many editors treat this as a word of four syllables, but it gives weight to the line to make it trisyllabic and upset the rhythm.

31 *idle*: Unemployed; frivolous.

32 *inductions*: Dramatic prologues (a quibble after *Plots*); preparations.

38 *mewed*: Shut.

41 *Dive, thoughts, down to my soul*: Descend, thoughts, down to my soul (that is, from my tongue). There is an unusual admission that soliloquy involves speech.

43 *waits*: Attends (ironical).

44 *Tendering*: Having regard for.

45 *conduct*: Guard.

50 *new-christened*: Dramatic irony: see I.4.273.

55 *cross-row*: Alphabet.

60 *toys*: Trifles; whims.

61 *Hath*: In Shakespeare the third person plural often ends in -s or -th (for example, 'has' or 'hath' for 'have'). Such archaic inflections, though they now appear to be 'false concords', have been silently retained in this edition.

64 *My Lady Grey*: The Queen, wife of Sir John Grey before her marriage to King Edward.

65 *tempers*: Moulds.

66 *worship*: Honour (ironical, as if speaking of a worthy citizen rather than a nobleman).

67 *Woodville*: Earl Rivers. The word has three syllables (Woodeville), according to the editors. But cf. II.1.69, and *Henry VI, Part I*, I.3.22: 'Faint-hearted Woodville, prizest him fore me?'

72 *night-walking heralds*: Secret messengers. Heralds carried messages between princes, and night walkers were not usually safe at this time.

73 *Mistress Shore*: *Mistress* could be a title of respect, but is not so intended here.

76 *her*: Jane Shore's.

77 *Lord Chamberlain*: Hastings.

80 *men*: Servants.

80 *wear her livery*: As her retainers.

81 *jealous*: Mistrustful; sexually jealous.
   o'erworn: Faded; the worse for wear.
   widow: Queen Elizabeth, widow of Sir John Grey.
   herself: Jane Shore.

82 *dubbed them*: Invested them with the status of. A malicious misrepresentation, for the Queen and her family, though acquiring titles with her marriage, were gentlefolk before it. Jane Shore was not given a higher rank, and the two women never became *gossips*.

83 *gossips*: Cronies; godmothers (see 50).

85 *straitly*: Strictly.

88 *An*: If.

   your worship: Ironic. Cf. *fellow* (98), *knave* (102).

92 *Well struck in years*: Well on in years. A set phrase, as in *The Taming of the Shrew*, II.1.353; ironically placed before *fair* (beautiful), it implies that the years have left their mark.

   jealous: So Q; F has the old form *iealious* (three syllables). Cf. 81.

98 *Naught*: Wickedness. 'To do naught' is 'to copulate'.

101–2 BRAKENBURY *What one ... betray me*: These lines may have been inserted in Q1 by the press-corrector and, though no copy of Q1 now survives in this state, taken over by Q2. But it is a strange coincidence that the lines do not scan, so they could be an actor's addition.

106 *abjects*: Servile subjects.

107 *Brother, farewell*: Clarence later (I.4.247–9) recalls that Richard wept and sobbed during this speech. Clarence's recollection has been dismissed as 'episodic intensification', but it should be noted that Richard *can* turn on his tears (II.2.23, III.5.24).

110 *enfranchise*: Set free.

111–15 *Meantime ... lie for you*: Dramatic irony; cf. I.4.249–51.

112 *Touches*: Hurts.

115 *lie for*: Go to prison for; tell lies about. Cf. 148, and note the jingle in (*de*)*liver you* and *lie for you*.

125 *brooked*: Endured.

138 *Saint John*: Though Richard usually swears by Saint Paul (I.2.36, 41, I.3.45, etc.), Shakespeare may not have decided on this characteristic touch so early in the play, and Q's reading here could be contaminated by Richard's later oaths.

139 *diet*: Course of life.

146 *with post-horse*: By express. Cf. Elijah's ascent to heaven, 2 Kings 2:11.

153 *Warwick's youngest daughter*: Lady Anne.

154 *husband*: Edward, Prince of Wales.
    father: Father-in-law Henry VI.

158 *secret close intent*: His intention to seize the crown.

160 *I run before my horse to market*: Proverbial for counting one's chickens before they are hatched.

I.2

Location: as before. After hearing, in I.1, of Richard's plans to kill those who stand in his way, we now see the funeral of one of his victims. Shakespeare brings together the events of 1471, 1472 and 1478 to create the impression that Richard not only talks but acts.

0 *corse*: Corpse.
  halberds: Halberdiers, guards with halberds. See 40, note.

2 *shrouded*: Concealed; buried.

3 *obsequiously*: Mourningly.

5 *key-cold*: Cold in death, as a metal key.

12 *windows*: Wounds (referring to the custom of opening the windows to allow a dying soul to pass).

13 *helpless*: Unavailing.

17 *hap*: Fortune.

21 *abortive*: Monstrous.

22 *Prodigious*: Abnormal, like a prodigy.

23 *aspect*: Appearance.

25 *unhappiness*: Evil; perniciousness.

27 *life*: This emendation is supported by IV.1.75. Q seems to have been contaminated by line 18, and F failed to correct.

29 *Chertsey*: Chertsey monastery, near London.

30 *Paul's*: Saint Paul's Cathedral.

35 *devoted*: Holy.

40 *Advance thy halberd*: Raise your halberd (so that I can pass). A halberd is a spear-like weapon, with a sharp-edged blade as well as a spear-point at the end.

42 *spurn upon*: Kick at; stamp upon.

46 *Avaunt*: Be off.

47–8 *Thou hadst but power . . . canst not have*: Cf. Matthew

10:28: 'And fear ye not them which kill the body, but are not able to kill the soul.'

49 *for charity*: For the sake of holy charity.
curst: Shrewish.

54 *pattern*: Example.

55–6 *Henry's wounds . . . bleed afresh*: It was a popular belief that in the presence of the murderer a murdered man's wounds bled again.

58 *exhales*: Draws out.

63 *O earth . . . revenge*: Cf. Genesis 4:11.

65 *earth gape*: 'Gape, earth!' was an exclamation of grief in *Tamburlaine* and other plays of this period.
quick: Alive. Cf. Numbers 16:30–33.

77 *By circumstance*: By explaining the details.

78 *diffused infection*: Anne describes Richard as a plague that has spread far and wide.

84 *current*: Genuine.

93 *In thy foul throat thou li'st*: Thou liest most foully.
Queen Margaret saw: In *Henry VI, Part III*, V.5, King Edward stabbed Prince Edward first, and Richard followed suit.

94 *falchion*: A slightly curved sword.

94 *smoking in*: Sending up a fine spray of.

102 *hedgehog*: Term of abuse applied to one regardless of others' feelings. Alluding to Richard's badge, the boar.

107 *holp*: Helped.

108 *fitter for that place*: Cf. Luke 9:62: 'apt to the kingdom of God'.

116 *something into a*: Into a somewhat.

117 *timeless*: Untimely.

126 *rent*: Rend.

127 *wrack*: Ruin.

147 *poison on a fouler toad*: Toads were popularly taken as types of the 'ugly and venomous' (*As You Like It*, II.1.13).

150 *basilisks*: Fabulous reptiles, supposedly able to kill with a look.

154 *aspects*: Appearances.

155 *remorseful*: Compassionate.

156–63 *No, when my father York . . . bedashed with rain*: See
        Henry VI, Part III, I.3 and 4, II.1.

165 *exhale*: Draw out.

168 *smoothing*: Flattering.

169 *fee*: Recompense.

182 *falls*: Drops.

192–202 *I would I knew thy heart . . . To take is not to give*: Anne
         and Richard now fall into the same rhythms, indicating
         that they are attuned. Notice that Richard allows her
         to dictate the rhythm, then seizes the initiative.

202 *To take is not to give*: I take your ring but make no
     promises in return.

203 *Look how*: Just as.

206 *servant*: Lover, as well as servant.

210 *designs*: Projects, intentions.

212 *Crosby House*: One of Richard's residences. (See also
     III.5.104.)

216 *expedient*: Speedy.

217 *divers unknown reasons*: Cf. I.1.158. Holinshed (p. 691)
     mentions that the body was moved from the Tower to
     Saint Paul's, then to Blackfriars ('Whitefriars', line 226,
     may therefore be erroneous), then to Chertsey
     monastery. That Richard took charge of the funeral is
     Shakespeare's invention – to demonstrate Richard's
     ascendancy.

227–8 *Was ever woman . . . in this humour won*: A common-
       place. Cf. *Henry VI, Part I*, V.3.78–9, *Titus Andronicus*,
       II.1.83–4.

234 *bars*: Obstacles.

243 *Framed*: Formed.

247 *cropped*: Lopped off.

249 *moiety*: Half.

250 *halts*: Limps.

251 *denier*: French coin, the twelfth of a sou.

254 *proper*: Excellent; handsome.

256 *entertain*: Maintain.

260 *in*: Into.

I.3

        Location: London. The palace. The scene opens with

a discussion of the King's illness. As this has already been mentioned (I.1.135–42) we need not imagine more than a brief lapse of time between I.2 and 3.

3 *brook it ill*: Suffer it impatiently.

6 *betide on*: Happen to.

15 *determined, not concluded*: Agreed, but not legalized.

20–21 *The Countess . . . amen*: The Countess, widow of Edmund Tudor, was mother of Richmond, who later claimed the throne and became Henry VII.

26 *envious*: Malicious.

36 *atonement*: Reconciliation.

39 *warn*: Summon.

48 *smooth*: Flatter.
   cog: Fawn.

49 *Duck*: Cringe.

53 *With*: By.

53 *Jacks*: Knaves. Jack was a generic proper name for any man of the common people.

54 *presence*: Company; royal presence. (He challenges Richard to accuse the Queen directly.)

60 *breathing while*: Short time.

61 *lewd*: Vile.

63–8 *The King . . . Makes him to send*: The syntax is confused: '(The fact that) the King guesses your hatred makes him send.'

65 *Aiming*: Guessing.

69 *I cannot tell*: I don't know (how things really stand).

70 *prey where eagles*: Cf. I.1.132–3.

81 *noble*: A gold coin, worth one-third of £1.

82 *careful*: Full of care or anxiety.

83 *hap*: Fortune.

88 *suspects*: Suspicions.

96 *lay . . . on*: Attribute to.

99 *marry*: Indeed (with quibble).

101 *Iwis*: Certainly.

108 *behind*: Here, and in her only other scene, Queen Margaret is not immediately noticed. As at IV.4.8, she *retires*.

111 *state*: Estate; rank; dignity.

113 *Look what*: Whatever.

115 *adventure*: Venture.

116 *pains*: Efforts.

117 *devil*: A monosyllable.

121 *packhorse*: Drudge. This continues the pretence (51–2) that Richard is *plain* and *simple*.

129 *battle*: Army.

134 *father*: Father-in-law.

135 *forswore himself*: Cf. *Henry VI, Part III*, V.1.81–106.

138 *meed . . . mewed*: Notice the jingle; *mewed* = shut, *meed* = reward.

143 *cacodemon*: Evil spirit.

144 *busy*: Active.

148 *pedlar*: Cf. III.1.128–31. To distract the others from the idea that he might want to be king Richard alludes to the load on his back, his hunchback, which makes him look like a pedlar.

157 *pirates*: Thieves.

158 *pilled*: Plundered.

160–61 *If not, that I am Queen . . . quake like rebels*: If you bow not as subjects because I am Queen, at least you quake because you have deposed me.

164 *repetition*: Recital.

169 *thou*: Richard.

170 *thou*: Queen Elizabeth.

173–9 *The curse . . . fallen upon thee*: Cf. *Henry VI, Part III*, I.4.111 ff., where the Duke of York, just before he is murdered, is offered a rag soaked in his young son's blood, and calls for revenge against Queen Margaret.

176 *clout*: Rag.

182 *babe*: Rutland was depicted as a young boy in *Henry VI, Part III*, but Shakespeare calls both him and the two princes (IV.3.9) *babes*, thus comparing Margaret and Richard as child-murderers.

184 *Tyrants*: Pitiless men.

193 *answer for*: Correspond to.
peevish: Silly, senseless.

196–226 *Though not by war . . . a hell of ugly devils*: All these curses are fulfilled, and are later recalled by those who

now disregard them. Shakespeare makes them an
important structural device.

205 *stalled*: Installed.

218 *them*: That is, heaven, treated as a plural as in V.5.21.

227 *elvish-marked*: Marked at birth by malignant fairies.

abortive: Unnatural.

rooting: To root is to dig up with the snout. The allusion is to Richard's twisted back.

hog: Referring to Richard's badge.

229 *The slave of nature*: The pre-eminent wretch in the
realm of nature.

232 *rag*: Term of contempt.

234 *I cry thee mercy*: I beg your pardon.

237 *period*: Conclusion.

240 *painted*: Feigned; unreal.

vain flourish: Empty ostentation.

241 *sugar*: Sweet words (alluding to the jocular advice given
to children to catch animals by putting salt on their
tails).

bottled: Shaped like a leather bottle; swollen (alluding
to Richard's hunchback).

spider: Because spiders were thought poisonous, and
appear swollen.

250 *duty*: Reverence.

254 *malapert*: Impertinent.

255 *stamp*: Design stamped on to a piece of metal during
process of minting: hence *fire-new*.

current: Current as coin; genuine.

258 *They that stand high have many blasts to shake them*: A
commonplace, often with an allusion to trees, as at 263.

263 *aery*: Brood of a bird of prey. Perhaps an allusion to
Ezekiel 17:3: 'There came a great eagle . . . and took
the highest branch of a cedar tree.'

264 *scorns the sun*: It was thought a sign of the eagle's
princely nature that it could gaze at the sun unblinded.
Cf. *Henry VI, Part III*, II.1.91–2: 'Nay, if thou be that
princely eagle's bird, | Show thy descent by gazing
'gainst the sun'; and *Love's Labour's Lost*, IV.3.330.

272 *BUCKINGHAM*: So Q, F. It has been suggested that

Buckingham has not injured Margaret (279–83), so 274–7 cannot be addressed to him, and so he cannot speak 272. But Margaret keeps turning from one person to another, and could address 273 to Buckingham and 274–7 to the rest.

276 *My charity is outrage, life my shame*: Either 'My most charitable feeling is one of outrage, my most shameful feeling that I am still alive', or 'The only charity shown to me is outrage, and a life of shame is all the life permitted me.'

276 *outrage*: Violent conduct or language.

281 *fair befall*: Fair fortune come to.

284–5 *curses never pass | The lips of those that breathe them in the air*: Cf. 'curses return upon the heads of those that curse' (proverbial).

288–93 *O Buckingham . . . attend on him*: This is treated as an aside by some editors. Margaret's other warnings are publicly delivered, however, so it may be best to take Richard's question (294) as a teasing pretence that he has not heard what was only too audible. He plays the same game later with Buckingham (IV.2.82 ff.): we must see it as connected with his deliberate misunderstandings (I.1.98, I.3.234, III.5.19).

289 *Look when*: Whenever.

290 *venom*: Poisonous.
    rankle: Cause a festering wound.

297 *soothe*: Humour.

303 *an end*: On end.

304 *muse*: Marvel.

310 *I was too hot*: A rather sudden transition to the thoughts of 120–24.

313 *franked up to fatting*: Shut up in a sty like a pig to be fatted for slaughter.

315–16 *A virtuous . . . scathe to us*: Such backing of Richard has been called inappropriate to Rivers 'except as bitter sarcasm'. Notice, however, that Rivers makes other conciliatory gestures (II.1.9, II.2.134).

316 *scathe*: Harm.

324 *abroach*: On foot.

325 *lay unto the grievous charge*: Make a grievous accusation against.

327 *gulls*: Fools.

334 *do good for evil*: Cf. Matthew 5:44.

336 *odd old ends*: Stale scraps.

339 *mates*: Fellows.

343 *about me*: In my pocket. Should Richard, perhaps, play with the (unrecognized) warrant earlier in the scene?

352 *drop millstones*: Proverbial, said of a hard-hearted person.
   fall: Drop.

I.4

Location: a room in the Tower. There is no time-gap between I.3 and 4.

 0 *Keeper*: See 75, note.

 1 *heavily*: Sorrowfully.

5–6 *spend . . . night . . . buy . . . days*: Double antithesis.

 9 *Methoughts*: methought, I thought. So 24, 58.

12 *tempted*: Induced; enticed.

13 *hatches*: Movable planks forming a kind of deck.

17 *giddy*: Rendering dizzy.

26 *Wedges*: Ingots.

27 *unvalued*: Invaluable.

37 *envious flood*: Spiteful water.

39 *vast*: Boundless; desolate.

41 *Who*: Which.

42 *agony*: Anguish; death-struggle.

45 *flood*: The river Styx.

46 *ferryman*: Charon.

50 *perjury*: See *Henry VI, Part III*, V.1.

53 *shadow*: Spirit, shade. He means Edward, Prince of Wales (see *Henry VI, Part III*, V.5.40).

61 *season*: Time.

68 *requits*: Repays.

75 *Enter Brakenbury, the Lieutenant*: So F. Q identifies Brakenbury and the Keeper from the beginning of the scene, and some editors follow Q.

80 *unfelt imaginations*: Things imagined but not experienced.

83 *two Murderers*: The two men are sufficiently individualized to be distinct: the First Murderer the more brutal
and aggressive, the Second Murderer more human. But
87–8 and 90–91 are not so characteristic as to point
unmistakably to one of the two, so I follow F; some
editors switch round these two speech-prefixes.

108 *urging*: Putting forward as an argument.

109 *remorse*: Pity.

119 *passionate*: Compassionate.

132 *thy conscience flies out*: Cf. 36–41. An ironic contrast.

134 *entertain*: Receive; take into service.

145 *live well*: A quibble on two opposed meanings: enjoy
life, live virtuously.

149 *Take the devil in thy mind*: Receive the devil (conscience)
in thy mind.

150 *insinuate*: Ingratiate himself.

154 *tall*: Valiant.

156 *Take*: Strike.
costard: Head (slang).

157–8 *malmsey-butt*: Cask for malmsey, a sweet wine.

159 *sop*: Cake or wafer dipped in wine.

163 *reason*: Talk, argue.

165 *You shall have wine enough*: This is ironic. But the tone
now changes. The murderers have to drop their profes-
sional heartiness: they respond, unwillingly, to a higher
ethos, and therefore speak in blank verse.

172 *darkly*: Frowningly; obscurely.

187 *quest*: Body appointed to hold an inquiry.

198 *Erroneous vassals*: Misguided wretches.

200 *do no murder*: Exodus 20:13.

201 *Spurn at*: Contemptuously oppose.

202 *vengeance*: 'Vengeance is mine' (Deuteronomy 32:35).

213 *dear*: Important.

219 *yet*: Now as always.

221 *indirect*: Unjust; round-about.

223 *minister*: Agent.

224 *gallant-springing*: Gallantly growing.

231 *hired for meed*: So Q, F. An alternative is 'hired, for
meed'.

243 *millstones*: See I.3.352.

244 *kind*: Could mean 'natural', and First Murderer so takes it.

245 *as snow in harvest*: 'As the cold of snow in the time of harvest' (Proverbs 25:13).

271 *Look behind you*: This is probably a genuine warning, as the First Murderer advances from behind, not a trick warning to allow the First Murderer to strike.

274 *desperately*: Recklessly.

275 *like Pilate*: Cf. Matthew 27:24.

285 *meed*: Reward.

II.1

Location: London. A room in the palace. Time: shortly after I.4.

1 *a good day's work*: Dramatic irony, after I.4.

8 *Dissemble*: Disguise.

14 *Confound*: Defeat.

19 *son*: Stepson.

33 *but*: Confused syntax; for 'but' understand 'nor'.

34–40 *God punish me . . . yours*: Cf. V.1.

38 *Deep*: Profound in craft.

44 *period*: Conclusion.

52 *swelling*: Inflated with anger.

54 *heap*: Company.

55 *intelligence*: Secret information.

57 *or in my rage*: This is thought to be an actor's addition by some editors, echoing *in thy rage* (I.2.187). It is true that the metre is regular without these words, but not that Richard, in his humble mood, would never admit to flying into a rage: he admits much worse things in I.2.101 ff., IV.4.291 ff.

68 *all without desert*: Wholly without my deserving it.

74 *I thank my God for my humility*: Perhaps an aside.

78 *grace*: Favour.

80 *flouted*: Taunted.

83 *KING EDWARD*: So F. Q assigns to Rivers, perhaps rightly.

90 *wingèd Mercury*: Mercury, the messenger of the gods, wore winged sandals.

92 *lag*: Late.

96 *current from suspicion*: Sound and not attacked by suspicion.

100 *requests*: Second person singular in -ts for euphony.

101 *forfeit . . . of my servant's life*: My servant's forfeited life.

105 *slave*: Wretch.

106 *his fault was thought*: His was a fault in thought but not in deed.

119 *thin*: Thinly covered (as in *Richard II*, III.2.112).

135 *closet*: Private apartment.

139 *still*: Always.

II.2

Location: as before. Time: shortly after II.1.

0 *two children*: Both were executed, when grown up, by Henry VII.

8 *cousins*: Grandchildren.

18 *Incapable and shallow*: Unintelligent and superficial.

22 *impeachments*: Accusations.

27–8 *shape . . . visor . . . vice*: With wordplay on the theatrical meanings: theatrical guise; mask; Vice or Iniquity in the older drama.

30 *dugs*: Breasts. Cf. the proverbial 'to suck evil from the dug'.

33 *with her hair about her ears*: The conventional expression of grief. Cf. Constance in *King John*, III.4.61.

38 *rude*: Barbarous.

47–8 *interest . . . title*: Right to share in . . . interest (legal metaphors).

50–51 *images . . . mirrors*: Likenesses, that is, children.

60 *moiety*: Half.

61 *overgo*: Exceed.

68 *reduce*: Bring.

69 *governed by the watery moon*: She compares herself to the tides. But why is the *moon* dragged in? Perhaps a quibble on 'moon'–'moan' (Q reads *moane*).

74 *stay*: Support.

77 *Was never*: A popular rhetorical construction found in *The Fairie Queene*, I.2.23, etc.

81 *parcelled*: Particular.

94 *opposite with*: Hostile to.

95 *For*: Because.

110 *butt-end*: Fag-end.

112 *cloudy*: Gloomy.

113 *mutual*: Common.

120 *train*: Troop.

121 *fet*: Fetched.

127 *green*: Unripe, weak.

128 *bears his commanding rein*: Takes charge of the rein with which it should be commanded.

144 *censures*: Opinions.

147 *God*: God's.

148 *sort*: Contrive.

149 *index*: Prologue.

151 *consistory*: Council-chamber.

II.3

Location: a London street. Time: shortly after II.2.

2 *promise*: Assure.

4 *seldom comes the better*: Proverbial: change is seldom made for the better.

5 *giddy*: Mad.

8 *God help the while*: Expression of pity.

11 *Woe to that land that's governed by a child*: Cf. Ecclesiastes 10:16: 'Woe be unto thee, O thou land, whose king is but a child.'

13–15 *in his nonage . . . govern well*: The council shall govern well under him during his nonage till he is of age, and he himself shall then govern well. (Some think that a line is lost.)

16 *Henry*: Three syllables?

17 *crowned in Paris*: He succeeded to the throne when nine months old, but was not crowned till later. See *Henry VI, Part I*, IV.1.1.

19 *famously*: Renownedly.

26 *touch*: Wound.

30 *solace*: Be happy.

36 *sort*: Ordain.

43 *proof*: Experience.

46 *to the justices*: Cf. line 2! – The three citizens differ

from the commoners in most of Shakespeare's histories and tragedies in that they are responsible men who
help in the administration of justice. They prepare us
for the coolness of the citizens reported in III.7, and
of the Recorder, one of the justices.

II.4

Location: London. A room in the palace. Time: some
days later.

1–2 *Stony Stratford . . . Northampton*: So F (and Holinshed).
Q reverses the names, probably because Stony Stratford
is nearer to London.

13 *herbs*: Plants.
grace: Virtuous property.

24 *flout*: Taunt.

25 *touch*: Strike at.

28 *gnaw a crust at two hours old*: Cf. Holinshed, p. 712.

35 *parlous*: Shrewd; dangerous.
Go to: Expression of disapproval.
shrewd: Sharp-tongued.

37 *Pitchers have ears*: Proverbial – the ears or handles of
small jugs are disproportionately large.

42 *Pomfret*: The castle at Pontefract.

46 *all I can*: Elliptical for 'all I can disclose'.

51 *Insulting*: Exulting proudly.
jut: Strut; swagger.

52 *aweless*: Inspiring no awe.

54 *map*: Picture.

60 *seated*: On the throne.

61 *overblown*: Blown away.

64 *spleen*: Malice.

71 *seal*: Presumably the Great Seal, of which he was keeper
as Lord Chancellor.

III.1

Location: a London street. Time: some days later.

1–2 *Welcome*: From II.2.146 ff. we learn that Buckingham
and Gloucester plan to fetch the Prince to London.
This, then, is not a *Welcome* to one they have not seen
for some time, but a formal congratulation to the boy-
king, virtually a prisoner, on entering his capital.

1 *chamber*: Capital. Holinshed has a gloss 'London the King's especial chamber' (p. 729).

2 *my thoughts' sovereign*: The chief of all my thoughts; with sinister implication.

6 *want*: Lack.

8 *dived*: Cf. I.1.41.

9–11 *Nor more can you distinguish . . . with the heart*: Cf. I Samuel 16:7.

10 *God He knows*: God knows.

11 *jumpeth*: Agrees.

22 *slug*: Sluggard.

28 *tender*: Young.

31 *peevish*: Senseless; perverse.

34 *presently*: Immediately.

36 *jealous*: Suspicious.

45 *ceremonious*: Scrupulous about forms.

46 *Weigh it but with the grossness of this age*: Weigh this act against the violent practices of these times, or weigh it as such actions are weighed in this gross age.

54 *charter*: Immunity granted by royal charter.

68 *I do not like the Tower, of any place*: I like the Tower less than any place I know.

75 *registered*: Recorded.

77 *retailed*: Repeated.

79 *So wise so young*: Those who are so wise when so young (elliptical).

81 *characters*: Writing.
fame lives long: Longer than Richard thinks!

82 *the formal Vice, Iniquity*: The stock Vice (also called Iniquity) of the morality plays.

83 *moralize*: Interpret; explain.

85 *With what*: With that with which.

91 *An if*: If.

94 *lightly*: Commonly.
forward: Early; pert.

99 *late*: Recently.

103 *idle*: Useless.

107 *beholding*: Beholden.

111 *With all my heart*: Dramatic irony.

118 *light*: With a quibble on light = trivial.

121 *I weigh it lightly, were it heavier*: I consider it as of no value, and would even if it were heavier.

122 *would you have my weapon*: Dramatic irony.

126 *cross*: Perverse; contradictory.

131 *on your shoulders*: Alluding to Richard's hunchback, and apparently to the saddle worn by those who carried monkeys about for exhibition.

132 *sharp-provided*: Quick and ready.

150 *sennet*: See note to IV.2.0.

151 *prating*: Babbling.

152 *incensèd*: Incited.

154 *parlous*: Shrewd.

155 *capable*: Gifted.

157 *rest*: Be.

169 *no more but this*: Do no more than this.

173 *sit about*: Meet and discuss.

179 *divided councils*: Cf. III.2.12–24. Richard apparently resorted to two councils to divide the opposition.

180 *highly*: In an important manner.

182 *knot*: Band (with quibble on knot = tumour).

183 *are let blood*: Are to be bled (surgically), that is, are to die.

192 *complots*: Plots.

194 *look when*: As soon as.

195 *movables*: 'Personal' as opposed to 'real' property.

200 *digest*: Arrange (with pun after 'sup').
      form: Good order.

III.2

      Time: early next morning.

  0 *to the door of Hastings*: So F. Later editors added 'before Lord Hastings' House'. A street scene is required, but it is odd that Hastings answers the door himself.

  4 *What is't a clock*: What time is it?

  7 *that*: What.

 10 *certifies*: Assures.

 11 *boar*: Richard.
      razèd off his helm: Plucked off his helmet.

 12 *two councils*: See III.1.179, note.

16 *presently*: Immediately.

24 *intelligence*: Secret information.

25 *instance*: Motive.

43 *crown*: Head. From here to III.4.66 Hastings's speeches are a series of dramatic ironies.

46 *forward*: Zealous.

52 *still*: Ever.

55 *to the death*: A common asseveration, 'at the risk of death'; dramatic irony.

58–9 *That they . . . tragedy*: That they who brought me into my master's hate (die while) I live (elliptical).

61 *packing*: Cf. I.1.146, *packed with post-horse up to heaven*.

70 *the Bridge*: London Bridge, where the heads of traitors were stuck up on poles.

75 *Rood*: Cross.

88 *The day is spent*: It's getting late.

92 *wear their hats*: Perhaps 'keep their offices': they, being true (loyal), have a better right to keep their heads than some who have (falsely) accused them who (should lose theirs but) do not even lose their hats.

93 *Pursuivant*: Junior officer.

Hastings: So Q. Here, and in lines 95, 98 and 105, it seems best to follow Q, which tallies with Holinshed, rather than F, which differs. Q must represent a Shakespearian version; F may do so too, but not so certainly.

104 *hold*: Continue.

105 *Gramercy*: God-a-mercy (expression of thanks).

108 *Sir*: A title prefixed to the Christian name of a priest.

109 *exercise*: Sermon; act of devotion.

111 *I'll wait upon your lordship*: Both here, and at 122, the words first appear in F. They may have been wrongly inserted here.

114 *shriving work*: Confession and absolution. Cf. III.4.95.

120 *stay*: Wait for.

121 *And supper too*: That is, you will never eat again. Cf. III.4.76, 94: Hastings is executed *before* dinner.

III.3

Location: Pomfret (Pontefract) Castle. Time: the same day.

0 *halberds*: See note to I.2.0.

4 *pack*: Conspiring gang.

5 *knot*: Band.

7 *limit*: Prescribed time.

10 *closure*: Enclosure.

12 *dismal*: Ill-boding.

23 *expiate*: Fully come (of an appointed time).

III.4

Location: a room in the Tower. Time: the same day.

0 *Norfolk, Ratcliffe*: Norfolk has nothing to say, and so is sometimes omitted. Ratcliffe was at Pomfret in III.3, a scene that takes place at the same time as III.4 – Shakespeare's oversight.

1 *are*: Have.

2 *coronation*: Of Edward V.

5 *nomination*: Appointing.

6 *happy*: Favourable.

8 *inward*: Intimate.

24 *neglect*: Cause neglect of.

39 *worshipfully*: Respectfully (said in contempt).

44 *provided*: Equipped.

45 *prolonged*: Put off.

49 *conceit*: Idea; fancy.

55 *livelihood*: Animation.

58 *I pray God he be not, I say*: Q only: perhaps an actor's addition.

63 *tender*: Dear.

69 *blasted*: Shrivelled.

70–71 *Edward's wife, that monstrous witch,* | *Consorted with that harlot*: See I.1.82, note.

76 *Saint Paul*: So Holinshed (alluding to Acts 23:12?). Shakespeare made *by Saint Paul* Richard's favourite oath.

84 *footcloth*: Ornamented cloth laid over the back of a horse and hanging down to the ground on either side.

96 *momentary grace*: Good fortune lasting but a

moment. Cf. Psalm 146:3: 'O put not your trust in princes . . .'

98 *in air of your good looks*: Upon the airy foundation of the favour of mortal men.

99–101 *Lives like a drunken sailor . . . of the deep*: Cf. Proverbs 23:34: 'Yea, thou shalt be as though thou layest in the midst of the sea, or sleepest upon the top of the mast of a ship.'

102 *bootless*: Unavailing.

III.5

Location: the same. Time: a little later.

0 *marvellous ill-favoured*: Remarkably ill-looking.

8 *Intending*: Pretending.

10 *offices*: Functions.

17 *o'erlook*: Inspect.

30 *apparent*: Manifest.

31 *conversation*: Intercourse (a quibble).

32 *from all attainder of suspects*: Free from all dishonourable stain of suspicions.

33 *covert'st sheltered*: Most secret and concealed.

34 *almost*: Used to intensify a rhetorical question.

39 *Had he*: Would he have.

46 *fair befall*: Good fortune come to.

54 *Something*: Somewhat.
    have: Plural influenced by *friends*?

55 *heard*: The emendation 'hear' is attractive, but *heard* wins support from the other deliberately awkward conditional clauses (39 ff.).

60 *Misconster us in him*: Misjudge us in his fate.

62 *as*: As if.

68 *Which . . . of our intent*: Who . . . in respect of our design.

70 *we bid farewell*: Very abrupt – almost contemptuous.

72 *post*: Haste.

73 *meet'st advantage of the time*: Most conveniently advantageous time.

74 *Infer*: Allege.

77 *house*: Shop.

79 *luxury*: Lust.

82 *raging*: Riotous.

94 *Doubt*: Fear.

97 *Baynard's Castle*: On the north bank of the Thames. One of Richard's London residences, like Crosby House (I.2.212).

102, 103 *Shaw, Penker*: Two well-known preachers who supported Richard.

105 *take some privy order*: Make some secret arrangements.

III.6

Location: London. A street, or a room in the Scrivener's house. Time: the same day. This brief scene was inserted to indicate the passage of time between III.5 and 7, and to prepare for the hostility of public opinion described in III.7.

2 *set hand*: Secretary handwriting, used in legal documents from the fifteenth to the seventeenth century.
fairly is engrossed: Is beautifully written out.

4 *sequel*: Sequence, series.

7 *precedent*: Original from which a copy is made.

9 *Untainted*: Unaccused.

10 *the while*: Just now.
gross: Stupid.

11 *device*: Contrivance.

III.7

Location: the courtyard of Baynard's Castle. Time: later the same day.

3 *mum*: Silent.

5 *Lady Lucy*: Dame Elizabeth Lucy.

6 *contract by deputy in France*: to Lady Bona.

8 *enforcement*: Violation.

9 *tyranny for*: Cruelty on account of.

15 *victories in Scotland*: Richard commanded the army that invaded Scotland in 1482.

16 *discipline*: Military experience.

30 *the Recorder*: The Recorder of London, a magistrate with criminal and civil jurisdiction.

32 *inferred*: Alleged.

33 *in warrant from himself*: On his own responsibility.

37 *vantage*: Opportunity.

44 *Intend*: Pretend.

48 *ground*: Plainsong or bass on which a descant is 'raised'. Cf. *Titus Andronicus*, II.1.70.

    descant: Melody, sung extempore; comment.

50 *answer nay, and take it*: Proverbial: 'maids say nay and take it'; maid = girl.

54 *leads*: Flat roof covered with lead.

55 *dance attendance*: Stand waiting in an ante-chamber.

71 *lulling*: Lolling.

    lewd love-bed: Vile bed for the indulgence of lust.

75 *engross*: Fatten.

76 *watchful*: Unsleeping.

80 *defend*: Forbid.

92 *much*: Hard.

93 *zealous*: Pious.

    between two bishops: So F. Hall mentions that Richard appeared 'in a gallery over them (the citizens) with a bishop on every hand of him'. As the two clergymen are never called bishops in the dialogue Shakespeare perhaps decided to replace them by Doctor Shaw and Friar Penker (III.5.102–4), whose summons to Baynard's Castle otherwise remains unexplained. Q reads *Enter Rich. with two bishops*: this may derive from the foul papers (cf. V.3.237, note).

96 *stay*: Support.

111 *disgracious*: Disliked.

118 *office*: Proper function.

119 *state of fortune*: High dignity assigned by fortune.

124 *want her proper limbs*: Lack its own limbs.

126 *graft*: Grafted.

127 *shouldered*: Thrust violently out of its place; immersed up to the shoulders.

129 *recure*: Make whole.

135 *empery*: Absolute dominion.

142 *degree*: Rank.

    condition: Position.

146 *fondly*: Foolishly.

156 *even*: Smooth.

157 *revenue*: Possession.

161 *brook*: Endure.

163 *vapour*: Implying worthlessness.

165 *much I need to help you*: I much need the ability requisite to give you help.

166 *The royal tree hath left us royal fruit*: See Matthew 12:33.

167 *stealing*: Stealthily moving.

170 *that*: What.

172 *defend*: Forbid.

174 *respects*: Considerations.
    nice: Unimportant; over-subtle.

178 *contract*: Contracted.

186 *purchase*: Spoil; booty.

187 *pitch*: Elevation.
    degree: Rank.

188 *declension*: Decline.
    bigamy: Marriage with a widow was bigamy in canon law. Here Edward's earlier contracts are meant.

193 *sparing*: Forbearing.

195 *benefit of dignity*: Bestowal of royal power.

197 *draw forth*: Rescue.

209 *tenderness*: Mildness.

210 *effeminate remorse*: Gentle pity.

212 *egally*: Equally.

213 *whe'er*: Whether.

219 *Exeunt . . . citizens*: Q omits this direction, and that after 225; F reads *Exeunt* and *Enter Buckingham, and the rest*. Only some of the citizens should leave the stage – or perhaps none.

232 *mere*: Downright.
    acquittance: Acquit.

233 *blots and stains*: Slanders.

IV.I

Location: before the Tower. Time: the following day.

1 *niece*: Granddaughter.

2 *in*: By.

3 *for*: On.

4 *tender*: Young.

9 *devotion*: Devout purpose.

10 *gratulate*: Greet.

15 *patience*: Leave.

20 *bounds*: Barriers.

25 *take thy office from thee*: Take on your official responsibility.

33 *lace*: Cord for fastening the bodice.

36 *Despiteful*: Cruel.

45 *Margaret's curse*: See I.3.196 ff.

46 *counted*: Recognized.

49 *son*: Stepson.

52 *ill-dispersing*: Scattering evils.

53 *bed of death*: Bed in which death was born.

54 *cockatrice*: Basilisk. See I.2.150, note.

55 *unavoided eye*: Eye when not shunned.

58 *inclusive verge*: Enclosing circle.

59 *round*: Surround.

64 *feed my humour*: Please my mood.

72 *so old a widow*: Because time has passed so slowly since her husband's death.

79 *Grossly*: Stupidly.

96 *teen*: Sorrow.

98 *tender babes*: See I.3.182, note; IV.3.9.

IV.2

Location: a room in the palace. Time: later the same day.

0 *sennet*: Notes played on a trumpet as a signal for the approach of a procession.

7 *Still*: Ever.

8 *play the touch*: Act the touchstone.

15 *consequence*: Sequel.

16 *true noble prince*: Whether taken as an interjected repetition ('live! – "True, noble prince"! –') or as part of Richard's sentence (live a true noble prince), we cannot miss his impatience.

19 *suddenly*: Swiftly.

22 *kindness*: Love, affection.

24 *breath*: Breathing-space.

26 *presently*: Instantly.

28 *iron-witted*: Obtuse.

29 *unrespective*: Unobservant.

30 *considerate*: Critical.

35 *close exploit*: Secret deed.

42 *deep-revolving*: Deeply considering.

47 *is fled*: Has fled. Though Richard appears not to heed the news, 84 proves that he took it in. His self-protective plans (49–64) betray the first traces of panic, and might be preceded by a hard look at Derby.

51 *close*: Shut up.

54 *foolish*: An idiot. Clarence's son was imprisoned by Henry VII (not Richard) and this apparently affected his mind.

57 *it stands me much upon*: It is of great importance to me.

64 *Tear-falling*: Tear-dropping.

69 *Please you*: If it please you.

71 *deep*: Deadly.

73 *upon*: With.

78 *token*: A ring? Or another warrant, as in I.3.341?

79 *There is no more but so*: that's all it is, dismissing the murder as a trifle.

80 *prefer*: Advance.

83 *in*: About.

89 *movables*: See III.1.195, note.

92 *answer*: Answer for.

96 *peevish*: Senseless.

98–115 *My lord . . . today*: This powerful passage was omitted by F, and is printed from Q. Perhaps one of the changes in the Buckingham material or omitted during the printing of F because another Buckingham was extorting favours from James I.

100 *I being by*: Richard was not present in *Henry VI, Part III*, IV.6.68 ff.

him: The prophet, Henry VI, whom Richard killed in *Henry VI, Part III* with the words 'Die, prophet', V.6.57. Yet, in context, *him* might here refer to Richmond.

104 *Rouge-mount*: Richard's superstition seems the greater since this is not the name foretold by the bard.

113 *Jack*: Figure of a man who strikes the bell on the outside of a clock.

keep'st the stroke: Goest on striking; keepest time.

114 *my meditation*: Despite this word, Richard's preceding speeches are probably not asides but a bravura exercise, to the effect that he recognizes his secret enemies, Buckingham no less than Richmond.

115 *vein*: Humour.

116 *resolve*: Answer.

118 *deep*: Weighty.

121 *Brecknock*: Brecon, Buckingham's manor in Wales.

IV.3

Location: as before. Time: a short time after IV.2.

2 *arch*: Pre-eminent.

5 *piece*: Masterpiece.
  ruthless: Pitiless.

6 *fleshed*: Inured to bloodshed.

7 *tenderness*: Sensitiveness.

9 *babes*: See I.3.182, note.

11 *alablaster*: Alabaster (white).

14 *book of prayers*: Cf. III.7.97!

18 *replenishèd*: Perfect.

19 *prime*: First.

20 *gone*: Overwhelmed.

24 *Kind*: Used like 'good'.

31 *after-supper*: Late supper.

32 *process*: Story.

33 *do thee good*: Be of use to thee.

38 *in Abraham's bosom*: See Luke 16:22.

40 *Britain*: Breton, of Brittany.

42 *by that knot*: By virtue of that marriage-tie.
  looks proudly on: Looks arrogantly towards.

46 *Morton*: Bishop of Ely.

48 *power*: Army.

49 *near*: Deeply.

51 *commenting*: Meditation.

52 *servitor*: Servant.

55 *Mercury*: *Herald* of Jove.

56 *My counsel is my shield*: My best counsel is to use my shield – to fight.

57 *brave the field*: Defy (us on) the battleground.

IV.4

Location: London. Before the palace. Time: a little later.

3 *confines slyly*: Regions stealthily.

5 *induction*: Cf. I.1.32.

10 *sweets*: Scented flowers.

12 *doom*: Death.

16 *night*: Death.

20 *doth quit*: Requites.

21 *a dying debt*: A debt that can only be cancelled by death.

26 *Dead life*: Oxymoron, typical of early Shakespeare. The duchess herself is probably the *Dead life*, etc., though Queen Elizabeth may be meant.

28 *abstract*: Summary account.

31 *thou*: Either the duchess, or *England's lawful earth*.

36 *seniory*: Seniority.

40 *Edward*: Her son, Prince Edward.

41 *Harry*: Her husband, Henry VI.

42, 43 *Edward, Richard*: Queen Elizabeth's two sons.

44 *Richard*: Her husband, the Duke of York.

49 *teeth*: Cf. II.4.28.

53 *excellent*: Surpassing (in bad sense).

56 *carnal*: Carnivorous (?).

57 *issue*: Offspring.

62 *cloy me*: Satiate myself.

64 *quit*: Requite.

65 *boot*: Something given into the bargain.

68 *frantic*: Insane.

71 *intelligencer*: Secret agent.

72 *Only reserved their factor*: Only retained on earth to do his work as the devil's agent.

79 *prophesy*: Cf. I.3.187 ff.

81 *bottled, bunch-backed*: Cf. I.3.241, notes, 245.

83 *shadow*: Semblance; player.

84 *presentation*: Semblance.

85 *index*: Prologue.

89 *shot*: Marksman.

90 *sign*: Mere semblance.

96 *troops*: Followers.

97 *Decline all this*: Go through all this in order.

101 *caitiff*: Wretch.

105 *wheeled*: Alluding, like 86, to the wheel of Fortune.

111 *half my burdened yoke*: Half the burden of my yoke.

128 *Airy succeeders of intestate joys*: Mere words that succeed as next of kin to an empty inheritance.

135 *Be copious in exclaims*: Make your exclamations with a rich command of language.
    train: Troop.

136 *expedition*: Warlike enterprise; haste.

142 *owed*: Owned.

144 *villain-slave*: Villainous wretch.

149 *alarum*: Call 'to arms'. Plutarch, in the *Life of Antony*, wrote that Lepidus 'commanded all the trumpets to sound together to stop the soldiers' ears, that they should not hearken to Antonius'.

152 *fair*: Courteously.

169 *Tetchy*: Peevish.

170 *frightful*: Full of terror.

171 *prime of manhood*: Early manhood.

172 *age*: Years of maturity.

174 *comfortable*: Cheerful, agreeable.

176 *Humphrey Hour*: Unexplained.

178 *disgracious*: Disliked.

193 *Whisper*: Whisper to.

196 *attend*: Serve; wait for.

203 *level*: Aim.

216 *opposite*: Adverse.

218 *unavoided*: Unavoidable.

219 *when avoided grace makes destiny*: When one has made it one's destiny to shun God's grace.

223 *cozened*: Cheated.

225 *Whose hand soever lanched*: Whoever it was whose hand pierced.

226 *indirectly*: Obliquely; wrongly.

230 *But that still use*: Except that the constant indulgence.

233 *bay*: (1) The position of a hunted animal when it turns to face the hunters; (2) Sea-bay. Note the hunting and sea imagery in the adjoining lines.

237 *success*: Issue.

245 *type*: Sign; badge.

247 *state*: Rank.

248 *demise*: Transmit.

250 *withal*: With.

251 *So*: Provided that.

    Lethe: At this time it was a commonplace that immersion in the river Lethe afforded forgetfulness.

254 *process*: Story.

255 *date*: Duration.

257 *with her soul*: With all her heart (ironic).

259–61 *from*: Ironic, either because his love is as unnatural as his soul, or taking *from* to mean 'at variance with', as in *Henry IV, Part I*, III.2.31.

269 *humour*: Temperament.

273 *haply*: Perchance.

274 *sometimes*: Once.

277 *sap*: Blood. Shakespeare overlooks that they were strangled.

283 *conveyance*: Removal (with quibble on legal conveyance of property, after his promises in 249–50).

290 *spoil*: Destruction.

291 *Look what*: Whatever.

292 *shall deal*: Cannot but act.

297 *quicken your increase*: Give life to your offspring.

300 *doting title*: Fond name.

302 *metal*: Substance; material.

303 *pain*: Labour; effort.

304 *bid*: Endured (the past of 'bide').

316 *Familiarly*: As a member of the same family.

322 *orient*: Specially lustrous.

335 *retail*: Relate.

340 *title*: Name.

342 *tender*: Youthful.

343 *Infer*: Adduce.

346 *forbids*: Marriage with a brother's daughter was prohibited by law (Book of Common Prayer, Table of Kindred; Leviticus 18).

348 *vail*: Let fall.

350 *title*: Word.

352 *fairly*: Without foul play.

360 *honest*: Honourable.

361 *quick*: Hasty. Taken by Queen Elizabeth to mean 'alive'.

366 *George*: Jewel, on which is a figure of Saint George, forming part of the insignia of the Order of the Garter.

369–71 *his*: Its.

370 *virtue*: Good quality; efficacy.

379 *unity*: Reconciliation.

390 *Hereafter*: Future.

402 *opposite*: Adverse.

405 *tender*: Have tender feelings for.

409 *decay*: Destruction.

413 *attorney*: Pleader.

416 *state of times*: Condition of the world.

417 *peevish-fond*: Obstinately foolish.

420 *forget myself to be myself*: Forget my former self, to become what I formerly was.

424 *nest of spicery*: The nest of the phoenix, in which this fabled bird burnt itself to give birth to another.

425 *recomforture*: Comfort.

434 *puissant*: Mighty.

438 *hull*: Drift.

450 *make*: Raise.

451 *suddenly*: Swiftly.

459 *Hoyday*: Exclamation of surprise or impatience.

464 *White-livered runagate*: Cowardly vagabond.

469 *chair*: Throne.
       sword: Symbol of regal power.

470 *empire*: State.

479 *power*: Army.

483 *north*: In Lancashire, Cheshire, etc.

495 *heart*: Disposition, hence loyalty.

496 *assurance*: Security.

499 *advertisèd*: Informed.

504 *competitors*: Associates.

507 *owls*: Cf. *Macbeth*, II.2.3: 'the owl ... the fatal bellman'.

513 *cry thee mercy*: Beg your pardon.

515 *well-advisèd*: Well-considered.

527 *Hoised*: Hoisted.

    Britain: Brittany.

533 *power*: Army.

535 *reason*: Talk.

IV.5

Location: Lord Derby's house. Time: some time later.

1 *Sir*: See III.2.108, note.

2 *boar*: See I.2.102, note.

3 *franked up in hold*: Shut up in custody.

15 *crew*: Band.

17 *bend their power*: Turn their forces.

V.1

Location: Salisbury. An open place. Time: some days later.

0 *halberds*: Cf. I.2.0.

7 *moody*: Angry.

12 *doomsday*: Death-day.

14 *fall on*: In retribution.

19 *determined respite of my wrongs*: Appointed time to which the punishment of my crimes was postponed.

23–4 *Thus doth He . . . their masters' bosoms*: Cf. Psalm 37:14–15.

29 *blame*: Culpability.

V.2

Location: Tamworth. Richmond's camp. Time: a little later.

0 *colours*: Military ensigns.

3 *bowels*: Middle.

5 *father Stanley*: Stepfather Derby.

7 *wretched*: Loathsome.

    boar: Richard.

9 *Swills*: Gulps down.

    wash: Hogwash.

10 *embowelled*: Disembowelled.

17 *Every man's conscience is a thousand men*: 'Conscience is a thousand witnesses' was proverbial.

21 *dearest*: Direst.

V.3

Location: Bosworth Field. Time: a little later.

1 *tent*: Tents could be erected on the Elizabethan stage, and in this scene two tents represent the two rival camps simultaneously.

5 *knocks*: Blows.

9 *descried*: Reconnoitred.

11 *battalia*: Large armed force in battle array.
   account: Reckoning.

12 *King's name is a tower*: Cf. Proverbs 18:10: 'The name of the Lord is a strong tower' (Genevan Bible).

16 *direction*: Capacity for tactics.

17 *discipline*: Military experience.

18 *tent*: See note to 1.

20 *tract*: Course.
   car: Chariot.

24 *form and model*: Military formation and plan.

25 *Limit*: Appoint.
   several charge: Separate post.

50 *beaver*: Face-guard of helmet, hence helmet.

59 *pursuivant-at-arms*: Junior officer.

62 *blind*: Dark.

63 *watch*: Clock; or possibly a special guard.

65 *staves*: Shaft of a lance (plural of staff).

70 *cockshut*: Evening twilight.

82 *father-in-law*: Stepfather.

84 *by attorney*: As proxy.

86 *steal*: Move stealthily.

87 *flaky*: Streaked with light.

89 *battle*: Body of troops in battle array.

91 *mortal-staring*: War is seen as a basilisk, able to kill with a look: cf. I.2.150.

93 *time*: World.

94 *shock*: Encounter.

96 *tender*: Young.

98 *leisure*: Time at one's disposal.

99 *ceremonious*: Punctilious.

105 *with*: Against.

106 *peise*: Weigh.

111 *bruising*: Crushing.

117 *windows of mine eyes*: Eyelids.

119 *sit heavy on*: Be oppressive to.

133 *fulsome*: Cloying; disgusting.

136 *fall*: Drop.

139 *battle*: Troops.

157 *boar's annoy*: Richard's molestations.

164 *fall*: Drop.

173 *Fainting*: Losing heart.

174 *for hope*: For hoping to support you.

177 *Exit*: Neither F nor Q gives exits for the ghosts. Most editors make them all leave the stage at this point, but producers will probably prefer separate departures.

181 *burn blue*: Traditionally supposed a sign that ghosts are abroad.

186 *fly*: Flee.

192 *I am a villain*: Cf. I.1.30!

194 *My conscience*: See V.2.17, note.

194–5, 199 *several*: Different.

199 *used*: Committed.

216 *shadows*: Illusions, things without substance; at 217, spirits.

220 *proof*: Impenetrable armour.
    shallow: Superficial.

222 *eavesdropper*: Cf. Queen Margaret's eavesdropping, especially in IV.4.3; and V.3.272 ff.

225 *Cry mercy*: I beg your pardon.

232 *cried on*: Invoked with outcry.

233 *jocund*: Cheerful.

237 *His oration to his soldiers*: Holinshed has a similar heading, 'The oration of king Henrie the seauenth to his armie' (p. 757). This suggests that those who prepared the Q text had access to an authorized manuscript, perhaps Shakespeare's (damaged?) papers. Cf. 314, note.

244 *except*: Being excepted.

249 *made means*: Used efforts.

251 *foil*: Setting of a jewel.

252 *set*: With a quibble.

255 *ward*: Protect.

259 *country's fat*: The fat of the land.
    pains: Efforts.

263 *quits*: Repays.

265 *Advance*: Raise.

277 *Tell the clock*: Count the strokes of the clock.

280 *braved*: Lit up; made splendid.

284 *lour*: Look dark.

288 *sadly*: Dismally.

289 *vaunts*: Brags unopposed.

290 *Caparison*: Put the trappings on.

291 *power*: Force.

293 *battle*: Body of troops.

294 *foreward*: Vanguard.

301 *wingèd*: Protected by a wing of an army.

302 *to boot*: To our help.

305 *Jockey*: Familiar for Jock, Jack.

306 *Dickon*: Dick (King Richard).
    bought and sold: Betrayed.

309–12 *Let not . . . swords our law*: Perhaps an aside, or spoken
    to Ratcliffe alone.

313 *join*: Join battle.

314 *His oration to his army*: So Holinshed, p. 755: 'The
    oration of king Richard the third to the chiefteins of
    his armie'. Cf. 237, note.

315 *inferred*: Stated.

317 *runaways*: Cowardly fellows, deserters.

318 *Britains*: Bretons.
    lackey: Serving.

319 *o'ercloyèd*: Overfilled with food.

323 *distrain*: Confiscate.
    distain: Defile.

325 *mother's*: Shakespeare followed a misprint in Holinshed.
    Richmond was aided by Richard's *brother* (brother-in-
    law), the Duke of Burgundy.

328 *whip*: English vagabonds were whipped by the parish
    beadle and sent home.

329 *rags*: Ragged persons.

331 *fond*: Foolish.

335 *bobbed*: Banged.

336 *in*: On.

341 *proud*: High-mettled.

342 *welkin*: Sky.

344 *deny*: Refuse.

348 *great*: Full with emotion.

349 *Advance*: Raise.

351 *spleen*: Fiery eagerness.

352 *helms*: Helmets.

V.4

Location: Bosworth Field. Time: a little later, the same day.

9 *Slave*: Wretch.

upon a cast: Upon one throw (of the dice, *die*).

10 *hazard*: Chance.

11 *six Richmonds*: Perhaps because some of Richmond's followers wore his 'colours': cf. *Henry IV, Part I*, V.3.25.

V.5

Location: Bosworth Field. Time: a little later, the same day.

0 *they fight*: This duel, in which Good overcomes Evil, is the play's supreme confrontation. It passes without a word, perhaps to emphasize its symbolic and ritual implications. Richard should be given all the violent physical action, and Richmond must bear himself calmly, with complete self-assurance.

Retreat and flourish: Trumpet signals.

4 *royalty*: Emblem of sovereignty, the crown.

7 *make much of it*: Turn it to great account.

19 *the White Rose and the Red*: The badges of the houses of York and Lancaster.

20 *conjunction*: Union.

21 *have*: Cf. I.3.218, note.

23 *scarred*: Disfigured, wounded.

24–6 *The brother . . . the sire*: Matthew 10:21.

35 *Abate*: Blunt.

36 *reduce*: Bring back.